# Playing Monopoly with the Devil

# Playing Monopoly with the Devil

Dollarization and Domestic

Currencies in Developing

Countries

**Manuel Hinds**

A Council on Foreign Relations Book

Yale University Press

New Haven and London

A Council on Foreign Relations Book

Printed in the United States of America.

Library of Congress Cataloging-in-Publication Data

Hinds, Manuel.
    Playing monopoly with the devil : dollarization and domestic currencies in
developing countries / Manuel Hinds.
        p. cm.
    "A Council on Foreign Relations Book."
    Includes bibliographical references and index.
    ISBN-13: 978-0-300-11330-3 (cloth : alk. paper)
    ISBN-10: 0-300-11330-7 (cloth : alk. paper)
        1. Money—Developing countries.    2. Currency question—Developing
countries.    3. Monetary policy—Developing countries.    I. Title.
    HG1496.H56 2006
    332.4'91724—dc22        2006006465

A catalogue record for this book is available from the British Library.

The paper in this book meets the guidelines for permanence and durability of the
Committee on Production Guidelines for Book Longevity of the Council on
Library Resources.

10 9 8 7 6 5 4 3 2 1

# Council on Foreign Relations

Founded in 1921, the Council on Foreign Relations is an independent, national membership organization and a nonpartisan center for scholars dedicated to producing and disseminating ideas so that individual and corporate members, as well as policymakers, journalists, students, and interested citizens in the United States and other countries, can better understand the world and the foreign policy choices they face. The Council does this by convening meetings; conducting a wide-ranging studies program; publishing *Foreign Affairs*, the preeminent journal covering international affairs and U.S. foreign policy; maintaining a diverse membership; sponsoring independent task forces; and providing up-to-date information about the world and U.S. foreign policy on the Council's website, http://www.cfr.org.

The Council takes no institutional position on policy issues and has no affiliation with the U.S. government. All statements of fact and expressions of opinion contained in its publications are the sole responsibility of the author or authors.

Para Carmen Beatriz, Eleonora y Eva María
Y para sus esposos,
Martin, John y Matthew,
que son también mis hijos
Y para sus hijos, mis nietos
Y Para Marielos

# Contents

# Acknowledgments

I am indebted to the Council on Foreign Relations. While writing this book, I was the Whitney H. Shepardson fellow at the Council, and benefited from the encouragement and comments of many of its associates. Chief among them, I would like to thank Council President Richard N. Haass and Director of Studies James M. Lindsay for their support, as well as Benn Steil, then acting director of the Council's Geoeconomic Center, who first invited me to become a fellow and guided me through all the steps needed to write and publish a book under the Council's imprint. He also provided valuable comments and ideas throughout the process. I also would like to mention the support I received from Janine Hill, the institution's associate director of studies.

Part of the process involved the formation of a study group to read my draft, discuss it, and provide comments in a meeting that convened on February 8, 2005, at the Council's headquarters in New York. The meeting was quite lively with useful comments and exceeded the three hours allotted for it. The group met under the competent chairmanship of Sergio J. Galvis. I am quite grateful to all of them for the time they took to read the draft and for the excellent comments they provided to improve it.

Before the study group, I presented the main ideas contained in the book to a distinguished audience on November 17, 2004, also at the Council's main offices. The meeting was chaired by John H. Biggs and the attendees were Wilder K. Abbott, Henry H. Arnhold, Frederick C. Broda, Robert J. Chaves, Jill M. Considine, D. Blake Haider, Jon K. Hartzell, J. Tomilson Hill, Nisha Kumar, Herbert Levin, Fritz Link, Michael S. Mathews, Irene W. Meister, Charlotte Morgan, Brian D. O'Neill, Diego Perfumo, Michael P. Peters, Thomas L. Pulling, Susan K. Purcell, Frank E. Richardson, Arthur M. Rubin, Benn Steil, Scott L. Swid, Paul A. Volcker, and James D. Zirin. The strong support I received from the Honorable Paul Volcker meant a lot to me.

In addition, I received detailed written comments from Millard Long and from one anonymous referee appointed by the Council.

## Prologue Playing Monopoly with the Devil

This is the tale of what happened to Dema Gogo, ruler of a poor country in an underdeveloped area of the world, when he discovered that he could issue his own currency. The tale starts with a conversation he had with the Devil himself, the day after his inauguration as President of the Republic. Drinking a glass of cognac and smoking a Cuban cigar on the veranda of the Presidential Palace, enjoying the sight of the luscious tropical plants that grew in the garden one floor below, he was pondering what he could do to assure his reelection five years down the road. He had many ideas but no money. It was in that placid moment that he saw a familiar character approaching him.

"Hello, Devil!" he said. "Join me in a cognac and a cigar."

"Hello, Dema!" said the Devil, helping himself to a glass of cognac and taking a seat alongside the ruler, so that both were looking at the garden. Sitting in this way, seeing not each other but instead

This prologue was first published in *International Finance*, Spring 2005. It is reproduced here with permission from Blackwell Publishing Ltd., Oxford, UK.

some common object, gave both of them a sense of intimacy, of common purpose.

"I have a proposal for you," said the Devil.

"A proposal? Maybe you mean a deal. That's what you're known for."

"A deal? I wouldn't dare. Your campaign said that you are incorruptible," the Devil said.

"Well, don't pay much attention to campaign language," said Gogo. "A politician always listens to proposals. That's politics, you know. I'd sell my soul for a reasonable price—say, the combined price of all the assets in the country. No credit, mind you. Cash only."

"I don't mean to sound offensive, Mr. President. I'll remember your kind offer but it'd be too much for me at this moment. Not much cash on hand at the moment. You'll understand."

Gogo laughed. "We share that problem. Let's drink to it!"

"If you'd allow me to address that problem," said the Devil, sipping some cognac, "let me tell you that I was just with Dr. Werner von Bankrupt down below, in my dominions. He has just arrived. Bright individual. Not quite reliable, though. He was a macroeconomist when on earth, you know."

"They're worse than us politicians. Never repeat this, please."

"I know, I have plenty of them down there. A great team, really. They have accomplished many a feat for me," said the Devil. Then he continued, "Well, in any case, he had a bright idea. I told him about my cash problems, and he said that I should issue Hell's own currency. I told him I didn't need a local currency because there are no transactions in Hell. I only needed cash for my operations abroad. That means dollars, you know. But, then, when he explained his ideas to me, I thought that maybe you could use them. You should issue your own currency, the gogo, with your face on each coin and bill."

"Oh, that's not such a brilliant idea. What's in it for me to print my own currency? I'm not quite sure I want my face all over the place. It's one of my weaknesses, you know, according to my Miami-based campaign advisors."

"Dr. von Bankrupt explained the benefits you could get. This is what he said. Imagine your country is a gigantic Monopoly game. You use Monopoly money to play Monopoly, right? Now imagine you force people to give you their dollars to get the money they need to play in the country. You get the dollars, they get Monopoly bills, and you can print as much as you want! It'd be as if you had the Monopoly bank for your exclusive use! You could land on Boardwalk with hotels and not worry at all. You just take money from the bank. If you want to buy property, just take more money. Get it? And on top of that, you can use their dollars! You can deposit them in New York and get interest on them. And that's real money. Dr. von Bankrupt told me it's called seigniorage: the ruler's right to extract an income from allowing people to use the local money. You win, Dema, no matter what!"

Gogo, openmouthed, turned his head to look at the Devil. "That's a brilliant idea!" Then he turned his eyes up, thought for a moment, and asked, "But what's in it for you? You've given it to me and I've signed nothing!"

The Devil looked at him with sweet innocence. "Consider it a bonus for a long and profitable relationship."

And so Dema Gogo created the gogo, and issued a decree mandating that all transactions in the country had to be denominated in the new currency. A central bank, managed by the eminent financier Don Santiago De la Insolvencia, was established to issue the gogos and manage the dollars obtained in the operation. Governor De la Insolvencia established the rule that the Central Bank would issue gogos only when the citizens surrendered their dollars to it. The exchange rate was 1 to 1, so that the Central Bank held one dollar for every gogo in circulation.

Dema Gogo was very happy when he saw the enormous amount of dollars going into the coffers of the Central Bank as the citizens exchanged them for gogos. His happiness turned into fury, however, when De la Insolvencia told him that he could only use the interest on the dollars, and not the total amount, for his pet projects.

"Why not the entire amount?" asked the ruler, suspecting that the governor was playing a trick on him.

"Because we have to hold reserves of true dollars, Mr. President. This Monopoly board is not self-contained. Not all the things that people need can be bought inside the board. We have to import things, people need to travel, and for this they need real money. Nobody takes gogos if not forced to do so. Therefore, we have to be ready to sell dollars back to them whenever they give us gogos."

"But I still can print as much local money as I want!" said Gogo, recalling what the Devil had told him.

"Not quite," said the governor. "The more you print, the more economic activity you have, and the more imported things are needed. So, the more money you print, the more dollars you need."

"So, what's the advantage of having gogos?"

"You still get the interest on the real dollars that remain in the country, which amounts to 5% of these. That's a lot of money, Your Excellency. The interest is so important that it has a name. It's called seigniorage: the ruler's right to charge for the use of money inside the country."

"I don't want to scale down my projects by 95%!" roared Gogo.

He called the Devil again. "This is a fraud," he said, "a mirage! I'm only getting 5% of the Monopoly bank."

The Devil smiled. "That's because Santiago De la Insolvencia is out of date. He established what's known as a currency board. This is not what Dr. von Bankrupt had in mind. De la Insolvencia is ignoring something that the experts call the 'float.' Not all the money leaves the country; there is always a certain amount that is left inside, which they call the float. You can spend that money, sure that nobody will ever withdraw it. Issue gogos against that float, and you'll see that nothing will happen, except that you'll be able to spend more money."

"And how much would that float be?"

"Von Bankrupt estimates that, on average, it's only 20% of the reserves that fluctuate. You can use the other 80%."

"I'm starting to develop a liking for you, Devil," said Gogo.

"You've always liked me. I know it in my heart," answered the Devil.

Gogo called De la Insolvencia and told him to get rid of the currency board and immediately issue a loan to the government equivalent to 80% of the reserves. The loan would finance the Gogo bridges, the Gogo roads, the Gogo statues, and so on—all the things that Gogo had dreamed of building to perpetuate his memory and win the next election. Within a few months, all these works were started. Not only that, the country was awash with money and a real estate boom was in progress. The Property Owners' Association gave him a golden decoration. The ruler was satisfied and enjoyed his late afternoon cigars more than ever.

Governor De la Insolvencia, always apprehensive, called him to say that dollar reserves were going down.

"Who cares, De la Insolvencia? Don't be a chicken. We knew they would decline. It's the float! Everyone loves gogos now!"

Gogo loved to say *float*. It was a technical word, like *seigniorage*, but he couldn't pronounce the latter.

One day, however, the Minister of Public Works, Mr. Rodrigo Diez Porciento, visited him. "Your Excellency," he said, "I'm having problems buying property and materials. Private citizens are demanding those as well, and they are offering increasingly higher prices. There have been a lot of gogos going around since the currency board was terminated. To ensure that we can buy these properties and materials, we have to offer higher prices."

"Don't worry, Diez Porciento, just pay a little more than the citizens are offering. That will suffice."

A few months later, Diez Porciento came back. He showed him a ledger with numbers. "Your Excellency," he said, "I come with bad news. Costs are outstripping our budgets considerably. We won't be able to finish any of your projects if we don't get more money. We're 25% short."

"How is that possible? I told you to pay only a little more than the citizens were offering for what you needed. Now you show me a 25% shortfall!"

"I've been paying just a tad over the private sector bids. But those bids have been increasing steadily. To outstrip them, I have had to bid increasingly larger amounts." Gogo called the Central Bank governor.

"Your Excellency, I've been trying to reach you. We're losing more reserves than we thought. The country is importing more than ever. I'm worried we might lose more reserves than we can afford. Also, with the continuous monetary creation, prices of everything are going up and people are protesting. They're calling your policies 'inflationary.' Could you tell Diez Porciento to cut his expenses?"

Then Gogo read a statement the Property Owners' Association had published in the newspapers. "President Gogo is playing the 'One million dollar cat for two half-a-million dollar dogs' game on us. We sold our properties at very high prices, but when we went into the market to replace them we found that all properties were equally expensive, and that the higher prices were only a mirage. We are as poor as ever."

Gogo summoned the Devil again. "Look at what's happening here! We've got inflation and we're losing reserves. Now Santiago De la Insolvencia says we should cut back expenditures while Diez Porciento says he won't be able to finish my projects unless he gets more money. I knew I couldn't trust you!"

The Devil feigned offense. "Dema, old friend, how can you tell me this? Dr. von Bankrupt says that all you have to do is devalue your currency."

"Devalue? What do you mean?"

"Today, you're selling one dollar for each gogo when people import things. Tomorrow you should charge two gogos for a dollar. People won't be able to buy all the dollars they're buying now."

Gogo looked at the Devil with wild eyes. "You're right, Devil! That's the solution."

And the next day he devalued the currency. Demand for dollars dropped immediately. Early in the morning, he got a call from the president of the exporters association. "We're very happy, Your Excellency. The gogo-equivalent of our export revenues has doubled. Since salaries have not gone up, exporting has become more profitable."

The ruler was elated, until he got a call from Ms. Tessa Bono, the Minister of Finance. "Your Excellency, we're in deep trouble. I enthusiastically endorsed the devaluation, but now I have realized that the burden of the external debt has increased twofold. Yesterday, we needed one gogo to pay one dollar, now we need two gogos, and our taxes are all in gogos. We have to keep on inflating the economy, so that our tax revenues increase enough to service our debts. What I'm saying is that you must tell the Central Bank to lend me more money. Of course, you can't devalue again. Just inflate, don't devalue. If you do, the dollars will be dearer again."

"Happiness is never complete," thought Gogo, one second before he got a call from Mr. Jaime Hoffa, the Minister of Labor.

"Your Excellency, we're facing a labor revolt. The workers claim that we've effectively lowered their salaries with the devaluation and demand an imme-diate adjustment, which would mean doubling their wages, so that they re-main the same when measured in dollars."

Then it was the Central Bank governor's turn. "Your Excellency, interest rates are going up, way up. They've reached 100%, almost twice those of Brazil. Banks say they have to increase them because, if they don't, people will take their deposits abroad. They think you'll devalue again. We can't afford this capital outflow. We don't have enough reserves, as you know."

"Reduce printing. Do as you want," said Gogo, tired of all this currency chaos.

The day proceeded with a call from Diez Porciento. "Your Excellency, Santiago De la Insolvencia tells me that you told him to stop lending to the government. Tessa Bono tells me that without such lending she can't give me the money I need. I'm sorry to say that we need further budgetary increases. The cost of all imported materials has doubled, and they represent a high percentage of the cost of new construction. Just think of oil."

Tessa Bono called immediately thereafter. "Your Excellency, the fiscal deficit is increasing rapidly because of the soaring interest rates. Our Treasury bills are paying 105%. We can't afford this."

"Sir, there is a demonstration coming to the Presidential Palace," inter-rupted his Chief of Security. "They say they want your head."

At 5 p.m., the ruler called the Central Bank governor and commanded him to increase the printing of gogos in order to lend more resources to the government. Immediately thereafter, he decreed that all salaries would be increased by 100%, effective immediately.

That solved most of the problems of the day, except the interest rates. Gogo was happy he had been able to find a solution without consulting the Devil. He then took a week's vacation on the beach.

When he came back he found the Central Bank governor waiting for him. "Your Excellency, we have a serious problem. Since we increased salaries, all prices have increased and we're in the same position as before, when we originally devalued the currency. Dollars are twice as expensive as they were before the devaluation, but incomes in gogos are also twice as much as they'd been before that date. We're losing reserves again, and quickly. Interest rates are also increasing rapidly, not because we've devalued but because people *think* we will devalue. Some of them are taking their money abroad, regardless of the interest rate. We have to devalue again."

Gogo looked at the governor. "But, De la Insolvencia, if we devalue today, we will have to devalue again tomorrow. This is like bicycling downhill without brakes."

"Yes, Your Excellency, I suppose it is."

Gogo's eyes went down to the newspaper that his assistant had left on his desk. The president of the exporters association was in the headlines. He looked indignant. The paper quoted him: "The government's policies are reducing the competitiveness of the country. Our labor costs are increasing fast and the prices of our exports remain the same. We demand another devaluation, and soon."

On the second page, there was a picture of the national labor leader. He also looked indignant. He was saying: "We'll strike if the government devalues further and doesn't increase our salaries proportionally."

Gogo steadied his nerves. He would talk with the Devil. The Devil always had solutions. He wished the Devil could be the governor of the Central Bank. It was a pity that he couldn't, on constitutional grounds. The Devil wasn't a national. He met all other requirements.

"Of course I have a solution," said the Devil. "Float the currency."

"What do you mean?"

"Don't have any official price for the currency. Just let the market set it. If you do this, you can keep on printing as much money as you want without having to announce that you'll devalue the currency. People selling and buying gogos will set that price in every transaction. Nobody will blame you."

The next day Gogo announced the flotation of the gogo. International institutions praised him. The *Timely Times*, the most influential newspaper in the country, published an editorial saying: "Our eminent President Gogo has entered the realm of enlightened rulers by adopting the most flexible of all monetary regimes. Now, according to what our macroeconomic advisors say, we will be free from the comings and goings of the international monetary markets. We are, at last, sovereign in monetary matters. We can exert what the experts call 'monetary policy' and let the market take care of itself."

Gogo felt happy again. But not much time passed before his calm was interrupted by a call from the governor of the Central Bank. "Your Excellency, our currency isn't floating but sinking. Inflation just keeps on increasing and interest rates are doing the same. Since the currency keeps on devaluing, the interest rates are too high for lending. Only bad customers borrow at these rates, and we face the prospect of a financial crisis, as bad loans are accumulating. At the same time, savers are taking their money abroad. We have to reduce the cost of money and give confidence to the people."

Gogo had never thought of such a possibility. "I don't want to go back to the Devil. I get into deeper trouble every time I do it. Besides, I don't want to give him the impression that I can't manage the country without his advice."

"I have a solution," said Mr. De la Insolvencia, "let's allow savers to deposit their money in our banks in dollar accounts. With that, they'll be protected against inflation and devaluations. The deposit interest rates on those accounts will fall. Then the banks will be able to lend at lower rates to good companies, in dollars of course."

This was done. Deposits increased in the dollar accounts, which paid interest rates much, much lower than those in gogos. People, however, didn't want to borrow in dollars, because as the gogo devalued the value of their debt increased in gogo terms. This time, Gogo forgot his pride and called the Devil again.

"Don't worry," said the Devil, "they'll soon discover that domestic inflation will allow them to repay their loans. If the currency falls by 100% and wage inflation is 100%, they can do it. Since the currency floats, it'll happen automatically."

Gogo felt happy, but he had the eerie feeling that something was wrong.

A voice told him, "You have gone back to square one. This is the same as not devaluing and having zero inflation. It is the same as when you didn't have a currency of your own, except that everything is more complex now."

Still, he called Mr. De la Insolvencia. He was already speeding downhill and there was no point in wishing he had never started doing so. "Pre-announce the rate of devaluation, which will be the same as expected inflation, 100%. This will be the rate at which you'll create money," said Gogo, repeating the detailed instructions he had received from the Devil.

The Governor was impressed. "This is what the international organizations say is best."

The Minister of Public Works called one month later. "Your Excellency, I need more money to finish the projects. Inflation is running ahead of me. When I try to buy things, prices increase before I have a chance to pay. One of my advisors tells me it's called rational expectations. At this rate, we won't be able to finish the public works in time for the election."

Gogo was seriously worried. He called the Devil again.

"Give them an unexpected shock to catch them off guard, something they wouldn't expect," the Devil said. "Give Diez Porciento a lot of money, so that he can finish the public works, but time this move so that the effect on inflation is delayed until after the election. This is called lags, you know."

In spite of the reassuring tone of the Devil, it was during those days that Gogo began to have a recurring nightmare of dismemberment. He was riding in between two bicycles, one called inflation and the other devaluation, and he had to keep them going at the same speed to avoid disaster. Later on, he began dreaming that the number of bicycles increased. In one of these dreams, he was holding inflation and devaluation with his hands, while he kept the other two going with his legs. Those were called interest rates and the debt service abroad. The worst nightmares came when he became an octopus, with a bicycle tied to each of his tentacles, which by now controlled the rate of capital flight, the spreads between loans denominated in dollars and gogos, the gains and losses to banks resulting from different rates of devaluation, the acquisitive power of wages, the levels of international reserves, lags, floats, rational expectations, seigniorage, unexpected shocks, and so on.

With only two months to go until the election, Santiago De la Insolvencia called again. There was anxiety in his voice. "Sir, we're in a mess. People can't repay their gogo debts. Interest rates are too high because people think that the rate of devaluation will accelerate. They can't repay their debts in dollars because inflation is depressing business and, for this reason, the gogo value of the dollar debts is increasing faster than their incomes with each devaluation. Depositors are changing from gogos to dollars and our reserves are plummeting. The black market is booming and there the price of the dollar is going up very fast. Now the official exchange rate is one billion to one, and in the black market 1.5 billion to one. I think the risk of a banking crisis is high and we don't have enough dollars to avoid it."

"But, why? We have guaranteed that we won't devalue the currency faster than 100%. And call me 'Your Excellency'!"

"The problem is that people don't believe that you'll be able to honor your word—Your Excellency. The crisis will explode if the public perceives that the government doesn't have enough dollars to back the gogos."

The Devil was back. "Don't worry. The Ministry of Finance should issue short-term dollar-denominated debt and pass the proceeds on to the Central Bank. This will give you the foreign exchange you need. This is more or less what Mexico did in 1994."

Since Gogo didn't know what Mexico had done in 1994, and didn't know what happened there afterwards, he felt optimistic. The Ministry of Finance issued 30-day notes paying 12% in dollars while U.S. Treasury Bills were paying 2%. Minister Tessa Bono, in a fling of vanity, called them Tessabonos. The government got a new influx of dollars.

Three days before the election, however, there was an editorial in the *Timely Times*. "As this paper went to print, the gogo fell off its predicted course by more than 200% and then went into a free fall in the black market, which is the only working one in the country, as the government has stopped selling dollars. Five years ago, we had a stable currency and, even if our growth rates were not sensational, we were making steady progress. Now, we have runaway inflation; there are no dollars to pay for our imports; interest rates are sky high; the value of the private sector dollar debts to the banking system is ballooning as the currency devalues, leaving the private sector as bankrupt as the government; and the government has defaulted on its dollar-denominated Tessabonos. Of course, the banks have plenty of gogos, which are printed by the Central Bank on demand, but cannot deliver what their depositors want: dollars. So much for the much advertised capacity of the Central Bank to act as a lender of last resort. We supported Gogo five years ago. We want to compensate the country for our mistake by offering a prize for his soul: one trillion gogos."

The phone rang as Gogo finished reading the editorial. "Gogo," said Mr. De la Insolvencia, "we have a run on the banks. People believe that the currency will devalue by more than any amount that you announce and they continue changing their gogos into dollars, now at a terrifying rate. I'm on board a plane that has just taken off, headed to a place I prefer to leave unknown. When I left, your reserves were fifty cents. There are riots in front of the banks. Please accept my resignation."

Gogo heard a deep rumble. First it was a faraway sound, but soon he realized that it was approaching him fast. The floor was vibrating with increasing force. Then he heard the horrible sound of windows breaking and pounding footsteps, thousands of pounding footsteps, running up the stairs. "What's going on?" he asked his assistant.

"A mob wants to get you," she said, rushing to the presidential helicopter, which took off as soon as she boarded, with Gogo's entire corps of bodyguards and the secret stash of dollars that Gogo had kept in his office for dire situations like these.

Gogo jumped into the garden and ran quickly, looking for a hideout. He found it inside a little grotto where he used to have drinks with friends. He sat there for a moment, head in hands, and then let out a muted cry. There was someone else there. It was the Devil.

"You really scared me!" he said.

"What's going on, my friend?" asked the Devil, smiling maliciously.

"A mob is chasing me."

"What did you do to them?"

"Nothing! They're unreasonable. They don't understand how difficult it is to manage the macroeconomy."

"What do they say?" asked the Devil.

"Look!" said Gogo, handing him the wrinkled page of the newspaper with the editorial printed on it.

"What can I do?" asked Gogo while the Devil read with deep concentration. "How can I make people trust my currency?"

"Oh, you should just abolish it at this point," said the Devil, "although I suppose it's a bit late for that." And before Gogo could respond, the Devil walked to the entry of the cavern and shouted, "He's in here!"

A startled Gogo ran from the grotto but, in his rush, stepped on a slippery stone, fell backwards and broke his neck. He died instantly.

Gogo woke up in another world. He expected to see a Court of Judgment, with God presiding, but he saw only his old friend, the Devil, who was tying him up with steel ropes while giving instructions to the minor devils as to the particular furnace he should be carried to. Once he finished tying him up, the Devil put a sign on top of him. " 'Devil's property," it said.

"Hey!" said Gogo, "I deserve a trial! I never sold my soul to you."

The Devil smiled. "Last night I bought out the *Timely Times* and, as you know, I tendered a public offer for your soul, which was delivered by the mob that chased you this morning. I paid a trillion gogos, which, when added to the trillion I paid for the newspaper, Dr. von Bankrupt tells me, is the combined price of all the assets in your country."

"I never signed anything!"

"There's no need for such trifling formalities. I have you on tape saying that you'd sell me your soul if I paid that amount. I just exercised the option."

As Gogo was being carried away by the minor devils, the Devil told him, "At today's exchange rate in the black market, I paid about a buck-fifty. That was a fair price."

# Introduction

Why should a developing country surrender its power to create money by adopting as its own an international currency?

This book addresses this question.

For most economists, the book should be very brief, a few paragraphs long. It should limit itself to state the conventional answer to this question, which would be that a country should never surrender this power. Such an answer would be based on impressive theoretical and institutional foundations.

Theoretically, there are arguments on trade, finance, and fiscal management grounds. On the side of trade, the argument is that flexibility to modify the exchange rate allows domestic authorities to shift domestic relative prices by devaluing the domestic currency in such a way that imports are discouraged and exports encouraged. This, an advantage in itself, also gives countries resilience against external shocks, such as negative turns in the terms of trade and natural disasters. On the financial side, the arguments are several. All are linked to the ability of central banks to print money and change the price of the currency, allowing them to keep their interest rates low even if they are high in the international market. The ability to print money would also ensure a plentiful supply of credit even if credit is tight abroad. Most important, the power to create money turns central banks into lenders of last resort when a crisis threatens the domestic financial system. On the fiscal side, the argument is that having a domestic currency allows the government to charge a tax on demand for money, called seigniorage. Whenever demand for money increases, the government can print it and spend the proceeds. All these theoretical advantages are lost when a country dollarizes. Moreover, the ultimate argument against dollarization is that a country can choose not to print money without having to resign from its ability to do so in the future.

The sad story of Dema Gogo's adventures contained in the prologue contradicts all these predictions. To Dema Gogo's chagrin, the local currency brought about high interest rates and runaway inflation, and far from turning financial resources plentiful, these dwindled as he printed more money. Quite dramatically, he was brought down not by an external shock but by one that he himself had engineered domestically through the manipulation of his own money. In addition, his central bank, which was supposed to be the lender of last resort, failed miserably when it ran out of the currency that people wanted when running against the banks: dollars.

Devil aside, his story is quite realistic. It contains the main elements of the path that many developing countries have taken to financial crises and political upheaval throughout their histories. Its realism illustrates the wide difference that exists between the sedate predictions of conventional theories and the crude monetary realities faced by people in those countries.

Many would suggest that the ultimate source of Gogo's fall was not the creation of a local currency in itself but its abusive manipulation to finance the government. This is partially true. Yet, the existence of a local currency not only provided the temptation to abuse it but also gravely complicated matters as the exchange rate acquired a dynamic of its own. While Dema Gogo was fiscally irresponsible and kept financing his pet projects throughout his adventures, he increasingly had to take actions to compensate for problems that the devaluations themselves were spurring in all dimensions of the economy. Each of these actions created new complications until everything got out of control.

Dema Gogo learned this lesson the hard way. Before he decided to create his own currency, things were quite predictable, even if they were not great. The economy was transparent. Prices gave reliable signals of the value of things. He knew that he had to increase taxes if he wanted to spend money. Debtors, including the government, knew the burden that debts imposed on their incomes. If overextended, they could plan to adjust their debts in a linear fashion, reducing their expenditures by a certain amount. They had no sudden increases in the amount they owed.

Suddenly, when he created his own currency, Dema Gogo found himself living in a nonlinear world where all the magnitudes that had been certain now moved wildly with each shift in the exchange rate. He also discovered that he had become a prisoner of the law of unintended results, as each of the actions he took to manage the exchange rate could have negative impacts on multiple variables. These included, among others, the level of output and the rate of inflation, the interest rates, the level and currency composition of bank deposits, the debtors' ability to service their obligations, and the health of the financial institutions. All these variables reacted so pronouncedly to movements in the exchange rate that he had to take all these and many other things into consideration each time he decided to pursue a certain monetary or exchange rate policy. As the population's standard of value and the value of the gogo drifted apart, the reactions of the population to these policies became increasingly weird, to the point that Gogo saw the effects of the same causes reverse themselves. In this way, he watched how increasing the amount of money in circulation led initially to a boom and then to depression. Interest rates increased when he devalued and when he did not, depending on what people thought would be his future devaluation policy.

With time, the unintended reactions of the economy to Gogo's monetary manipulations became treacherously sudden. Before the introduction of the gogo, for example, a bank with bad loans representing, say, 5 percent of its portfolio, knew that it had a problem of that magnitude and could plan its solution with reasonable certainty. With the gogo and its exchange rates in place, this amount could explode to 20, 30, or 50 percent as a result of a single devaluation. This happened, if not because their loans were denominated in dollars, then because the interest rates on the gogo loans increased so much that the borrowers could not afford to service them. Thus, as it has happened in so many developing countries, banks could find from one day to the next that they were bankrupt, not by actions they have taken but by decisions made in the central bank.

Dema Gogo realized that the divergence between the inflation and devaluation rates introduced serious complications because the gogo was no longer the population's standard of value. Then he tried to keep the two rates going at the same pace, although he did not understand why keeping the two variables moving at the same pace was better than stopping both of them.

Yet, keeping the balance of the rates of change was also hard because the possibility of having the rates of inflation and devaluation diverging opened the door for political pressures coming from groups that could benefit or suffer from such divergence. In this way, for example, workers found that just keeping the level of salaries constant in real or dollar terms required continuous pressure on the government to keep wage inflation ahead of devaluations. At the same time, he had the pressure of the exporters, who demanded reductions on the real wage, which required higher rates of devaluation than inflation.

These problems are alien to the current generations living in developed countries, even if their currencies routinely devalue and appreciate against each other. Being large and widely diversified economies, the main impact of currency depreciations on their economic activity is a substitution, not an income, effect. That is, if the dollar depreciates relative to the yen, producers using inputs imported from Japan can replace them with inputs produced in the United States at similar prices and quality. People can realize this substitution in consumption as well. For this reason, the inflation rate does not increase with currency depreciations and wages, while reduced in foreign currency terms, remain constant in real terms. Thus, the currency retains its domestic value even if losing it in terms of other currencies for very long periods. Because of these reasons, people in developed countries think of value in terms of their own currency, so that the public in general does not even notice the fluctuations of the exchange rate. By contrast, developing economies are weak and poorly diversified, so their ability to replace imports with local products is very limited. Therefore, the domestic currency prices of imported goods increase when there is a devaluation. The main effect is an income, not a substitution effect. Because of these reasons, people in developing countries use the domestic currency but think of value in terms of a foreign one, most often the U.S. dollar.

This difference is crucial to understand the monetary behavior in developing countries. People in developed countries have two services provided in one single currency—the standard of value and the means of exchange. In developing countries, these two services are divorced, the first being provided by a foreign currency and the second provided by the domestic currency. Because of this divergence, people think in terms of ratios of domestic to dollars prices and adjust their behavior to the rates of change of these ratios. This gives the local currencies of developing countries their nonlinear behavior, which in turn results in the endemic financial and macroeconomic insta-bility that characterizes most of them. That is why, for example, savers demand a compensation for the risk of devaluation in the interest rates in local cur-rencies. The result is that, rather than falling, equilibrium interest rates tend to increase when the currency depreciates. The ultimate loyalty to a foreign standard of value is also the reason why people in these countries rush to exchange their local currency for dollars whenever there is a crisis or the prospect of one. This does not happen in developed countries. If banks fail, people rush to get their deposits cashed, but they do not turn around to buy foreign currencies with them, as they do in developing countries. The differ-ence is that people in the developed countries do not think that the failure of a bank will negatively affect the currency. People in developing countries do, and frequently the reason why they withdraw their deposits from the banks is not that they are afraid that the bank will fail but that the currency will be devalued. They want their deposits to buy dollars, not to put their local currency in another bank or to store it under their mattresses, as they do in developed countries.

The costs of the divorce of standard of value and the local currency are staggering even when countries do not slip into crises. These costs include high interest rates, very low levels of financial intermediation, high depen-dency on foreign credit to finance their long-term investments and, ironically, high vulnerability to external shocks. Sadly, countries that desperately need financial resources to finance their development lack access to the interna-tional financial markets, where they could get resources cheaply at the long maturities needed for productive investment. They are also left out from the services now offered by the globalized financial markets. This happens because creditors and investors get scared at the possibility of currency crises and the endemic instability of domestic currencies. It also happens because govern-ments in developing countries are quite reluctant to allow the private sector to get too close in touch with the international markets. Their reluctance comes from two sources. First, they are afraid that allowing this would create dangerous exchange rate risks. Second, having such access would free the population from the grip of the currency monopoly they enjoy inside their countries. Governments would then turn around to make sure that the com-peting standard of value would be kept outside the borders of the countries, banning the contact of all sectors with such currency.

Of course, this means that people wanting to have a stable standard of value must be encircled in a maze of controls that would prevent their access to save and enter contracts denominated in a currency that would provide a reliable link connecting past, present, and future. Perversely, the problem becomes worse the more the central bank exercises its powers to create money. This is one of the highest costs of the ability to print money in the developing countries.

Central banks could live by these rules in the fragmented world of the mid-twentieth century. In those days, central banks enforced their monopolies through strict controls imposed on the flows of capital and could deny their citizens access to foreign exchange. Exporters were forced to surrender their dollars to the central bank at the price it established, and importers, even if they were also exporters, had to buy their dollars from the central bank as well, also at its fixed price. For everything else, they had to use the domestic currency. This was the ideal setting for a local currency. Of course, for decades, people exported their savings to developed countries and even those who could not do it kept in mind the value of the dollar as their measure of value. However, the restrictions imposed by these leakages on the management of the currency were not visible.

Today, however, the power of central banks to enforce their monopolies is being eroded by financial globalization, which facilitates the transfer of money at very low costs of transaction. As this process advanced, domestic banks in many developing countries created offshore facilities to carry out domestic financial transactions in dollars. They were very successful in attracting customers. Faced with the reality that people preferred to use dollars, many central banks of developing countries allowed the creation of dollar-denominated deposits and credits in their local financial system. These deposits have taken over substantial portions of the banking operations in those countries in a very short time, even if many countries impose substantial restrictions on them. In the last few years, the ratio of foreign currency–denominated deposits to total deposits has surpassed 25 percent in most regions in the developing world. In three regions—Latin America, the formerly communist countries of East Europe and Central Asia, and the Middle East—the ratio has gone beyond 40 percent. In South America, it is 56 percent.[1] In all countries where this practice is allowed, the interest rates on the foreign currency operations are much lower than on those in the domestic currency, showing clearly where the standard of value resides.

The coexistence of two currencies in the same domestic market, one weak and the other strong, complicates monetary management, presents high risks of currency mismatching, and drastically reduces the power of the central banks to control their countries monetarily. While this phenomenon, which we may call "spontaneous dollarization," is not the cause of the divorce between the standard of value and the currency that people use in their normal transactions, it greatly facilitates the arbitrage between the two currencies, rendering useless many of the monopolistic powers previously held by the central banks. When central banks try to reduce the value and yield of the domestic currency, people escape into the other currency. This possibility of substitution establishes a lower limit to the interest rates that central banks can set in the local currencies if they want to prevent the shrinking of their own source of power. In numerical terms, this limit is equal to the interest rate in the foreign currency, plus a premium for the country risk, plus a premium for the risk of unexpected devaluations. Because of the latter, to attract deposits in local currency, banks must always offer a substantial interest rate premium on them over the rates paid in foreign currency deposits. This happens even if the country risk is the same because domestic banks operate with the two currencies in the same country. Thus, the difference is entirely attributable to the risk of a divergence between the future path of the value of the local currency and that of the standard of value.

You cannot control an economy with a currency that people can desert. These countries have lost what people like to call "monetary sovereignty." In fact, however, these countries had lost their economic sovereignty a long time ago. Ironically, they lost it through the instrument that would give such sovereignty to them, their domestic currencies. Unable to print a currency that would meet the needs of the population in terms of carrying value, these countries became hostage to the dictates of the real lender of last resort, the International Monetary Fund (IMF). In many, if not most developing countries, governments are forced to negotiate their monetary and exchange rate policies with this institution. However, the IMF is not to be blamed; dramatic problems emerge when the countries themselves run out of real cash, which is dollars. These problems in turn force them to bend their backs to the IMF to get more money. The fact is, however, that when countries come to depend on the IMF for the supply of dollars, they effectively transfer their power to decide about their economic policies to that institution. Through this, they surrender their true sovereignty, which does not reside in the nationality of the people portrayed in the currency, but in the ability to determine autonomously their country's economic policy. In most cases, they are forced to do this because of currency problems.

Many believe that all these problems would disappear if only developing countries learned to manage their own currencies in a prudent way, so that they could become standards of value for their populations. That is, the problems are attributed to the countries' bad management, not to problems caused by their inherent weakness. There are three problems with this argument, however.

First, governments of developing countries have promised to do this for decades on end and failed. This has eroded their credibility to the point that people have started to use an international currency as the yardstick to measure the extent to which they honor their promise. As the growing spontaneous dollarization all over the developing world clearly shows, restoring credibility to a currency is a very difficult task. There are very few countries that have been able to do it. Once the population's standard of value has shifted, restoring credibility involves fixing, or close to fixing, the exchange rate relative to that currency. This, in turn, implies that central banks would have to abandon their ability to exercise independent exchange rate and monetary policies. The exchange rate would be fixed, and monetary policy would have to be determined by the overwhelming objective of keeping it fixed. Thus, these countries would be renouncing the possibilities that having a domestic currency would afford them.

Second, by doing that, they would be trying to convince people that an image in a mirror is better than the real thing, which is obviously not true. Why should you take a currency that mirrors the dollar if you can have the dollar? To encourage people to do it, central banks would have to convince them that all governments in the future would manage the currency in accordance with the policies set by the acting one. Otherwise, long-term intermediation would not take place. The financing of investment in infrastructure, productive facilities, and housing, so fundamental for the economic and social development, would remain as difficult as it is today. Even if central banks could convince the population that they would always behave prudently, and that they would never contradict with their monetary policies the objective of keeping the exchange rate fixed, people would always wonder why they should not take the real thing. To convince them not to do it, banks would have to pay higher interest rates on the domestic currency. And people would always hedge. They would keep a portion of their savings in the real thing.

These two problems are related to the past or current mismanagement of a local currency. The third, however, is not. This problem is that central banks in those countries, even if well behaved, would not be able to provide a currency that people can use throughout the world. This would seem to be a triviality, just a point about the transaction costs of exchanging the local currency for an internationally tradable currency whenever you have to travel or import something or sign a contract with foreigners. In fact, these costs are not trivial. Infinitely more important, however, is the fact that without an internationally tradable currency, you have no access to the globalized financial system and all the services that it offers in addition to credit and deposits. These operations require a financial market size that no developing country can have. Without an international currency, you cannot manage your risks in the efficient ways that have become the standard in countries with internationally tradable currencies. The lack of international stability is also a problem in trade. The trade of intermediate goods is expanding enormously as connectivity and globalization are creating global chains of production, in which a component of any given product is produced in one country, the other components in other countries, and then they are assembled together in still another country. Entering into these chains with internationally tradable currencies is definitely an advantage, because costs can be estimated more accurately in the long term, transaction costs can be minimized, and risks against other international currencies can be hedged.

It is unrealistic to think that the sophisticated services now available through the international currencies, which require enormously deep markets to develop, will appear in the small, weak, and poorly capitalized markets of developing countries. Keeping a country away from these services, always costly, is becoming more so in the increasingly globalized economy. Companies in the developing countries would have to enter the global competition with a crucial disadvantage. While their competitors would be able to hedge, swap, and obtain financing wherever it is cheaper and most convenient, they would be forced to rely on the credits and services provided in their weak, shallow financial systems.

These and many other complications do not arise from the abuse of currency creation, although they become nonlinearly worse when such abuse takes place. They are imbedded in the existence of a dual standard in the economy: The standard of value that the population uses to plan their actions and the value of the money they are forced to use in their domestic transactions because their salaries, their savings, and the prices of the things they sell and buy are denominated in that currency. People throughout the developing world are showing, through spontaneous dollarization, that they want to escape from this situation.

By doing so, they are invading a field that hitherto had been dominated by macroeconomists: They are redefining the criteria that would determine what currency should predominate in a given geographical region. This belongs to a field called the optimal currency area theory. Up to now, the criteria had been that a region should have a local currency when its economy is big, moves together in the business cycles, is relatively closed to the rest of the world, trades mostly within its borders, is vulnerable to the same shocks, and enjoys free mobility of people within its borders. These conditions would allow the central bank of that region to conduct the monetary and exchange rate policies most appropriate for the circumstances.

Obviously, the theory has been developed on the assumption that the main purpose of money is to serve as an instrument of macroeconomic control. Yet, with spontaneous dollarization, people around the developing world are replacing this theory with an overwhelming criterion, that a currency should be used wherever it is the standard of value of the population. In this way, they have redefined what an optimal currency area should be: It should carry with it a standard of value.

Thus, the case for replacing the domestic currency with an international one (which, for the sake of simplification of the language I call dollarization, even if the international currency is not the dollar) exists for three main reasons, two of them having to do with the past and current performance of local currencies and the third with their ability to help in the future process of development. First, a review of the evidence shows that local currencies have failed to deliver their promised benefits. Second, they have burdened their economies with substantial costs that gravely impair their capacity to integrate into the global economy and grow. Third, dollarization brings about many benefits that are not captured in the limited conceptual framework that supports the adoption of local currencies. Those benefits are crucial in helping countries to take advantage of the unprecedented opportunities of development that the new economy of the twenty-first century is offering them. The first two reasons weaken substantially the arguments in favor of the local currencies to the point of questioning whether such benefits exist; the second reason provides strong arguments in favor of dollarization.

These are the issues I discuss in this book. Before starting the discussion, however, it is necessary to clarify some issues regarding the subject and the scope of the book. First, throughout the book, I trace a sharp distinction between dollarization (the elimination of the local currency accompanied by the adoption of a foreign one), partial or spontaneous dollarization (the partial substitution of the local currency by a foreign one), and currency boards and other schemes of fixed exchange rates. It is amazing that people frequently refer to all these regimes as "dollarized." For example, many people believed that Argentina was dollarized, either because it had a currency board (which is a way of institutionalizing a fixed-rate regime) or because it allowed dollar deposits in its banking system. The essential feature of a dollarized economy is that there is no exchange rate between the dollar and the local currency, which is also the dollar. This eliminates the foreign exchange risk, something that exists in the spontaneously dollarized and the fixed exchange rate regimes. The difference elicits completely different responses from the population in their monetary behavior precisely because the central bank cannot play with the value of their money. Monopoly currency is not the same as true currency, even if the player controlling the board promised to give back the true currency to the other players at the same exchange rate when they needed it. Imagine how confident you would feel in trusting the word of casino managers that they would not depreciate their chips once you tried to cash them at the end of a gambling night, knowing that if they wanted to, they could depreciate them with impunity.

Second, this book does not contain a review of the literature on the subject. I wrote it as a practitioner for the use of practitioners. The arguments I present here were the basis for a concrete action, the dollarization of El Salvador.

Third, while there is a difference between devaluing a currency (which refers to fixed exchange rate regimes) and allowing it to depreciate (which refers to floating currencies), I used the terms interchangeably in the book. I did this because trying to be precise sometimes results in awkward drafting, particularly when referring to countries with different foreign exchange regimes in the same sentence.

Fourth, the book deals with the problems associated with the choice of a currency regime. Thus, although I analyze the short-term problems that are so important when considering such a choice, I do not discuss whether one country should have devalued and in what magnitude in such and such conditions. The focus of the discussion is on the way different regimes react to those problems, aiming at distilling criteria that would be useful in the choice of regime.

Fifth, while many could argue that the problems arising from bad monetary management should not be taken against the domestic currency regime, I take the position that the incidence of bad management should be a criterion in the choice of regime for two main reasons. First, a regime that is prone to being badly managed in a set of countries is less likely to be the optimal one in any country belonging to such set. Second, the bad management of the past creates problems of credibility that are crucially important in monetary matters, particularly in terms of the ability of a currency to play the role of a standard of value. Such effects then condition the responses of the population to the currency regime in ways that may become structural. This has important pragmatic consequences. If the population of one country has transferred the role of standard of value to a foreign currency, that is a fact that should be taken into consideration in the choice of regime. Of course, this does not mean that the choice should be dollarization. However, if the chosen regime is that of a local currency, the accompanying policy should aim at recapturing such role for the domestic currency. The probabilities of being able to do so should be one of the criteria of the choice.

Sixth, while dollarization may be the only practical solution in some crises, I do not dwell on this argument for dollarization. A decision on whether to keep one's country currency or adopt a hard currency needs to be taken in good times. This was the way it was done in El Salvador. Quoting an anonymous referee we can say that for many developing countries, the good times are now, when international capital is flowing into the countries, and the world is showing strong economic growth. I wrote the book mainly for people who are not rushing to resolve a crisis and have the time to ponder all the presented arguments.

Seventh, when writing the book, I tried to avoid one of the pitfalls so common in the literature about monetary regimes: attributing the entire economic performance of countries to the choice and management of such regimes. Reading many of the papers on the subject, one gets the idea that the entire field of economics has collapsed to the choice of monetary regime and its proper management. In many countries, the term "economic policy" is a synonym for "macroeconomic policy," comprising mainly the manipulation of price levels, devaluation rates and their impact on the financing of the fiscal deficit, the international reserves of the central bank, and the competitiveness of the country.

There is no doubt that these issues are crucially important. There are, however, many other dimensions to economic policy. These are often neglected on the idea that a country will grow and develop if only it devalues this much, or if it chooses that monetary regime or that new band to keep the exchange rate within. Collapsing economics to exchange rate issues is done not just by professional economists but also by the population at large. To an extent unknown by the citizens of developed countries, people in most of the developing ones are acutely conscious of the main macroeconomic variables, particularly the exchange rate against the dollar and the level of international reserves. In fact, giving so much preponderance to the monetary regime and the exchange rate is natural for countries that have suffered so much from them. The stability that the citizens of the developed countries take for granted is not guaranteed in the developing ones and, because of this, keeping the economy out of catastrophic rates of inflation and devaluation is the main objective of economic policy in most developing countries.

Attaining such stability should be the minimum requisite of an economic regime, so that economic policy could turn toward the other dimensions that determine economic growth and development. The monetary regime should provide a stable and predictable scenario, so that the play of development can be staged. While such play cannot be staged in the midst of the chaotic movements of all variables so common in many developing countries, it requires much more than simple stability. This, which has been true throughout history, is becoming more so in the new world that is emerging with connectivity. Mired in the exhilarating challenges of managing monetary policy, the exchange rate and many other variables to attain an elusive path to development, many developing countries have missed the importance of the revolutionary changes that the world economy is experiencing. Economic policy must focus on taking advantage of the opportunities that this new world is opening for the developing countries. Countries should choose their monetary regime as a means to attain this objective.

It is in this context that I set the discussion of the subject in this book. However, when writing a book on the choice of monetary regimes, the emphasis should be placed on the observed differences between countries with different regimes. Otherwise, the focus of the book would be lost. It would become a book on the diversity of developing countries. For this reason, the readers will find that, while I tried to remind them about the many factors influencing development, the focus is on comparisons in terms of the exchange rate regimes.

In this respect, I tried to be fair in portraying the arguments in favor of having domestic currencies in the developing countries. This requires sharpening those arguments in the relevant aspects of the discussion, expressing them in terms of having all other things equal. Doing this opens the book to criticisms that it exaggerates the theoretical claims, oversimplifying them to the point of building a straw man to then destroy it. My sharpening of these arguments, however, does not go further than that done by their expounders. For example, most readers will have read that having access to a domestic currency allows countries to conduct independent monetary policies, or that the ability to devalue their currencies allows them to be competitive, or that the ability of central banks to issue currency allows them to control financial crises. However, when it is demonstrated that these theoretical promises have not come true, many people, including some of those who had made the assertions listed above, respond that stating these promises in this way grossly misrepresents them.

If such promises had never been made, dollarization would not raise so many eyebrows and would not attract the all-too-frequent criticisms that it would result in losing the ability to set interest rates at the optimal level, determine at will the competitiveness of the country, or save the banks in cases of crisis. Moreover, the ultimate foundation of the arguments in favor of domestic currencies, the theory of the optimal currency area, which I discuss in the last part of the book, asserts very clearly that such currencies enable the authorities of these areas to set their interest rates optimally, independently of those prevailing in the international markets, and to absorb external shocks by varying the rates at which they export and import—which is the main measure of competitiveness for those who defend the ability of devaluing or depreciating the currency. Correctly, this theory is sharp and assumes that other things would be equal. Otherwise, it could never be contradicted by reality and, because of this, it would be valueless. This, of course, does not deny that there are many theoreticians who see competitiveness from different points of view, mainly those who see it as a feature of production functions. However, they do not tend to say that a country would lose competitiveness if it could not devalue its currency.

Finally, in most international comparisons of income, I use the international dollars with purchasing power parity (PPP). I do this even if these indicators have the problem analyzed by Werner von Bankrupt in the epilogue: They have a built-in bias in favor of countries that devalue in real terms. This, of course, distorts international comparisons in favor of these countries. Still, I used these indicators because most economists use them and because I could make specific points even with the built-in bias against countries that do not devalue their currencies.

I split the discussion into three parts. In the first part, I show how local currencies have failed to deliver the promises that conventional theory made on their behalf, focusing on trade, the financial system, and the overall rates of growth. In the second part, I show how local currencies increase the financial risks of a country, focusing on the currency and financial crises that have affected developing countries in the last several decades. In the third part, I analyze the issues of currency choice through two different conceptions of what is an optimal currency area. At the end of the book there is a chapter with conclusions and an epilogue in which Werner von Bankrupt discusses the art of buying countries with a buck and a half.

Part One   **The Unfulfilled Promises
of Local Currencies**

# Chapter 1 The Standard of Value and the Reversed Liquidity Trap

Money started its long career in history as a means of exchange: the currency that everyone accepts in payment. With time, however, it evolved into something much broader than this in three steps, each larger than the precedent. First, it led to the creation of the banking system, which multiplied the money actually printed by the sovereign so that in addition to the currency bills, people could use checks and other drawing instruments against their deposits in the banks. In modern times, money exercises its payment function in many other ways, including credit and debit cards, as well as the electronic impulses needed to effect payments on the Internet. Second, people started to use money not just as a means of exchange but also as an asset with a rental price. This rental price is the net result of the interest rate and the rate of inflation, the latter being measured in terms of the change in the price at which people can exchange monetary assets for other things—which produce either capital gains or capital losses, depending on whether the prices of the other things are going down or up, respectively. People choose to keep money as currency bills, checking accounts, and interest-bearing accounts in the banking system or to spend it depending on the interest rate, the capital gains or losses afforded by money, and the cost of converting one of these forms into the other. Third, money became the standard of value for the population and, through this, the abstract indicator giving meaning to the economic obligations established in the main mechanism that society has to control economic activity: contracts. When developing this dimension of its functions, money became the main economic instrument linking the past, the present, and the future.

Money multiplied its impact on the economy in each of these steps. With the development of new payment mechanisms, it reduced transaction costs. When it became an asset, it propelled the development of financial intermediation, leading to the creation of credit and, through this, to the separation of the identity of the saver from that of the investor. This multiplied exponentially the possibilities of funding investment. Because of the existence of credit, an investor with an idea did not need to have money to turn it into reality.

While crucial for the functioning of the economy, money is linked inextricably to the financial system in the first two functions. By becoming the standard of value, however, it became central to the operation of all economic activity, independently of whether the financial system is involved or not. Of course, this dimension of money is also essential for the functioning of the financial sector, which is a system of contracts. Yet, its impact on the economy overspills the realm of financial operations and far exceeds what we can measure through the monetary and financial statistics, which focus on the size of the contracts held by the financial system. The future performance of the economy does not depend solely on these financial contracts. They are, in fact, subsidiary to other, more important contracts that establish what people will do with the money intermediated by the financial system, regulating the flow of real goods and services across the economy. All of them are denominated in monetary units. When money becomes the standard of value, it gets ingrained in the brains of people, providing them with the main source of market information and the means to plan for the future. Playing this role, money floats in the environment without having been created. It is an abstract measure of value, but it exists with full reality in people's minds, in the contracts they engage in, and in the daily calculations they make about the size and composition of their consumption and saving. In spite of its abstractness, people trust in it to denominate their pensions, to transfer legacies to their children, to plan their future. It is the blood of the economy.

Thus, for people, money is not just a currency but also a yardstick that they use to measure value, carry out transactions, keep their accounts, and provide the denomination of all their contracts, including those related to their savings and investments. To play those roles, money should *keep* its value through time.

The fact that money is so central to the operation of the entire economy makes it possible for the issuer of the means of payment to manipulate practically all aspects of economic behavior by changing the rate at which it creates money. If, for example, the central bank creates more money than the public demands, the people spend it, and this increases demand for goods and services. The increased demand can have two different effects on the economy, depending on the ability of the economy to react to it. If it cannot augment its production, the expanding demand leaks into the balance of payments with other countries, increasing imports and reducing exports (as enterprises sell in the domestic market goods that otherwise they would have exported). If the economy doesn't have enough foreign exchange to pay for the trade deficit, the value of the currency falls relative to other currencies and the excessive demand is turned into inflation through devaluation. None of this, however, would happen if the capacity utilization in the economy were lower than 100 percent. That is, if enterprises are not using their machinery to the full, there is unemployment, *and if this is not the result of a shift in the composition of demand*, additional demand spurs more production without creating much inflation or balance of payments problems. I have emphasized the condition in italics. It simply means that if the low capacity utilization were due to a shift in the composition of demand, higher monetary creation would also lead to inflation and balance of payments problems. Think, for example, of a country producing horse carriages in the 1910s. Its capacity utilization would have fallen to almost zero with the popularization of the automobile, and no monetary policy would have been able to increase it.

John Maynard Keynes, one of the greatest and most conservative monetary economists in modern history, was the first to expound on the possibility of expanding production by creating money. He noted that in some circumstances, which he defined very specifically, the activity of the economy could be constrained by the lack of money. That is, when money itself is scarce, its value keeps increasing relative to that of all other goods in the economy. In such circumstances, people prefer to hold on to money rather than spend it. On the other side of the financial system, potential borrowers cannot find investments that would be more attractive than holding money. This, in turn, leads to low investment in real assets, high unemployment, and depression. The solution to this problem was to create additional money, thus lowering its relative value and enticing people to spend it. Inflation, the normal effect of rapid monetary creation, would not take place because capacity utilization would be low. Thus, the greater demand for goods and services would not increase prices but would stimulate production.

This insight created macroeconomics, the art of manipulating real variables through a nominal instrument, monetary policy. For the macroeconomist, money is a policy variable that governments can use to affect the level of production, prices, and the aggregate relationships with other economies. To do this, governments should be able to *change* the value of money, relative to the goods and services traded within and without the economy.

Thus, conducting monetary policies requires a balance between two contradictory objectives, so that its macroeconomic manipulation, aimed at *changing* the value of money, does not destroy the essential role of money, which is *keeping* its value through time. If money loses this essential property, it also loses its ability to affect economic behavior in the ways intended by the central banks. Instead, people react in ways that introduce serious instability in the economy and constrain its ability to function normally and grow.

This contradiction is at the core of the problems of developing countries. Through excessive manipulation, their currencies have lost the ability to provide a standard of value to their populations with grave consequences that I explore in this part of the book.

Keynes was quite conscious of the need to keep the value of money through time, and he made this clear in his writings. Even if this is not widely recognized, Keynes's recommendations to overcome the Great Depression were rooted on the idea that money should keep a constant value. He based his advice to create money on the fact that during the Depression money was becoming dearer. He developed his main arguments in two great books, *A Treatise on Money* and *The General Theory of Employment, Interest and Money*. In the second book, he claimed that the root of the Great Depression was that the value of money relative to produced goods and investment was increasing. For this reason, people preferred to keep their wealth in monetary assets rather than invest it in increasing production. In an ideal world, this problem would be resolved by decreasing interest rates. In reality, however, there is a floor to the interest rates, which cannot be lower than the cost of financial intermediation. In the 1930s, he argued, the rate of interest that would attract investment in capital goods was below the cost of intermediation. That is, money had become too expensive for the good of society as the world was in a *liquidity trap*—people preferred liquidity to investment. He advised monetary creation through the financing of fiscal deficits to cheapen money to a reasonable level.

Keynes's two books dealt with closed economies; that is, economies that had no contact with the rest of the world. He was consistent with the same advice when addressing open economies. In a popular tract, *The Economic Consequences of Mr. Churchill*, he advised the devaluation of the pound sterling, which Winston Churchill had grossly and arbitrarily revalued against other currencies at the end of the 1920s. In this and in many of his other actions, he kept in mind the damage that devaluing or appreciating money could cause to the economy. That is, he appreciated monetary stability and showed this in his writings and in the creation he coauthored, the Bretton Woods system, which regulated the international monetary relations from the end of World War II to the late 1960s.

This system linked currencies through fixed exchange rates, which countries could change only through certain procedures managed by the International Monetary Fund (IMF). The emphasis, however, was not on the possibility of change, but on the desirability of keeping the value of the different currencies internationally. This would give predictability to international trade, investment, and their associated capital flows. To work, this system demanded consistency between the rate of domestic money creation and the exchange rate. This meant that the rate of monetary creation had to be the same around the world, corrected by some domestic factors, prominent among them the rate of growth of production of each of the economies. This correction was needed because an economy demands more money the more it grows, and having the same growth rate for all of them would result in imbalances in the exchange rates, as the currency of the fastest growing countries would become domestically dearer and could generate depressing pressures in the domestic markets. Thus, to make sure that exchange rate stability existed, the system focused on regulating the rate of domestic money creation so that it would be consistent with keeping a fixed exchange rate, even if such rates could diverge across countries. The United Nations created the IMF to make sure that this happened. To emphasize further that money should keep its role as a standard of value, the United Nations established that the worst offense a country can commit against the rules of the IMF is having multiple exchange rates for its currency.

The system allowed changes in the exchange rate as exceptional events. Successful exporters experienced an increasing demand for their own currency in terms of the international currencies, creating a wedge between the official exchange rate and the one prevailing in the private markets. This demanded an official revaluation of the currency, which countries carried out under the oversight of the IMF. The same happened when the price of the currency in the private markets was lower than the official one. In both cases, the country had to unify the exchange rate by appreciating or devaluing it, according to the case.

Thus, in Keynes's view, there should be only one international standard of value. Domestic standards would be linked to it by fixed, predictable exchange rates. At the time, gold was the standard of value across the world. Central banks kept gold as well as the two international currencies—the U.S. dollar and the pound sterling—as international reserves to carry out transactions across borders and protect the value of their currencies. With time, the dollar became the only international currency. It based its international role on the credibility of the United States' promise to deliver gold at a given price if other countries presented dollars for collection.

Events superseded Keynes in two main ways. First, during their recovery from the devastation of World War II, Europe and Japan experienced high rates of export growth and accumulated dollar reserves much in excess of what the United States could back with its gold reserves. One country, France, began to demand its gold in exchange for the dollars it kept in its central bank. The U.S. government decided to demonetize the gold—that is, to sever the link between its gold reserves and the value of the dollar. From that moment on, a dollar was no longer a claim on a certain amount of gold, but just a dollar. As the common saying states, a dollar is a dollar is a dollar. That effectively floated the dollar against the gold. The other countries floated against the dollar, and the international system that prevails today came into being.

Flotation came none too soon because a second factor had come into play that rendered impractical the general system of fixed exchange rates. Before the late 1960s, inconsistencies between the domestic rates of monetary creation and the exchange rates were common, creating opportunities for monetary arbitrage. For example, people could deposit money in countries with higher inflation and interest rates to enjoy the latter and then convert their funds to the international currency at the fixed exchange rate, which ensured that the gains obtained by the higher interest rates in the domestic currency would become gains in the international currency. The magnitude of these inconsistencies, however, was not enough to endanger the exchange rates across countries because the costs of transaction of international capital movements were too high. In fact, most countries imposed controls on the international flows of money. Then, in the 1960s, the development of communications allowed for the transfer of money through countries at very high speeds and with low transaction costs. At the same time, the Eurodollar market, a market for international dollar financing, was created in London with part of the excess dollars that floated around the world, providing resources for capital flows that were not under the control of any government. With costs of transaction amounting to practically nothing and with plenty of dollars to move across borders, the margin of inconsistency that would be admissible by the system of fixed exchange rates collapsed too. Capital flowed between countries at lightning speed, arbitrating interest rates, and eventually speculating against the ability of countries to keep their exchange rates fixed. Governments recognized that they could not win the war against technology and gradually dismantled their controls on capital movements across countries.

The emergence of these new capital flows caused a structural transformation of the international markets. Prior to the late 1960s, international economic relationships were led by trade, and financial capital flows mainly settled trade transactions. While there were autonomous capital flows, they were mainly related to direct foreign investment in productive facilities. Financial capital flows (money transferred from one country to another to invest in financial assets) were almost inexistent. For this reason, the exchange rate was mostly determined by trade flows and the relationship between domestic monetary creation and such flows. That is, currencies tended to appreciate when they ran current account surpluses in the balance of payments, and to depreciate when they ran deficits. Then, in the 1970s, capital flows predominated and their autonomous determinants, mainly the differences between the interest rates in different countries, became the major determinants of the *market* exchange rate. When the dollar-equivalent interest rate of a currency increases relative to the dollar rates, the currency tends to appreciate, and the other way around, so that if a country wishes to change its exchange rate for trade or other reasons, it has to act through financial variables.

Flotation presented several theoretical advantages when seen from the point of view of using money as an instrument to control the rate of expansion of demand and, through it, the performance of the economy. The ability to print their own money would allow countries to devise their own monetary policies, independently of the conditions of other countries, and let the exchange rate absorb the differences across countries, not occasionally, but continuously. These gradual adjustments would prevent the violent shifts in the exchange rates that had prevailed in the last few years of the Bretton Woods system, which had produced some disastrous results not just for developing countries but also for some developed ones. Moreover, monetary creation seemed to provide the means to eliminate or drastically alleviate the business cycles, diminishing volatility and keeping the economy growing at its maximum potential. Countries experiencing a slowdown in their economic activity could print more money to lower interest rates and stimulate domestic demand. Of course, the domestic demand would increase for both domestically produced and imported goods and services. Yet, increasing the supply of the domestic currency would result in its depreciation relative to other currencies. With the currency devalued, demand for imports would fall and the newly created demand would concentrate on the domestic production. Additionally, devaluation would increase the profitability of exporting, which would give a further boost to domestic production.

Of course, there is another side to this logic. When domestic demand is growing too fast relative to its potential, the central bank must reduce the rate of monetary creation to slow down the growth of demand, generating the reverse of the process launched by increasing the rate of monetary creation. Inevitably, when you make money scarcer, it tends to appreciate, domestically and in the international markets. Following the same logic, the export growth rate would decline and your imports would increase. Rather than spurring demand for goods and services, you would induce a certain degree of recession. Manipulating domestic demand required both kinds of actions. The idea, however, was to use the capacity to do it moderately. Care had to be taken not to spur too much demand in the troughs of the business cycle, so that it would not have to be repressed too much in the peaks. In this way, monetary policy would smooth out the costly fluctuations of the economy, increasing its efficiency.

Theoretically, flotation would make countries more resilient to external shocks as well. These are unpredictable events that affect the economy positively or negatively, such as natural disasters and shifts in the relative prices of the goods and services that the country exports and imports. For example, a fall in the prices of the country's main exports would be a negative shock. Because of this, the production of such goods would become less profitable, the less-efficient producers would fail, and unemployment would soar. Yet, if the government were able to shift the domestic relative prices in such a way that production remained profitable, employment would be sustained. Devaluations can have this effect by reducing the burden of wages (which are denominated in local currency) on the sales price of tradable goods (which is denominated in dollars in the international markets). Of course, the rate of devaluation has to be kept higher than the rate of inflation until a new equilibrium is reached, sustained by higher exports and lower imports. Otherwise, the devaluation would only increase the rate of inflation and the relative prices between wages and tradable goods would remain the same. Thereafter, the two variables can be kept moving in a synchronous fashion.

These theoretical advantages, however, were lost in the developing countries, mainly because there, Keynes's followers distorted his ideas so that *Keynesianism* became the synonym of loose monetary policies. Forgetting that he had advised monetary looseness as a means to resolve a particular problem—the liquidity trap—many developing countries, particularly in Latin America, kept on creating money at full throttle throughout their business cycles. By doing that, they debased their currencies and trapped themselves in a world where Keynes's insights are still true but they work in reverse. As experience clearly shows, in that world, the liquidity trap becomes worse the more money you create.

Most frequently, countries get into crises after creating an artificial divergence between the rate of inflation and devaluation for a prolonged period, with the former exceeding the latter. They come to this situation by creating money in excessive amounts. Rather than spurring growth (except maybe in the very short run at the beginning of the process), this generates high rates of inflation and wide current account deficits in the balance of payments, which become depressive after a while. Central banks then intervene to reduce the rate of currency depreciation, which they do by selling dollars in exchange for domestic currency. When doing so, they lose their dollar reserves until they disappear. Then they call the IMF to get more dollars.

By that time, the official exchange rate is grossly overvalued in terms of what its price would be without the intervention of the central bank because the rate of devaluation has been lower than the rate of inflation for too long a period. In this situation, since local wages and prices directly linked to them increase at the domestic rate of inflation while the prices of goods and services produced abroad increase at the slower rate of devaluation, domestic producers cannot compete with cheaper imports. Exports collapse for the same reason. Production declines. Unemployment is high. The recessive trends that Keynes noted are already at play. Typically, people suspect that the government will have to devalue the currency much faster and, having their concept of value tied to the dollar, withdraw money from the banks to convert it into dollars. This further accelerates the rate at which the central bank loses reserves, which in turn leads to higher devaluation. The devaluations themselves confirm the expectations of the people who turned their local currency holdings into dollars, making capital gains in local currency terms when the currency is devalued. The central bank could compensate for this effect by increasing its interest rates. Yet, as it happened to Dema Gogo, if interest rates are increased beyond a certain limit, the government loses its credibility. In fact, very high interest rates confirm the suspicions of those who believe that the rate of devaluation will continue to be high. People keep on buying dollars, further depressing the economy, while the reserves of the central bank plunge.

When the door of this peculiar liquidity trap shuts, the IMF comes in and normally says that there is no way it would lend the country dollars to finance further the excessive monetary creation. It offers to provide the dollars only if the government meets two conditions. One of these is to devalue the currency, so that its price reaches equilibrium in the free markets, without the dollar sales of the central bank. The other is to impose a restrictive monetary policy, so the growth of domestic demand is constrained to the level that would give equilibrium to the new exchange rate. These measures go in the direction of, first, finding the true value of the domestic currency in foreign currency terms and, then, give consistency to it, so that demand for it firms up at the new price. That is, in this moment, the IMF goes back to the old principles established by Keynes, although in our times of flotation, equilibrium in the exchange rate does not mean keeping the same value but devaluing at the same rate as inflation.

No politician likes such conditions. As with Dema Gogo, in most cases, the excessive monetary creation was directed to finance the government deficits, so that reducing the rate of such creation means stopping most, if not all, of the pet projects. Moreover, large devaluations mean reducing the real wages to the workers and, in the interconnected modern world, causing terrible losses to the banking system. The IMF offers help with the banks, which, in any case, also need dollars desperately.

With no other means to obtain dollars, countries agree to meet the IMF's conditions. At that time, they experience a catastrophic devaluation and then the central bank puts the brakes on monetary creation. Now the objective is to make domestic money dearer in a sustainable way, domestically and internationally, so that people do not spend it as freely as before the arrival of the IMF. While before this arrival the rate of inflation was higher than the rate of devaluation, now the rate of devaluation must be higher. This is necessary to ensure that inflation does not dissipate the effect of devaluation, leaving the economy as unstable as before. The population impoverishes. The prices of all exportable and importable goods and services increase, while their wages and the prices of the other goods and services increase at a slower pace.

Eventually, the economy recovers. Hopefully, after the currency has reached its equilibrium, the government will keep the rates of inflation and devaluation running together, so that they do not fall into another grave inconsistency unless the government is forced to create a new wedge between the two by external shocks. If everything goes well, the country begins to grow again, the central bank gains reserves, and stability returns.

There is a lingering effect, however. The population does not easily forget the traumatic effect of crises and devaluations. Through time, the repetition of these cycles increasingly alienated the population of developing countries from their currencies. Having lost their fundamental role, serving as standards of value, these currencies failed to honor the promises that theory had made on their behalf.

What has just been described is the developing countries' version of Keynes's liquidity trap. As in the case that he described, the people's preference for liquidity depresses production—except that in this case, *the liquidity they prefer is denominated in a foreign currency.* For this reason, Keynes's logic works in reverse when seen from the point of view of the local currency. In the case he studied, the Great Depression, people preferred to hoard money because doing so was more profitable than investing in productive assets. This happened because money was appreciating relative to other assets. In the developing countries' case, people prefer to hoard foreign currency because doing so is more profitable than holding assets denominated in domestic currency *and* productive assets. The problem is not that the interest rate in the local currency cannot decrease as much as people would demand to invest in real assets, but instead that such rate cannot increase as much as people would demand to stop hoarding a foreign currency. Interpreting Keynes's prescriptions in a naïve way to overcome the depressive state of the country only worsens the situation. The more domestic money you create, the more you increase the value of the dollar in domestic currency terms and the more people spend the local currency in exchange for dollars.

People react in this reversed way because their standard of value is the foreign currency. I could have presented the argument in Keynes's way, saying that people cling to dollars because they are becoming dearer, and the only way to resolve the problem is to lower the benefits of having dollars, so that people would turn to invest in real goods in the country. I did not do this, however, because developing countries do not have the power to create dollars and make them more plentiful. The only way they can shift the relative price of the two currencies is to make their own scarce by stopping its creation. This is ironic because many people believe that the ability to print local currencies is useful to resolve crises in those countries.

The two versions of the liquidity trap also diverge in terms of their likely frequency. In the developed countries, the liquidity trap is a rare occurrence, the result of relatively rare qualitative changes in behavior, while it is endemic in the developing ones. Of course, people in both kinds of countries always tend to cling to a certain amount of liquidity for transaction and precautionary purposes. Such amount is a function of the probabilities of needing different amounts of liquid resources at any given moment in the near future and the costs of transforming illiquid assets into liquid forms. Financial development tends to reduce the demand for strictly liquid assets (currency bills and coins), as payments can be realized through checks and credit or debit cards, or electronically, debiting accounts kept in a less liquid form. Yet, they always prefer to keep liquid a certain portion of their resources, and this is normal.

The problem begins when people start demanding money for speculative purposes—that is, because they believe that money will appreciate relative to all other assets in the economy. This is what can effectively lead to a downward spiral in economic activity. This happens only in quite special circumstances in developed countries. However, it happens endemically in developing ones, where the speculative motive to hold money is always there, but associated with an international currency. It is endemic because the possibility of incurring in capital losses by holding the local currency is not a risk but a certainty in countries where the currency sinks continuously. People hedge against this capital loss continuously, too, keeping part of their resources abroad or, at least, denominated in dollars. When doing that, they create a liquidity trap in which the door is always half shut, ready to fully close if a currency crisis takes place.

The endemic presence of this liquidity trap gravely reduces the ability of the local currency to provide financing and, therefore, reduces the power of the central banks in ways that frequently are not visible. To understand what is happening, you have to see what is *not* happening, what local currencies do not do in those countries.

In this part of the book, I show some of the main consequences of this reversal of realities and how such consequences invalidate many of the arguments to have a local currency in those countries. In the next chapter, I review one dimension of the unfulfilled promises of floating local currencies: their ability to provide plentiful financial resources at low financial costs. Then, in the following chapters, I analyze their ability to spur export growth in the long term, their ability to keep economic growth strong through the years, and their ability to provide a lender of last resort.

In this discussion and throughout the book, I use the dollar as the international currency to express the exchange rates and the rates of devaluations when dealing with groups of countries. I do so for two main reasons. First, the dollar is the international currency at this time. Most of the international reserves of developing countries are in dollars, 62 percent of their outstanding long-term debt is in dollars,[1] and all major indicators (such as income and income per capita in international currency with purchasing power parity, balance of payments accounts, international flows of money, and international price quotations of most products among them) are also in dollars. When asked about the income per capita of a country, people answer in dollars, so that it is the international standard of value as well. The second reason is that the behavior of groups of developing countries shows a distinct correlation with their exchange rate against the dollar in all dimensions of economic activity. I use the exchange rates against other currencies only in some particular cases when dealing with specific countries.

## Chapter 2 The Unfulfilled Promises
## in the Financial System

International currencies can play the role of standards of value for several reasons. The main one is that they cover large and diversified areas, which can meet all the economic needs of their inhabitants with world-class quality and efficiency. Because of this diversification, substitution effects predominate over the income effect when they depreciate relative to other currencies. In this way, for example, when the dollar devalues relative to the yen, people buy fewer Japanese and more American goods and services. The income effect is practically zero because prices and real wages measured in the domestic currency remain the same. Thus, even if their exchange rates are unstable, the inflation rates in these economies are low.

In other words, people living inside the area of an international currency do not feel the fluctuations of the exchange rate in their daily activities. Their perceptions of value are not affected by such fluctuations. The behavior of the euro and the dollar in recent times provides a clear example of this. While their exchange rate fluctuated by more than 20 percent in both directions since 1999, the inflation rates have remained low in the two areas. The same can be said about the fluctuations of the exchange rates of the pound sterling and the yen against the dollar and against each other. The inflation rates in the United Kingdom and Japan have not been affected by these movements. Equally, their domestic interest rates have not been affected by the exchange rate fluctuations.

In contrast, if a local currency is devalued in a poorly diversified economy, as all the developing ones are, the cost of the many goods and services that it does not produce will increase by the magnitude of the devaluation. There would be no substitution effect in those areas of the economy, which include not just finished but also intermediate products used in the local production. Even the prices of nontradables experience increases because they use tradables as inputs. Sometimes, as in the case of domestic transportation and electricity and water supply, most of the inputs of the nontradables are tradables (equipment, oil, and other similar products). Thus, due to their poor diversification, the economies of developing countries experience strong inflationary pressures when devaluing their currency.

Government may react to such pressures either prudently or imprudently. First, if it behaves prudently, it would impose a restrictive monetary policy, aimed at keeping nominal wages constant. In this case, the real wage would decline and the growth rate of domestic demand would drop. The rate of devaluation would be higher than the rate of inflation, and a real devaluation would have taken place. If the government behaves imprudently, its monetary policy would be expansive, wages would increase, inflation would pick up, and the impact of the devaluation would be nullified.

The nature of the problem with the currencies of developing countries can be appreciated by realizing that in any of these cases, people would link devaluations with the erosion of value—in one case, the value of their wages; in the other, of their nominal currency. In any of them, prudent and imprudent, events would create the incentives for people to transfer the standard of value to an international currency.

Thus, the first reason leading to the transfer of the standard of value from the developing countries to international currencies is the poor diversification of their economies, which makes domestic prices highly sensitive to the fluctuations of the exchange rate.

A second reason for this transfer is that local currencies in the developing countries have a very limited purchasing power in geographical terms. They are not accepted beyond the boundaries of their countries. Thus, people in those countries need at least two currencies: their own, which is accepted only in the national territory, and an international one—most commonly the dollar—which is accepted both inside and outside that territory. It is only logical that the currency with more acceptance should impose its standard of value.

The third reason for the transfer of the standard of value is that for a long time the model of floating currencies was interpreted asymmetrically in the developing countries. Floating means going up and down, gently if possible. In nearly all developing countries and for most of the last several decades, however, the benefits of the system were seen largely on the side of devaluation. That is, within flotation, they chose to pursue a policy of weak currencies, under the assumption that weakness implies more flexibility.

This is understandable. According to the conventional model, devaluations are associated with low interest rates and expansionary monetary policies, which in the short term are always politically preferable to the stringent ones associated with sustainable currency appreciations. On the trade side, real devaluations are supposed to lead to export booms. According to the model, these are advantages that cannot be attained with a fixed exchange rate. Thus, the policy of expansionary monetary policies and devaluations (weak currency) seemed much more attractive than keeping the exchange rate fixed or appreciating it (strong currency).

Developing countries responded to this appeal, until very recently, with a twist. All of the supposed benefits of weak currencies are associated with real devaluations—that is, those that take place when the rate of devaluation exceeds the rate of inflation. As Dema Gogo discovered, devaluing and then letting the inflation rate catch up with the rate of devaluation leaves everything the same as before the devaluation, except for a higher inflation rate. Thus, the art of devaluing in real terms efficiently consists in minimizing the inflationary impact of devaluations, so that the changes in the real variables are very close to those in the nominal ones. For instance, if you want to devalue by 5 percent, it is much more efficient to do it by devaluing in nominal terms by that magnitude with zero inflation than devaluing by 105 percent while allowing the inflation rate to increase to 100 percent.

Yet, since at least the late 1970s, developing countries have shown a marked preference for managing their real exchange rates through large nominal devaluations, which they carried out even when their objective was to have much smaller or zero real devaluations. To see this point, three main periods during the last two decades can be identified: a period of real devaluations from 1985 to 1997; one of stability of the real exchange rate, from 1997 to early 2003; and a very short one of real appreciation from that date to the end of 2004.

Except for the last period, the rates of nominal devaluations exceeded by an ample margin the changes in the real exchange rate.

During the first period, a sample of seventy-five developing countries (which excluded the twenty-two countries that devalued the most in a larger sample) devalued so enthusiastically that the average nominal exchange rate at the end of the period was 336 percent of its initial value. Yet, the average real exchange rate depreciated by only 9 percent, which means that about 97 percent of the nominal devaluation was wasted in inflation. It was as if to get from one place to another nine miles away you took a train and ran against the direction of its movement, but a little slower, so that by the time you reached your destination, you would have jogged 336 miles. You would be justified in asking if it would not be easier to run the nine miles in the right direction. The question would be even more justified for the twenty-one countries that appreciated their currencies in real terms while depreciating them in nominal terms by allowing the rate of inflation to overcome the rate of devaluation.

From 1997 on, the rate of devaluation in both nominal and real terms tended to abate, so that the countries in a similar sample of seventy-six developing countries kept their real exchange rate constant from January 1997 to February 2003.[1] To do this, however, they devalued their currencies by 80 percent in nominal terms while allowing domestic prices to increase by the same amount. That is, they ran eighty miles to stay in the same place. Then, from March 2003 to December 2004, they allowed their currencies to appreciate in real terms by 17 percent. They did that, however, while appreciating their nominal rates at only 6 percent.[2] If they had appreciated their currencies by 17 percent in nominal terms (the rate at which they appreciated in real terms) their inflation rates would have been about 10 percent lower.

Thus, on average, and for most of the last several decades, developing countries went down the slope that terrified Dema Gogo so much, trying to devalue at a faster pace than the inflation that their devaluations in turn induced, attaining real devaluations that were just a tiny fraction of their nominal ones. By the time the currencies of developing countries began to appreciate in early 2003, their value was just a very minor fraction of what it had been twenty years before. It should not be a surprise that the people suffering from their debasement chose an international currency as their standard of value.

In summary, therefore, the local currencies of developing countries face three formidable obstacles to become standards of value. Only one of them is related to mismanagement of the currency. The other two are related to the limitations of currencies covering weak and poorly diversified economies, which offer a very limited supply of goods that can be exchanged for them.

Today, the problem is that regardless of its origins, the transfer of the standard of value to other currencies has introduced structural changes in behavior that gravely impair the ability of the local currency regimes to deliver their theoretical promises.

In this chapter, I review one dimension of the unfulfilled promises of floating local currencies: their ability to provide plentiful financial resources at low financial costs. For this purpose, I begin by analyzing the behavior of interest rates, then that of the volumes of resources intermediated, and then how these two variables interact with each other to give shape to the financial systems of the developing countries.

According to conventional theory, the main advantage of having a local currency is that you can detach your monetary environment from that prevailing in the rest of the world. In this way, if the interest rate in the international markets is too high for your position in your business cycle, you can print domestic money, which would at the same time increase the supply of credit and reduce the local interest rate. Given that the supply of the domestic currency would increase relative to that of foreign currencies, another effect would be that the first would depreciate relative to the second. The effect of the increased supply of money would be taken by the exchange rate. This, however, would be immaterial. The crucial fact would be that interest rates and supply of credit would be disconnected from the conditions prevailing in other financial markets.

Of course, for this to happen, the local interest rate should not be influenced by the rate of devaluation. This is what happens in countries where the local currency is the population's standard of value. In the developing countries, however, interest rates tend to increase along with the expected rate of devaluation because savers measure the yield they want from their deposits in the international currency, which is their standard of value. This breaks the model on the side of the interest rates. In these circumstances, the freedom to increase the supply of money and let the exchange rate take the adjustment does not result in a reduction of interest rates. On the contrary, it results in their increase.

In fact, the rates of interest in developing countries tend to be equal to those in an international currency, most commonly the dollar, plus a country risk, plus the risk of expected devaluations. Of course, the interest rates may be set below that level, but then the volume of intermediated resources would fall. Thus, when we say that the interest rate must increase when the currency is devalued, we refer to the interest rate that attracts a given percent of gross domestic product (GDP) in resources, which we may call the equilibrium rate of interest. As explained later in this chapter, this equilibrium rate varies widely across developing countries and it varies in accordance with the rate of devaluation. That is, the amount of resources attracted for intermediation as a percent of GDP by any given interest rate tends to decline as the rate of devaluation increases.

Does this happen in reality? Do the equilibrium interest rates in developing countries tend to increase with the rate of devaluation?

We can start our analysis by emphasizing the crucial role of interest rates in the determination of exchange rate movements. This can be done by examining a phenomenon that has been the subject of substantial controversy: the deep depreciation of the dollar that took place from 2001 to roughly the end of 2004 and its subsequent recovery in 2005.

Quite frequently, the depreciation of the dollar is blamed on the large current account deficits of the United States, which in turn are blamed on its large fiscal deficits. This explanation, however, ignores the fact that the current account deficit started in the late 1990s, when the country had a large fiscal surplus and when the dollar had a tendency to appreciate against other international currencies. It also ignores the fact that the dollar started to recover from its depreciation in 2005, when the twin deficits were still raging and actually increasing. That is, tracing the depreciation of the dollar to the fiscal and current account deficits would require assuming that the sign of the relationships among the three variables shifted from positive to negative to positive again in the last few years.

Figure 2.1 shows a relationship that held through periods of fiscal surpluses and deficits and of dollar appreciation and depreciation against the euro: that existing between the ratio of the central bank interest rates in the United States and the euro area and the *subsequent* rate of annual appreciation or depreciation of the dollar against the euro. As shown by the figure, the dollar initially appreciated against the euro because the central bank interest rate in the United States (the federal reserve discount rate) was substantially higher than its counterpart in the euro area (the marginal lending facility). The

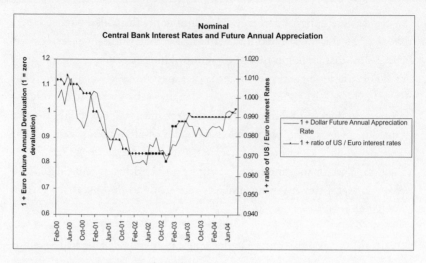

Figure 2.1: Central Bank nominal interest rates and future annual rates of currency appreciation/depreciation. *Source:* International Financial Statistics of the International Monetary Fund.

dollar's rate of appreciation began to decline in early 2001, when the spread of the U.S. interest rates over those in the euro area began to fall. By mid-2001 (shown in the figure as mid-2000), the dollar's rate of appreciation had turned negative because the spread had fallen below a certain critical value one year before. After that moment, the dollar depreciated at an accelerating annual rate until, around early 2002, the rate of depreciation stabilized along with the spread. Then, the spread started to enlarge again in early 2003, and the dollar's rate of depreciation declined until, by May 2005, it became a rate of appreciation.

Of course, the fiscal and the current account deficits may have an effect on the rate of appreciation/depreciation of the currency. The point is that, other things equal, the rate of change of the exchange rate against another currency tends to vary in direct proportion to the spread between the local currency interest rates and those prevailing in the other currency. Other factors influencing the rate of appreciation/depreciation include many other variables that can prompt shifts in the perceptions of the relative country risks, which of course may include the fiscal and *balance of payments* deficits. (I emphasize the balance of payments deficits because they could affect the international monetary balances. Current account deficits by themselves do not affect these balances if they are counterbalanced by capital inflows.)

Changes in risk would be reflected in the relationship between the interest rates and the rates of appreciation/devaluation as a shift in the level of the spread over foreign interest rates that would be needed to keep the exchange rate in equilibrium. As discussed below, changes in the exchange rate do not tend to generate shifts in the perceptions of risk in the United States. In contrast, they do so in developing countries, in such a way that while interest rates influence the rate of devaluation, the devaluation in turn affects the equilibrium rate of interest.

We can now examine the effect of changes in the exchange rate on the local economy in two dimensions: the rate of inflation and the interest rates. Figure 2.2 shows how the inflation rate responds differently to the rate of devaluation in the United States and the developing countries. As visible in the top panel, the inflationary impact of the exchange rate movements of the dollar against the euro on the U.S. economy is so negligible that the two variables moved in the opposite direction during January 2000–June 2004, a period that included interludes of substantial dollar appreciation and depreciation against that currency. In contrast, as seen in the lower panel, the average rate of inflation in a sample of seventy-six developing countries tended to increase when their currencies devalued against the dollar.

We can now see what happens with the domestic interest rates as a consequence of the shifts in the exchange rate. To do this, we compare the domestic nominal interest rates with the rate of currency depreciation/appreciation of the previous twelve months. The top panel of figure 2.3 shows that the interest rates in the United States declined while the dollar depreciated against the euro. In contrast, the lower panel shows that the domestic rates of interest tended to increase with the rate of devaluation in the developing countries. The bulge on top of the curve shows the increases in interest rates over the average trend caused by the Asian crisis and the 2001 events. Combining the results of the two panels, we may conclude that the domestic rate of interest increases with the rate of devaluation in developing countries and that sometimes, when something happens, as in the case of the Asian crisis or 2001, the effect is worse. These results did not change materially when the outliers were removed, leaving a sample of seventy-six instead of 114 countries.

Thus, it is clear that the responses of the economies of developing countries to shifts in the exchange rate are quite different from those of the U.S. economy. While the monetary environment in the United States is impervious to such shifts, those of the developing countries are deeply affected by them, both in terms of inflation rates and in terms of interest rates. In other words,

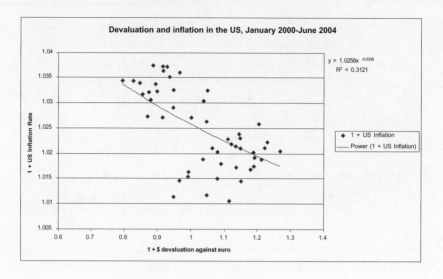

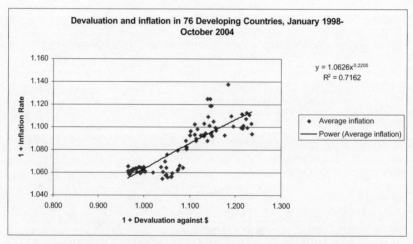

Figure 2.2: Devaluations and inflation, United States and developing countries. *Source:* International Financial Statistics of the International Monetary Fund.

the evidence shows that the behavior of the currencies of developing countries is conditioned by the dollar, which remains the standard of value in most of them. As in the United States, when central banks in these countries reduce their interest rates relative to those prevailing in the dollar markets, the effect is a depreciation of their currency; in contrast to the United States, however, their inflation rates go up as a result of the devaluation itself. Worse still, the equilibrium rate of interest also goes up, forcing them to keep their dollar-

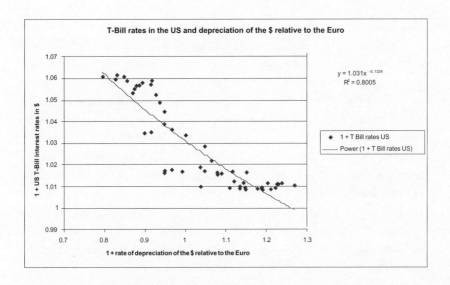

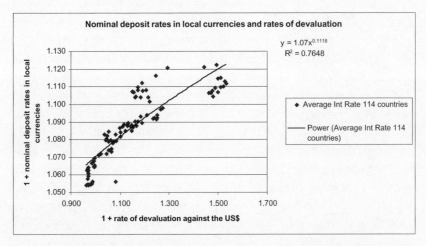

Figure 2.3: Domestic interest rates and devaluation rates. *Source:* International Financial Statistics of the International Monetary Fund.

equivalent rates (the domestic rates deflated by the rate of devaluation) higher than those prevailing in the international markets if they do not want to lose deposits. In such an environment, the independence of the developing countries' central banks is seriously compromised. They do not have the freedom to set interest rates independently from those prevailing in the dollar markets.

This point is frequently misunderstood. Many people identify the recent reduction in the interest rates in developing countries, and particularly in

Latin America, as proof that these countries have at last attained monetary independence. The fact that the interest rates have fallen, however, does not contradict my argument because it has happened as the currencies in these countries have tended to appreciate due to high commodity prices. The relationship remains the same. The only difference is that instead of getting higher interest rates as they devalue, they are getting lower rates as they revalue. This can be seen in figure 2.4, which shows the case of two sets of countries: a sample of 114 developing countries and Latin America, where the interest rates have fallen the most. The figure clearly shows that interest rates did not fall because there was a structural shift in the behavior of these countries. Rather, they fell because their relationship with depreciations against the dollar held, and these depreciations were lower or turned into appreciation.

In the case of the 114 countries, the top panel also hints at another of the developing countries' problems: the escalation of the spread of their interest rates over those of the United States that took place in 2001. In that year, such spread went up by about four hundred basis points even if these countries' rates of devaluation were steadily declining, most probably as a result of the uncertainties generated by the collapse of the stock exchanges in the developed countries and the contemporaneous fall in the prices of commodities. After that jump, as in the case of Latin America, the spreads of these countries fell as their currencies appreciated, confirming the dependence of the local interest rates on the shifts in the exchange rate against international currencies.

We can draw three conclusions from this analysis. First, developing countries can reduce either the international-equivalent or their domestic interest rates, but not both. They react in opposite ways. Second, the only way these countries can reduce their domestic rates below the dollar rates is to appreciate their currencies against the dollar—that is, of course, if the appreciation is sustainable. (They can also reduce their country risk to levels below those of the United States, but this is unrealistic.) Otherwise, as the case of Chile clearly shows at the end of this chapter, they run the risk of seeing their deposits in domestic currency stagnate or decline in nominal terms. Also, in what is essentially a manifestation of the same flight from the local currency, they run the risk of seeing spontaneous dollarization emerging in their midst. Third, barring continuous currency appreciation, the lowest equilibrium interest rate that a country with a local currency can attain in a sustainable way is the rate that it would get if it were dollarized.

Thus, we should note that an economy with a local currency does not enjoy any advantage over a dollarized one in terms of reducing its interest

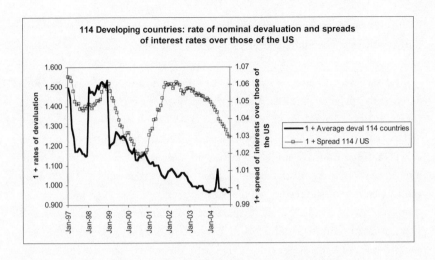

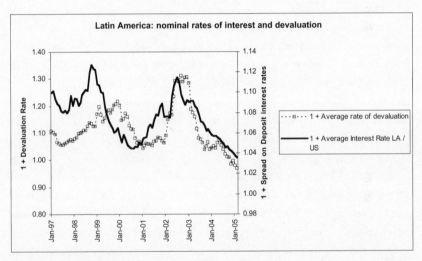

Figure 2.4: One hundred fourteen developing countries and Latin America: Divergence of nominal deposit rates relative to those in the United States and nominal devaluation against the dollar. *Source:* International Financial Statistics of the International Monetary Fund.

rates. In fact, the best that the first regime can do without continuously appreciating its currency is to reach the level of the second one. As history has proven so many times, however, it can do much, much worse.

This actually destroys the financial argument in favor of local currencies. We could stop here. However, we must look at the dual interest rates—the amount of resources intermediated by the financial system in developing countries—and review the main way that people are abandoning the local currencies when their interest rates do not compensate for the risks of devaluation: spontaneous dollarization.

The ability of financial systems to intermediate resources is usually measured through what is called financial depth—the ratio of deposits or M2 (deposits plus currency in circulation) to GDP. There are substantial regional differences in terms of this ratio across the developing countries. The main one is between East Asia and the Pacific and the rest of the developing world. The financial depth of that region is now about 140 percent of GDP, more than twice that of the rest of the developing countries and even much higher than the average in the OECD (Organization for Economic Cooperation and Development) countries, which is 80 percent. While, at 25 percent, the poor performance of Latin America is evident, the financial depth of other regions, particularly the Middle East and South Asia, has been increasing to average between 40 and 60 percent.[3] Thus, it would seem that the performance of most of the local currencies is not as bad as I have been suggesting up to this point.

Yet, before jumping to a conclusion, we should note that these data include both local and foreign currency deposits, so that the figures should be adjusted to measure the capacity of the domestic currency to attract deposits. Spontaneous dollarization must be deducted. Unfortunately, only a few countries publish the amount of deposits denominated in foreign currencies in their banking systems. Nevertheless, data compiled in a special report issued by the International Monetary Fund (IMF), shown in table 2.1, show that the share of these deposits in the developing countries has been rapidly increasing in the last few years, so that by 2001, it had reached more than 25 percent in practically all developing regions. The only exception is the Caribbean, where most of the islands have kept a credible fixed exchange rate against the dollar for decades. In two of the regions, South America and the former communist countries in transition, the share was already around 50 percent of total deposits, while in the Middle East, it was close to 42 percent of them.

Table 2.2 shows the financial depth of the different regions after correcting for the share of foreign currency deposits in the banking system. It is evident from the table that taking away the dollar deposits makes a big negative difference in the financial depth of the regions. Moreover, on average, the financial depth of the developing world did not increase noticeably during the period. Practically all the financial deepening was attributable to the spontaneous dollarization.

The magnitude of the reduction of the developing countries' financial

Table 2.1: Spontaneous Dollarization Worldwide (in Percent)

|  | 1996 | 1997 | 1998 | 1999 | 2000 | 2001 |
|---|---|---|---|---|---|---|
| South America | 46 | 46 | 49 | 53 | 54 | 56 |
| Formerly Communist | 37 | 39 | 44 | 44 | 47 | 48 |
| Middle East | 37 | 37 | 38 | 38 | 38 | 42 |
| Africa | 28 | 27 | 28 | 29 | 33 | 33 |
| Asia | 25 | 28 | 27 | 29 | 29 | 28 |
| Central America & Mexico | 21 | 21 | 22 | 22 | 23 | 25 |
| Unweighted Average | 32 | 33 | 35 | 36 | 37 | 39 |
| Caribbean | 6 | 8 | 7 | 7 | 6 | 6 |
| Industrial Countries | 7 | 8 | 8 | 7 | 7 | 7 |

*Source: Financial Stability in Dollarized Economies*, prepared by the Monetary and Exchange Affairs Department of the International Monetary Fund (IMF) for the Board of Directors of that institution, Washington, D.C.

Table 2.2: M2 in Domestic Currencies as a Percent of GDP

|  | 1996 | 1997 | 1998 | 1999 | 2000 | 2001 |
|---|---|---|---|---|---|---|
| South America | 15 | 16 | 16 | 16 | 15 | 15 |
| Formerly Communist | 15 | 15 | 14 | 14 | 14 | 15 |
| Middle East | 37 | 38 | 39 | 40 | 40 | 39 |
| Africa | 26 | 22 | 18 | 18 | 18 | 19 |
| Asia | 33 | 33 | 35 | 35 | 36 | 37 |
| Central America & Mexico | 23 | 26 | 27 | 29 | 27 | 27 |
| Unweighted Average | 25 | 25 | 25 | 25 | 25 | 26 |
| Caribbean | 47 | 48 | 49 | 51 | 54 | 58 |

*Source:* Author's calculations based on the World Tables of the World Bank for the ratio of M2 to GDP and, for the shares of foreign currency deposits, *Financial Stability in Dollarized Economies*, prepared by the Monetary and Exchange Affairs Department of the IMF for the Board of Directors of that institution, Washington, D.C.

depth is confirmed by the data we have on individual countries. Table 2.3 shows the magnitude of spontaneous dollarization in a sample of thirty-eight countries with dual currency deposits, plus three fully dollarized, using data from Moody's Investment Services.

Notice in the table that the ratio of quasi-money to GDP of the countries with a local currency, on average a healthy 37 percent, falls to a paltry 13 percent when the foreign currency deposits are deducted. Also notice that, with few exceptions, foreign currency deposits are high as a percent of the

Table 2.3: Foreign and Local Currency Deposits, 2003, for 41 Countries for Which Data Exist

| | | | % of GDP | |
|---|---|---|---|---|
| | Total deposits % of GDP | Share of $ in total deposits (%) | Dollars | Local currency |
| 1 Jordan | 83 | 66 | 55 | 29 |
| 2 Nicaragua | 67 | 77 | 52 | 16 |
| 3 Uruguay | 54 | 94 | 51 | 3 |
| 4 Bahrain | 68 | 53 | 36 | 32 |
| 5 Croatia | 50 | 68 | 34 | 16 |
| 6 Bolivia | 32 | 91 | 29 | 3 |
| 7 Turkey | 45 | 55 | 25 | 20 |
| 8 Egypt | 66 | 35 | 23 | 43 |
| 9 Paraguay | 28 | 69 | 19 | 9 |
| 10 Barbados | 51 | 31 | 16 | 35 |
| 11 Peru | 21 | 73 | 15 | 6 |
| 12 Philippines | 47 | 32 | 15 | 32 |
| 13 Romania | 18 | 83 | 15 | 3 |
| 14 Honduras | 41 | 34 | 14 | 27 |
| 15 Bulgaria | 25 | 55 | 14 | 11 |
| 16 Costa Rica | 26 | 48 | 12 | 13 |
| 17 Vietnam | 29 | 33 | 9 | 19 |
| 18 Jamaica | 30 | 30 | 9 | 21 |
| 19 Trinidad & Tobago | 33 | 26 | 8 | 25 |
| 20 Mauritius | 70 | 12 | 8 | 62 |
| 21 Indonesia | 45 | 18 | 8 | 37 |
| 22 Dominican Republic | 26 | 27 | 7 | 19 |
| 23 Saudi Arabia | 25 | 23 | 6 | 20 |
| 24 Kazakhstan | 9 | 60 | 5 | 4 |
| 25 Moldova | 12 | 42 | 5 | 7 |
| 26 Belize | 39 | 12 | 5 | 34 |
| 27 Lithuania | 13 | 33 | 4 | 9 |
| 28 Russia | 10 | 35 | 4 | 7 |
| 29 Oman | 25 | 14 | 4 | 22 |
| 30 Chile | 33 | 10 | 3 | 30 |
| 31 Pakistan | 22 | 10 | 2 | 19 |
| 32 Malaysia | 77 | 3 | 2 | 75 |
| 33 South Africa | 27 | 6 | 2 | 26 |
| 34 India | 41 | 4 | 1 | 40 |
| 35 Guatemala | 18 | 8 | 1 | 17 |
| 36 Thailand | 87 | 2 | 1 | 86 |
| 37 Mexico | 13 | 5 | 1 | 13 |
| 38 Venezuela | 8 | 0 | 0 | 8 |
| 39 Panama | 74 | 0 | 0 | 0 |
| 40 El Salvador | 40 | 0 | 0 | 0 |
| 41 Ecuador | 17 | 0 | 0 | 0 |
| Average non-dollarized | 37 | | 23 | 14 |

*Source:* Moody's Investor Services for the share of foreign currency deposits and International Financial Statistics of the International Monetary Fund for deposits.

total deposits or as a percent of GDP, or both. For example, foreign currency deposits represent only 4 percent of GDP in Russia but this is equivalent to 35 percent of its total deposits. In Chile, where these deposits amount to only 3 percent of GDP, they represent 10 percent of the total deposits. More recent figures provided by the country's central bank show that by 2004 they represented more than 20 percent of total time and savings deposits.[4] Mexico has only 5 percent of its deposits in foreign currencies, but its total deposits represent only 13 percent of GDP. Moreover, many of these countries impose drastic restrictions on the foreign currency deposits. For example, in Turkey, where they represent 55 percent of total deposits, they can be held only by Turks living abroad. In other countries, like Jordan, prudential regulations mandate that banks should not encourage currency mismatching by lending foreign currency to borrowers who have their income denominated in local currency.

The table understates the degree of spontaneous dollarization in many countries in at least two additional dimensions. First, in many of these countries, medium- and long-term contracts are denominated in a foreign currency, so that their value in domestic currency is adjusted continuously to devaluations. Second, in many countries, there is a parallel financial system, located offshore, which operates in foreign currencies. Quite frequently, these parallel institutions are owned by the local banks and are therefore a part of the local financial system. They, however, are beyond the regulating power of the local authorities. The volume of their operations is not reported to anyone, so that the total extent of the participation of the foreign currencies in the domestic market is not known. These offshore facilities played a crucial role in the Venezuelan crisis of 1994 and the Dominican one of the early 2000s.

Of course, deposits in foreign currency put their holders out of the reach of the local central bank, even if they are deposited locally. They are not just immune to inflation and devaluation; they actually gain in local currency terms whenever there is a real devaluation. This makes monetary management much harder for central banks. If, for example, they want to reduce the acquisitive power of deposits by 20 percent as a way to reduce domestic demand, and the share of foreign currency deposits is 50 percent, they have to devalue the currency by at least 40 percent because half of the deposits are not affected by the devaluation.

The presence of a competitor currency in their own backyard establishes very strict limits to the actions of central banks in other crucial dimensions of policy. To compete, the local currency must equal the expected yield offered by the dollar. If the central bank wants to devalue the currency, it will have to put up with higher domestic nominal and real interest rates. If it wants to expand the supply of money, it faces the stark reality that expanding it would reduce the relative value of their local currency, prompting people to move to the foreign currency. Of course, it is clear that the local currency interest rates in the spontaneously dollarized countries are below their equilibrium levels. If they were at those levels, there would be no spontaneous dollarization.

Spontaneous dollarization also reduces the power to shift relative prices in the real economy. If, for example, the central bank wants to reduce the relative price of nontradables (as they do whenever they devalue the currency), many of the prices of these products would not react as desired in an economy where spontaneous dollarization is substantial. The dollars inside the economy produce this result in two ways. On the side of deposits, the acquisitive power of people with deposits in dollars in terms of nontradables would increase. The resulting increase in demand coming from them would nullify a part or the total of the desired reduction in the relative price of these products. The results on the side of loans could be more worrying. If some nontradable activities have been financed with foreign currency loans or provide their services through long-term contracts denominated in foreign currency, their prices in local currency would increase or, if they do not, they would experience financial problems. In this way, for example, the already contracted rental prices of housing, office, and industrial space would increase in domestic currency terms when the currency is devalued. Equally, companies producing tradables or nontradables for the domestic market with machinery financed with foreign currency loans would see their financial costs increase with the devaluation, to the point that they can become insolvent even if their payrolls have declined.

Thus, it is clear that spontaneous dollarization severely constrains the power of the three instruments that central banks have used to manage the economy: the interest rates, the rate of expansion of the money supply, and the rate of real devaluation of the currency. Certainly, the same variables determine the movement of funds between local banks and banks abroad in an economy without foreign currency deposits. Yet, the transaction costs incurred by the population when escaping from central bank policies are infinitely lower when the competitor currency is inside the banking system and embedded in other contracts. More people react with higher volumes of resources when the costs of moving from one currency to the other are practically zero. These problems are among the reasons why it is so difficult to prevent a surge in interest rates when the currency is devalued in a developing country.

Theoretically, countries should be able to compensate for any rate of devaluation by increasing the local currency interest rates in order to maintain the yield of the local currency deposits higher than the foreign one. Through this mechanism, they would eliminate the foreign currency deposits in a natural way. Of course, the relevant yield determining the depositors' choice of currency is the expected one, a quantity that is not observable except through the choices of currency that people are making. Still, by trial and error, central banks should be able to reach the yield that would shift the preferences of the people from the foreign to the local currency. In reality, however, they have not been able to do it for two main reasons. First, the banks have two constraints in adjusting the interest rates. They cannot reduce the rates they pay on their dollar accounts below a certain limit, given by the interest rate in the United States plus some adjustments (adding the country risk and deducting the additional transaction costs of depositing in the United States). If they go below this level, dollar deposits will go to the United States. At the same time, banks cannot increase interest rates in domestic currency beyond a certain limit, which would be given by the resulting level of the real rates of interest. If this rate increases too much, the lending risks of banks become imprudently high. In fact, countries become highly dollarized in a spontaneous way when, because of the instability of the currency, they fall outside this range of feasible differentials between the two rates. Most deposits move to dollars because the banks cannot offer a differential of rates high enough to attract savers to domestic currency deposits.

The second reason why central banks cannot compensate for high rates of devaluation through the interest rates is that people feel insecure when the yield of the local currency is offered through very high interest rates with high rates of devaluation. Feeling apprehensive, people hedge by saving in the foreign currency, even in cases where the yield of the local currency seems to be adequate to compensate for the risk of devaluations.

The impact of these motivations to shift to dollars is such that we can observe a clear relationship between the rate of devaluation and the share of foreign currency deposits in partially dollarized countries, even if we ignore the differential between the interest rates in the two currencies. Figure 2.5 shows this in the case of two individual countries. The top panel shows the share of dollar deposits and the rate of devaluation in Peru, a country where spontaneous dollarization has become pervasive. As is evident in the figure,

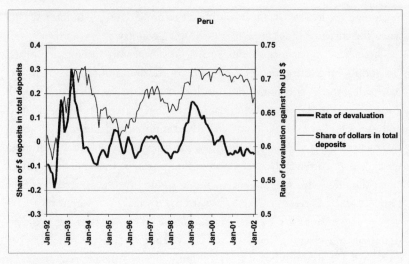

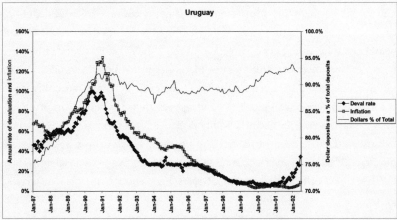

Figure 2.5: Share of dollar deposits and rate of devaluation in Peru and Uruguay. *Source:* Central Banks of Peru and Uruguay.

the share of dollar deposits has fluctuated in accordance with the rate of devaluation, although with some tendency to remain high for a while after the devaluation rate drops. The lower panel shows another feature of this phenomenon. In Uruguay, the share of dollar deposits in the total deposits of the country increased along with devaluation in the late 1980s, going from 75 percent to more than 90 percent during the period. In this case, however, when the rate of devaluation declined, the share of dollar deposits remained high, as if people decided that it was not worth going back and forth between currencies. We can call this phenomenon "local currency fatigue."

The positive correlation between devaluations and the share of dollar deposits in the total time and saving deposits also held for Dominican Republic from January 1966 to June 2004, a period that includes the financial crisis that started in 2002–2003. In this case, the ratio of deposits in dollars to total deposits increased from 25 percent to 40 percent from November 2002 to November 2003 when the rate of devaluation increased from 3 percent to 150 percent. It stayed there even when devaluation slowed down to 50 percent after the latter date.[5]

The same relationship between devaluation and spontaneous dollarization is visible in comparisons of different countries during a certain period. Figure 2.6 shows that the share of foreign currency deposits in total deposits had a positive relationship with both nominal and real devaluations against the dollar in 2000–2002 in a sample of thirty countries for which data exists. That is, the more a country devalued against the dollar, either in nominal or real terms, the higher was the share of foreign currency deposits.

It could be argued that this association between devaluations and the share of dollar deposits could be expected in the very short term because there is a mathematical relationship between the two variables. The devaluation automatically increases the share of the dollar because it increases the value of the dollar in domestic currency terms. Yet, the fact that, as shown in figure 2.6, the new composition tends to remain in place for at least the two years covered by the data reveals that the population prefers this composition. They could move back to the local currency if they wished. It may seem that this would be a silly thing to do when the local currency is devaluing. Precisely. That is the point. People save in foreign currency to protect themselves against devaluations.

Quite tellingly, figure 2.6 shows that the relationship of the share of foreign currency deposits and devaluations is stronger in the nominal than in the real devaluations. That is, volatility in the nominal exchange rate deters saving in the domestic currency, independently of its impact on the real exchange rate.

The interest rates may now be included in the analysis of spontaneous dollarization. Figure 2.7 shows how the spread between the domestic rates and the dollar rates have tended to fluctuate in accordance with the rate of devaluation in Peru and Uruguay. If the spreads do not increase when the local currency is devalued, people shift to the foreign currency.

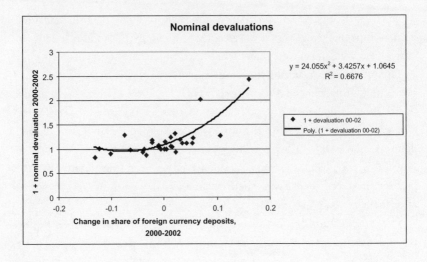

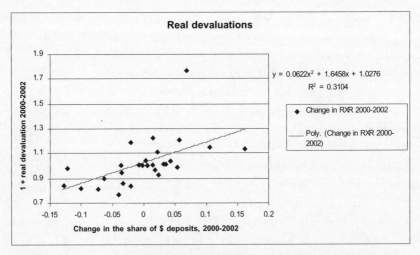

Figure 2.6: Change in share of foreign currency deposits and devaluations against the dollar, 2000–2002, sample of thirty countries. *Source:* Moody's Investor Services for the share of foreign currency deposits and International Financial Statistics for the exchange rates.

That is, as it would be expected from theory, the evidence shows that the share of dollars in total deposits depends on both the rate of devaluation relative to the dollar and the spread between the interest rates in local currency and dollar deposits. Central banks have to increase such spread to prevent increases in the spontaneous dollarization when they increase the rate of devaluation.

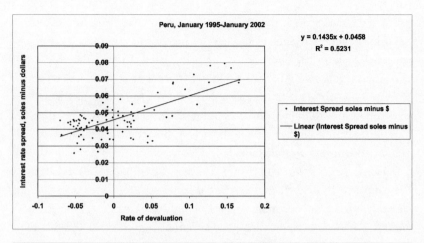

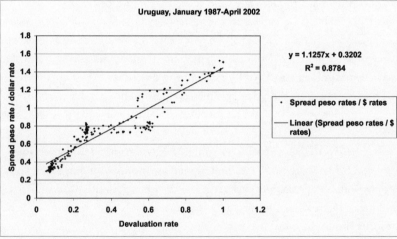

Figure 2.7: Spread of peso rates over dollar rates in Peru and Uruguay. *Source:* Central Banks of Peru and Uruguay.

Having gone through this analysis, you would expect that the rate of interest in the local currency would have to increase in the average developing country whenever the devaluation rate is increased. I tested the proposition that interest rates would move along with the rates of devaluations with a sample of seventy-six countries with monthly data from 1997 to 2002. There was a trend toward higher real rates of interest in countries that devalued the most in the previous five years. This trend, however, depended mostly on outliers. When these were eliminated, the correlation rapidly collapsed.

This, however, is not surprising. The fact that spontaneous dollarization has happened is a clear sign that central banks have not increased the local currency interest rates as much as they should to compensate for their devaluations. The size of spontaneous dollarization suggests that the difference between the actual interest rates and those that would be needed to keep the dollars away must be substantial. The fact that the share of dollars in the domestic deposits varies across countries suggests that such difference also varies across countries. Moreover, as discussed below, the same interest rate may attract 40 percent of GDP in deposits in one country and only 5 percent in another. Thus, we should expect that a regression linking devaluations with domestic interest rates would be much weaker than what the reasoning suggests.

In other words, testing observed interest rates against devaluation rates is pointless for two reasons. First, interest rates are meaningful only when knowing the volume of resources they attract to the financial system. Second, when looking at the resources attracted by the interest rates, only the local currency deposits should be considered.

Thus, to ascertain the impact of devaluations on financial costs, adjustments must be made in these two dimensions. Regarding the first adjustment, we should notice that the same rate of interest may attract higher amounts of resources in one economy than in another, so that an economy may settle in a lower equilibrium than another in terms of financial resources intermediated. This may happen because, as already discussed, the deposit rate that banks offer is a function of the amounts they can lend safely. As the risk of lending increases with the rate of interest, there is a maximum rate that is consistent with a reasonable probability of collection. Once they reach that rate, banks are unwilling to increase further their lending operations and do not have to increase the deposit rate because they do not need more resources. They settle on their desired level of intermediation, defined by the deposit and the lending rates. On the other side of the ledger, the amount of resources that depositors are willing to deposit at the settled rate would be lower in an unstable than in a stable country. Thus, the same rate of interest may result in quite different levels of intermediation across countries. One moment of reflection would indicate that this affects the cost of funds, because higher instability means fewer resources available for lending, which in turn means that many activities that would be viable at the lower interest rates of a stable country could not get credit in the unstable one.

Figure 2.8 illustrates this crucial point that, even if evident, is not taken into account in the comparison of interest rates across countries. The figure shows two supply curves of deposits. In the way I have drawn the picture, which is wholly justified by the evidence presented later, the supply of funds in unstable economies (those that devalue frequently and by substantial magnitudes) tends to have a steeper slope than in stable ones, so that the same interest rate attracts much fewer resources in the former than in the latter. To attract the same amount of resources than the stable country, banks in the unstable one would have to move their deposit rates to the higher horizontal line, which represents a higher level of risk in the lending operations. In these circumstances, it is better to intermediate a lower amount of resources with a reasonable expectation of repayment than a larger one with high uncertainty of repayment. For this reason, unstable countries tend to have a lower level of equilibrium than the stable ones.

Thus, as shown in the figure, two countries may settle in the same rate of interest. However, as shown along the horizontal axis, many activities that would be profitable in the stable economy become unviable in the unstable one. The financial costs that they would have to pay would render them too risky or unprofitable. Because of that they cannot get credit. This is the hidden financial cost that you cannot see when just looking at the level of the interest rates across countries.

To compare interest rates across countries, therefore, an indicator should be used that normalizes the rates in terms of the resources intermediated as a percent of GDP. For this purpose, the percent of GDP attracted by one point of the interest rate may be used.

Regarding the second adjustment that is needed to compare financial costs across countries, it is obvious that we cannot include the foreign exchange deposits as part of the resources attracted by the domestic currency interest rate. We should remember that these deposits exist because the banking system cannot attract them at the interest rate paid in the domestic currency.

Once the two adjustments are made, we find that the capacity to attract

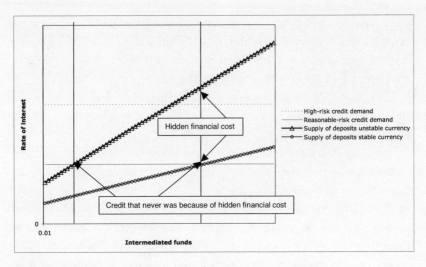

Figure 2.8: Interest rates and the supply of deposits in two countries.

deposits in domestic currency is negatively correlated with devaluation. The top panel of figure 2.9 shows that the amount of deposits (as a percent of GDP) attracted by one percentage point of nominal interest in the domestic currency decreases sharply with the rate of nominal devaluation in such a way that a country devaluing by 10 percent more than another would attract 15 percent fewer deposits per point of the interest rate.[6]

The lower panel shows that an almost identical relationship exists when the comparison is made between the amounts attracted in deposits by the *real* deposit interest rates and the rate of *nominal* devaluation.[7] If we reverse the relationship, and estimate the points of interest that are needed to mobilize 1 percent of GDP, we realize that the equilibrium rate of interest increases with the rate of devaluation across countries. This was the relationship we expected in accordance with our reasoning.

These results could have been explained with a simpler reasoning. The financial system is a system of promises. The basis of its performance—its ability to mobilize resources—crucially depends on the credibility of those promises, which has two obvious dimensions. One is the guarantee that the financial obligations will be honored, which requires the enforcement of property rights and collections. The other is that the acquisitive power of these obligations will be maintained. The idea that this should be assured by the

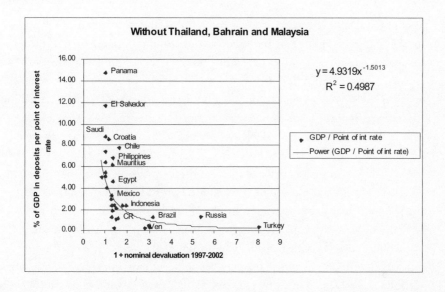

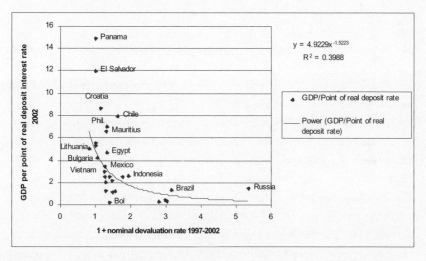

Figure 2.9: Percent of GDP attracted in deposits by one percentage point of nominal and real interest rates, in local currency, sample of thirty-six countries. *Source:* Moody's Investment Services for the share of local currency deposits and the International Financial Statistics of the International Monetary Fund for the deposit rates, quasi-money, exchange rates, and GDP.

level of the real interest rates is quite common. Reality shows that this is not so. As visible in figure 2.9, the same real or nominal interest rate attracts different volumes of resources depending on the rate of nominal devaluation.

This is an interesting point because it shows the importance of nominal variables. Twenty years ago, before the liberalization of the financial systems, the idea was that the levels of financial intermediation were low in developing countries because central banks fixed the rate of interest below the rate of inflation, so that they were negative in real terms. The expectation was that liberalization of interest rates would solve this problem because any rate of devaluation or inflation could be compensated with a higher interest rate. Yet, the previous data shows that even in liberalized financial systems with high real rates of interest, people fly away from financial instruments denominated in the local currency when this is weak in nominal terms. That is, contrary to what is commonly assumed, people react not just to real but also to nominal variables. Like Dema Gogo, they do not like to speed down a slope without brakes. They do not think that a real rate of interest of 5 percent embedded in a nominal rate of 47 percent when the inflation rate is 40 percent provides the same security as a rate of 7.1 percent when the inflation rate is 2 percent. Any slip in the rate of inflation (which happens quite frequently at high levels of inflation because the variability of inflation increases with its level) would turn your real interest rate negative.

The nominal instability of domestic currencies has also destroyed the long-term financial markets in developing countries. In most cases, financial operations are not longer than one or two years; in many countries, most of the financial contracts are in the range of 180 to 360 days. It is frequently assumed that this happens because developing countries are too poor to have the capacity to save in long-term financial instruments. For this reason, it is stated that they face a stark choice if they want to have long-term credit: They either have maturity mismatching (using short-term deposits to finance long-term loans) or currency mismatching (using a strong foreign currency for that purpose).

Nevertheless, some cases suggest that the potential for long-term savings in developing countries is large, even in the poorest ones. In Pakistan, for example, the government sells securities of up to ten-year maturities to the public under a program called the National Savings Scheme (NSS). The securities are sold in government agencies throughout the country, located in even the most distant and isolated places. They are not only a convenient instrument for saving but also the only such instrument available for many people. Propelled by a high yield (16 percent against 10 percent for T-bills and 7 percent for bank deposits), these securities grew at twice the rate of bank deposits during the late 1990s, and by 2000, they represented about half of those deposits. This happens in a low-income country. Pakistan, however, is a country with relatively low inflation rates. They averaged 7.8 percent from 1976 to 2002 and 8.2 percent from 1990 to 2002. In contrast, savers are extremely reluctant to tie their resources in instruments with long maturities in richer countries with high inflation rates.

More fundamentally, high inflation rates, beyond a certain threshold, make long-term lending in the weak currency irrelevant, directly contradicting the fallacy of the real interest rates I mentioned before. According to this fallacy, only the real rates of interest are important because people can see that even very high interest rates can be very low or even negative in real terms if the inflation rate is also very high. In this way, for example, a nominal interest rate of 35 percent is equal to just 3.8 percent in real terms if the rate of inflation is 30 percent. Charging 3.8 percent in real terms through a 35 percent nominal rate, however, kills long-term credits.

This is so because high nominal interest rates, even if they are low in real terms, reduce the real maturity of loans, forcing borrowers to refinance frequently even if their obligations are nominally long-term. This, in turn, happens because inflation erodes the principal of the loan, and interest rates include a portion aimed at covering such erosion as it takes place. For example, if the inflation rate were 30 percent, the real value of a principal of one hundred at the end of one year would be approximately 76.9. To avoid losses, lenders would then demand the immediate payment of the amount lost to inflation. This goes into the interest rates, in such a way that if the real yield that the banks desire from their loans is 5 percent, the interest rate will be approximately 36.5 percent. Since 30 percentage points would be aimed at covering the loss of the principal caused by inflation, the borrower will amortize 30 percent of the loan in real terms every year, regardless of the nominal maturity established in the loan agreement. To make this payment the borrower would need refinancing—which is what happens when long-term projects are financed with short-term loans. Thirty percent is not an unrealistic rate of inflation when we remember that Colombia, a country that was praised for its relative stability, experienced rates close to this level for several decades.

Thus, it is monetary instability, not poverty, that makes for extremely short financial operations in developing countries. Indexation can eliminate the acceleration of real amortizations in a highly inflationary environment. For example, long-term financial operations in Chile are denominated in a currency different from the peso, the Unidades de Fomento (UFs). This virtual currency is indexed to several variables with an emphasis on the inflation rate, in such a way that the interest rates in UFs are quoted in real terms. When inflation goes up, the principal goes up, but the impact on current payments is much lower. If, say, the rate of inflation were 30 percent and the real rate of interest were 5 percent, the nominal balance at the end of the year would increase by 30 percent. The interest payment would be 5 percent of that increased balance, or 6.5 percent of the original loan. The resulting payment would be much lower than that under a nonindexed regime, which would be of 36.5 percent of the original loan.

While resolving this problem, however, the system poses some problems of its own. First, people may not trust that the government will keep the integrity of the index. That is, people must believe that the government will not manipulate the index or change its basis. This might be difficult for governments that have already eroded the public's confidence in the local currency.

Second, indexation is vulnerable to disintermediation. It works well as long as the relevant variable in the decisions to save and invest is the variable used in the index. If the relevant variable shifts, for example from the rate of inflation to the rate of devaluation, the system may become unstable.

Third, it may be politically difficult to convince people that the earnings of the savers should be indexed while the incomes of the wage earners should not. While there are many economic arguments to support this discrimination (in its absence, inflation becomes uncontrollable), politically it sounds awful. In Chile, the discrimination was instituted under the dictatorship of General Pinochet. This feat may not be replicable in other countries.

Fourth, while providing domestic credibility, the system fails internationally. That is, the need to use a third currency for international transactions remains in place. Certainly, the UFs protect the acquisitive power inside Chile. Yet, since Chile is not a widely diversified economy, it is difficult to believe that people outside its borders would buy international instruments denominated in UFs. To finance itself internationally, Chile needs instruments denominated in an international currency. As a result, the currency markets become more complex, as the economy plays daily with at least three currencies: the local one, the indexed one, and at least one foreign currency.

For these reasons, the generalized indexation of long-term financial operations has not been tried in other countries. Some countries, however, have tested indexation in some specific financial markets and with some specific instruments. Some of these experiments have failed.

One example of such a failure is the Unidad de Poder Adquisitivo Constante (UPAC) system of housing financing in Colombia. Within that system, savings and loans institutions indexed their deposits and loans to the UPAC index, which started linked to the rate of inflation exclusively. The problem came during a period when the inflation rate largely exceeded the rate of devaluation. In those circumstances, the peso nominal rates of interest fell relative to those charged on the housing loans, the borrowers protested, and demand for loans declined. The government yielded and changed the basis of the UPAC from inflation to devaluation, just in time to catch a period when the situation reversed and the rate of devaluation became much higher than the rate of inflation. The result was a serious crisis in the savings and loan system.

Some governments issue debt instruments indexed to the exchange rate. This is equivalent to introducing spontaneous dollarization through the back door, with one important flaw: The fact that the promise to repay is given in local currency terms induces the suspicion that the government is letting the door open to repay and devalue immediately thereafter, thus diluting the indexed debts.

Because of these problems, most developing countries depend on funds denominated in international currencies for long-term financing. The foreign exchange risk, however, makes this financing unattractive for both the international banks and the local borrowers. The most common result is that long-term credit for the private sector practically does not exist. This is true even in the case of Pakistan, which demonstrated that long-term resources can be attracted even in very poor countries. There, the long-term resources in local currency are too expensive for the private sector.

The lack of long-term credit is one of the most difficult problems to overcome because, even if a country succeeds in stabilizing its currency, people wonder whether another government would keep the currency stable. We must remember that a simple twenty-year loan for housing or investment extends through four or five presidential administrations, and experience shows that it is hard for developing countries to attain policy continuity. How many administrations would you have to watch in a developing country to invest part of your pension fund in its currency?

All these problems push countries in the direction of spontaneous dollarization. It is worth noting that while Pakistan provides a good example of the availability of long-term savings in very poor countries, it has not been free from this kind of dollarization. As shown in table 2.3, above, 10 percent of the country's deposits are denominated in foreign currencies, mostly dollars. The Pakistani government created the foreign currency deposits in the mid-1990s as a way to finance its own needs for foreign exchange and the balance of payments. It allowed the banks to receive such deposits, but forced them to deposit the proceeds with the central bank, which offered high returns for them. The central bank in turn transferred most of the dollars to the government and used the remainder to settle the balance of payments. By 1998, it had become obvious that the central bank was unable to service its foreign currency obligations to the local banks, and a crisis developed. The crisis was resolved by converting the foreign currency obligations into local currency, lowering the interest rates, and extending the maturity of the obligations to several years. Today, the banks are free to use their foreign currency deposits in operations with the private sector. That is, as with most other developing countries, the relatively low rates of inflation have not isolated Pakistan from the generalized problems caused by spontaneous dollarization.

Understandably, the IMF is extremely concerned about spontaneous dollarization and is advising countries to eliminate it altogether, although by the summer of 2005, it had not yet produced a clear methodology to do it. Just prohibiting dollar deposits could be dangerous because people could transfer their money to offshore banking facilities, which, in many cases, are just another façade of the local banks. The data in table 2.3 above shows the magnitudes that the central banks would be risking.

Of course, exporting their savings may not be within the reach of the simplest citizens, who, as usual, are the ones who pay for the inefficiencies of the monetary system. Still, even they can defend their savings by storing them in nonfinancial instruments like durable consumer goods or real estate, leading to an increase in the prices of those assets. The actions of the two groups combined—those who would export their savings and those who would increase the prices of assets—would result in a drastic reduction in the size of the financial system relative to GDP and a contraction of the system's ability to provide credit. This would worsen the endemic scarcity of credit in the developing countries.

Spontaneous dollarization can also be controlled with a regulation mandating a strict matching of currencies in the banking system—not only between their assets and liabilities but also between the denomination of loans and that of the incomes of the borrowers. This would also eliminate the risk of currency mismatching inside the banking system, thus improving its reliability. Some countries have this regulation in place, but this of course limits the amount of deposits that central banks can attract back to the country, which is why many other countries do not establish such regulation.

Furthermore, even if it were feasible to ban the foreign currency deposits the dangers of mismatching would still exist through capital flows. Of course, capital flows can also be banned, as many economists have been advising for some time now, focusing on the short-term ones. Yet, as I discuss later, imposing increasing limitations to your private sector is not what would be desirable or logical. It does not make much sense to isolate the private sector from access to the international financial markets in order to protect a system that produces a scarcity of local resources. Thus, it would be better to act through market mechanisms aimed at improving the appeal of the domestic currency in a credible and sustainable way, domestically and abroad.

There are two interrelated ways of doing this while keeping in place the domestic currency. Partially dollarized countries could reduce or even eliminate their dependence on foreign currency deposits by either stabilizing their currencies—which is a long and painful task—or by increasing the spread of local currency deposits over dollar deposits, which seems to be easier. As discussed previously, however, there is a limit to the power of the central bank to change the currency composition of deposits through setting the interest rate differential between the two currencies.

Hence, to reduce the share of foreign currency deposits in a banking system, its currency must be strengthened against the competing one. There is no other way out. This means that to reduce the foreign currency deposits, the rate of nominal devaluation must be reduced to levels close to zero and, if possible, the currency appreciated in a sustainable way. This would increase the yield of the domestic currency over the foreign one, and people would move into it even if the difference in interests were not as large as today. The problem is that this must be done in a credible way, meaning that the appreciation or reduction in the rate of devaluation must be sustainable and apparently so. The role of appearances is essential because when currency appreciates in a credible way, the share of foreign currency deposits declines, while if credibility is lacking, it will increase. One example of this kind of behavior was provided by Argentina, where the share of dollar deposits increased very rapidly, from 59 percent in 1999 to 71 percent in 2001 when the country was not devaluing the currency but many people believed that it would have to do so.[8]

Even more important, pursuing a policy consistently aimed at reducing the share of foreign deposits (this certainly would not happen in one go) would commit countries to peg for a long time their currencies to the foreign currency that has become the standard of value. This would tie the hands of the central banks completely because in those circumstances, the peg must be the only objective of monetary policy. Central banks would be controlled by one single objective: Do nothing with the nominal exchange rate. To meet this objective, they would have to let the market set the interest rate in isolation from any central bank's policy; they would not be able to conduct monetary policies except those necessary to keep the exchange rate fixed. Central banks would then have to resign their powers to keep them.

Furthermore, even if they attained a reduction in the interest rates, these would remain higher than in their domestic dollar markets today for the reason discussed in the introduction: People would have to be provided with an incentive for them to prefer saving in their currencies than in the currency that is their standard of value.

There is another problem. Advising the revaluation of currencies or stopping devaluations as a permanent policy to increase the appeal of the currency is something that the IMF would find difficult to do. It would contradict the doctrine of flexible exchange rates that has guided its advice to developing countries since the collapse of the fixed exchange rate system in the 1960s.

The other alternative is to dollarize, which is much simpler. This, however, would have momentous consequences beyond the behavior of the central banks themselves. The international model would evaporate and, therefore, the need to maintain it. There would be no demand for learned papers on how to manipulate the savings and the wages of people while maintaining stability or on how to survive healthily without it. There would be no need to calculate the optimal exchange rate regime or the optimal rate of devaluation. The realities of fiscal policies would become too transparent, and all wisdom would collapse to a simple dictum: Do not spend more than you earn in the long term. This dictum is insultingly identical to that which governs lower worlds, those of businesses and average citizens. Everybody would understand the finances of the government and the country. Financial crises would not be associated with currency crises. The thrill of macroeconomics would go.

Thus, central banks have driven themselves into a trap. The only ways they have to eliminate the threats to their own power are: to abrogate their own ability to conduct monetary, interest rate, and exchange rate policies at will; or to surrender their power altogether to their competitor currencies.

This is happening because the players are abandoning the board and taking the real money with them. It seems that the era of all-powerful central banks issuing money at will is coming to an end in the developing countries. In fact, it is difficult not to think that the improved macroeconomic management of the last few years in the developing countries is related to the emergence of spontaneous dollarization, which, for all its problems, imposed discipline on the central banks and forced them to think in ways of increasing the appeal of their currencies.

What about a counterfactual, one that would show how a developing country can have a local currency that is the standard of value for its users? Regarding these issues, many people have argued that the Chilean peso is the standard of value of the population it serves. They point out that the interest rates have fallen dramatically in the last few years even if the currency has depreciated also dramatically against the dollar and other major currencies.

In fact, Chile seems to have attained true monetary independence. As in the United States, the inflation rate has been declining while the currency experienced high rates of depreciation up to May 2003. Thereafter, it kept on falling as the currency appreciated up to February 2004, to the point that the country experienced a short period of deflation. Subsequently, it went up as the currency depreciated; however, it escalated only to 2.9 percent.

Moreover, unlike Brazil, which I discuss in a subsequent chapter, Chile did not have to pay a price in high interest rates for this feat. On the contrary, the country's interest rates are among the lowest in Latin America and the whole world. The ratio of the Chilean nominal deposit rates to those of the certificates of deposit (CDs) in the United States went down from the very high levels that prevailed after the Asia crisis to be lower than one in early 2005. That is, at some moments in the recent past, deposit rates in Chile have been lower than in the United States. Different from most other developing countries, Chile did not miss the low interest rates prevailing in the international markets in the early 2000s.

Yet, as previously discussed, just comparing interest rate levels can be meaningless if the effects of these rates are not examined. Figure 2.10 shows that the Chilean rates were not able to prevent a rapid and substantial increase of

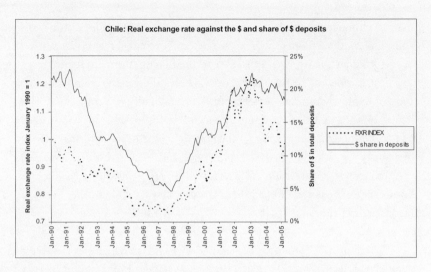

Figure 2.10: Chile: Real exchange rate against the dollar and share of dollars in total deposits. *Source:* International Financial Statistics of the International Monetary Fund and the Central Bank of Chile.

the share of the dollar deposits in total deposits. They were not high enough to clear the market, and therefore the dollar gained market share.

The relationship between dollar deposits and real depreciations in Chile is very similar to that prevailing in countries like Peru and Dominican Republic. The dollar interest rates set a floor for the domestic currency rates. If you go below it, you risk losing ground to the dollar. The figure does not suggest that there has been any drastic change in this behavior. If anything, it seems that the share of the dollar deposits is falling sluggishly in spite of the rapid appreciation of the peso—although it is too early to say whether this would be a manifestation of a shift in the coefficient linking the two variables.

Moreover, figure 2.11 shows that the Chilean interest rates not only failed in preventing the increase in the share of dollar deposits but actually failed to attract deposits in pesos at the margin during the long period of real depreciation. When the trend toward currency appreciation that prevailed from 1990 to early 1998 ended, the growth of peso deposits went flat, so that the total savings and time deposits grew only because dollar deposits were increasing. Then, when currency depreciation peaked in 2003, peso deposits actually declined in nominal terms, bringing down total deposits. That is, the growth of dollar deposits was not enough to compensate for the peso decline. It was in this period that the spreads of the Chilean rates relative to the United States

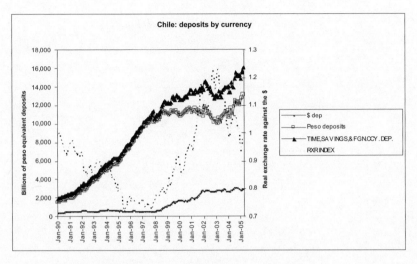

Figure 2.11: Chile: Deposits by currency. *Source:* International Financial Statistics of the International Monetary Fund and the Central Bank of Chile.

rates went down, in both peso and dollar terms. Peso deposits only recovered when the peso began to appreciate in real terms.

The low interest rates that have prevailed in Chile in the most recent past have elicited different responses from depositors. During 2002, they led savers to withdraw deposits in net terms. Later on, they enticed them to increase their deposits only because the currency began to appreciate. Moreover, while the rate of depreciation against the dollar seems to be unrelated to the rate of inflation in the short term, when looking at five-year averages, as in figure 2.12, the relationship becomes visible.

When discussing these issues, some economists have pointed out that it is unfair to take into consideration the period from 1997 to 2000, which was distorted by the Asian crisis, and the years immediately after 2001, which show the effects of both the worldwide collapse of the stock exchange and 9/11. Those events negatively affected all countries in the world. Even the dollar began to depreciate in 2001. However, this is not relevant for our discussion, which is centered on the question of whether the Chilean peso is the standard of value of the Chileans. The point is that people in the United States did not turn to deposit 20 percent of their resources into euro accounts when their currency depreciated against the latter. Furthermore, the Asian crisis was not even noticeable in the monetary performance of the United States or the dollar internationally. In fact, it was not noticeable in Panama, either. Looking

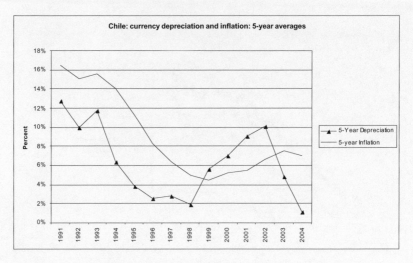

Figure 2.12: Chile: Currency depreciation against the dollar and inflation, five-year averages. *Source:* International Financial Statistics of the International Monetary Fund and the Central Bank of Chile.

at the performance of monetary systems only in times of fair weather is not a reasonable proposition.

In summary, it is clear that the Chilean peso is still vulnerable to spontaneous dollarization and is not yet the standard of value for its population. It still does not behave like the euro and the dollar. In fact, I could not find one currency among the developing countries that behaves like those. Even if we ignore these problems, it is also clear that the peso is not accepted as a means of payment beyond the frontiers of the country. It has no international liquidity. If you have pesos, you can buy things only in Chile. This is the same that happens with the currencies of all developing countries. As discussed in the last part of the book, this deficiency is crucial in the increasingly globalized world of today.

Thus, currency flexibility, which in developing countries has mostly meant flexibility to devalue, has resulted in low levels of financial intermediation, high financial costs for both the government and the private sector, and very short maturities of the financial operations. Moreover, it also weakened the power of the central banks to conduct the policies that supposedly would bring about the promised benefits of the local currencies. This is the opposite of what most people take for granted that floating currencies would do.

We can now examine whether weak currencies help in promoting exports and economic growth.

## Chapter 3 The Unfulfilled Promises in Trade and Growth

The idea that real devaluations promote the growth of exports is probably the best known of the arguments in favor of having a local currency. The idea is so entrenched that the word "competitiveness" has been associated with the weakness of the currency even in the popular press. People say that a country becomes more "competitive" when it devalues more than its trade partners. When discussing dollarization, the people's first reaction is to say that a country lacking the power to devalue the currency would become uncompetitive. The underlying logic in this assertion is that devaluations reduce wages in terms of those prevailing in other countries. The lower wages would reduce production costs, also relative to those in other countries, and, through this, they would increase the export growth rate. The increasing exports, in turn, would give an impulse to the economy in general.

In this chapter, I argue that real devaluations fail to deliver on their promises in terms of fostering the growth of exports and economic activity in general in the developing countries. To prove this point, I would only have to show that there is no correlation between the rates of real devaluations and the rates of growth of these variables. In fact, I found that in most cases, the correlation exists, but it is of the opposite sign—that is, exports and economic activity decline when devaluations increase. This proved to be true both when dealing with long-term rates of growth across countries and with changes in the performance of a single country. Of course, many cases of individual countries with no relationship or with a positive one can be found. Overall, however, the relationship tends to be negative.

The fact that the correlation between devaluations and exports is negative in most cases may seem puzzling, perhaps paradoxical. Yet, this behavior can be explained in three steps. First, in all cases, it is clear that other factors, different from the real exchange rate, are much more important in the determination of the rates of growth of both exports and gross domestic product (GDP). Second, in many cases, these other factors are negatively affected by devaluations in such a way that their deterioration more than compensates for the supposed advantage given by the reduction of wages. Third, the currencies of successful exporters tend to appreciate, so that the value of the currency is not a cause, but instead an effect, of their success. The first step would eliminate the correlation between real devaluations and the growth of exports and GDP. The second and third would turn it negative. In the rest of this chapter, I argue that the facts fit this explanation.

I must clarify that there are cases in which countries, through the abuse of their powers to set monetary and exchange rate policies, bring their currencies to unsustainably high levels of overvaluation. This, for example, happened to Dema Gogo. Devaluations are unavoidable in these circumstances. They, however, arise from the previous abuse of the central bank powers and are thus linked to the possibility of conducting monetary and exchange rate policies. I deal with this issue in the second part of the book. In this chapter, I consider devaluations that are not forced by these circumstances but instead are carried out as a manifestation of trade policy.

Our discussion begins by noting that associating devaluations with competitiveness, as when saying that a country becomes "more competitive" when it devalues its currency, goes against common sense in the environment of the developing countries. When you devalue in a developed country, you reduce the wages only in terms of other currencies. Their real level remains the same. In contrast, when you devalue in a developing country, you reduce the wage in real terms as well. From a national point of view, the workers are your partners. In the business world, a company is labeled uncompetitive when it is forced to reduce the share of the partners to keep on selling. A competitive company is one that can sell the same things at the same or a lower price but with higher value added; or even better, the same thing but designed, produced, and marketed in such a way that it commands a higher price. If a company is forced to sell its products at lower prices and profits because they are not as well designed or marketed as those of its competitors, that company has a problem of competitiveness. Thus, saying that you become more competitive because you reduce your earnings does not make sense from a business point of view.

The concept does not make economic sense, either. As any investor can tell you, what matters is not the level of the wages but, instead, their relationship with the production that workers carry out in exchange for them. If a worker produces one hundred with a salary of forty, he is much more competitive than a worker who produces one and a half with a salary of one. Singapore, for example, is much more competitive than African countries with salaries less than a tenth of its wages. From an economic point of view it makes much more sense to aim policy at increasing the numerator in the ratio of production to wages than to aim it at reducing the denominator, which is what real devaluations do. The concept does not make sense even in plain English. What is the purpose of being competitive if that means you have to keep on repressing the real wage of your population?

In fact, it is becoming increasingly clear that competitiveness does not depend on the exchange rate or any other macroeconomic variable—except in the trivial sense that macroeconomic instability detracts from competitiveness. The important question is what determines competitiveness once this minimum requirement—stability—has been attained.

Research on this question started on two parallel tracks that are converging in their identification of microeconomic variables as the sources of competitiveness. One of the tracks was inaugurated on the side of business studies by Michael Porter with his book, *The Competitive Advantage of Nations*.[1] This approach gave prominence to microeconomic aspects of the business environment from the very start. The other track began with the analysis of total factor productivity (what remains unexplained in models trying to explain economic growth with the changes in the volumes of capital and labor applied in the process of production). This remainder proved to be crucially important in the explanation of growth and development—potentially more so than the capital and labor inputs. For example, Stephen L. Parente and Nobel Prize winner Edward C. Prescott argue in their book, *Barriers to Riches*, that most of the difference in income per capita between the richest and the poorest societies in the world, which is on the order of twenty-seven times, can be is explained by the fact that the total factor productivity of the latter is a third of that of the former.[2] The question is, What makes for this difference? Increasingly, research is turning toward microeconomic variables of difficult measurement, such as the rule of law, the strength of institutions, the use of available knowledge, the ease of creating new enterprises and closing failing ones, and so on.

Still, it is very common to listen to statements that link competitiveness with currency depreciations. The popularity of this idea among economists and the public in general is puzzling because it does not fit with the facts. If we insisted in saying that countries become more competitive by devaluing their currency in real terms, we would have to say that Japan became immensely less competitive than most of Latin America during the last forty years. During that period, the yen appreciated by 176 percent in real terms against the dollar while, on average, Latin America depreciated by an amount that cannot be calculated because the nominal exchange rate and the consumer price indices of some of the countries were so small relative to today that they disappear in the tables. The data allows the calculation for some cases, however, and we can choose to compare the appreciation of Japan with the depreciation of Colombia. The latter's currency depreciated in such a way that by 2004 its real exchange rate was only 48 percent of its value in 1960. Thus, according to the definition, Colombia became 5.6 times more competitive than Japan during the last forty years. This, of course, is not true. Annual exports in Japan increased twice as fast in a compounded fashion as those of Colombia during the period, diversifying and increasing in value added at a rate incalculably higher than those of Colombia.

In fact, figure 3.1 shows that in the long-term, the export growth rate in Japan has been closely related to real devaluations, but in a negative way. Since the curve drawn on the figure is logarithmic, it shows the relationship between the changes in the two variables. A real appreciation of 1 percent has been associated with an increase in exports of 3.7 percent. Adjusting this elasticity for the percent of the export growth rate that the equation explains, almost 90 percent, we find that 1 percent of currency appreciation corresponded to an increase of 3.3 percent in exports.

The top panel in figure 3.2 shows that the relationship holds when the real unit labor costs are used to measure the real exchange rate.[3] In this case, the

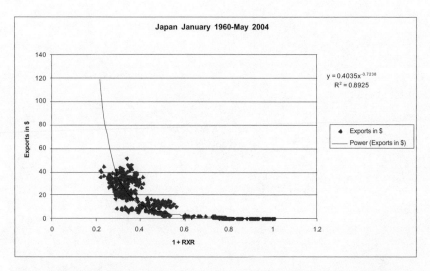

Figure 3.1: Japan: Real exchange rate and exports January 1960–May 2004, calculation based on exchange rate and difference in rates of inflation. *Source:* International Financial Statistics of the International Monetary Fund.

curve goes up, showing that Japan exported more when its real unit labor costs were higher. The lower panel shows the same relationship in the case of Germany. The top panel covers monthly data from 1960 to 2004 and the lower one from 1978 to 1998.

The behavior of these successful exporters could be taken as a paradox; these two countries exported more the higher their real wage was. Of course, it is not. What happened in Japan, for example, is that the country's success as an exporter flooded the country with dollars, appreciating its currency even in nominal terms. The nominal exchange rate of the yen was 362 yen for the dollar in 1960 and 110 in May 2004. When currency appreciation rendered unprofitable some exported products, Japanese enterprises abandoned these and moved toward other activities that could be profitable at the higher levels of salaries. In this way, Japan moved from cheap toys to cheap steel and cheap cars, and then to high-quality steel and cars and electronic goods, increasing the value added in each stage of the process. Thus, the success of Japan was based not on devaluing its currency but instead on shifting from lower- to higher-value-added production when the currency appreciated in real terms. Germany did the same. That is true competitiveness. That is also development. After all, increasing the income of the population must be the aim of economic policy.

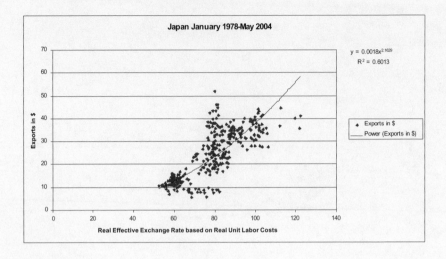

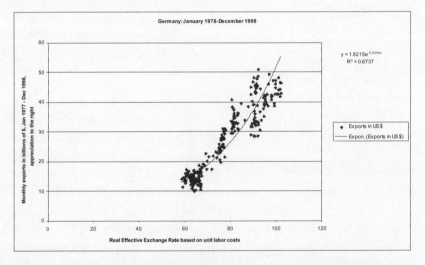

Figure 3.2 Real exchange rate and exports: Japan, January 1978–May 2004; Germany, January 1978–December 1998; calculation based on labor unit costs. *Source:* International Financial Statistics of the International Monetary Fund.

Japan is a good example because, at the end of World War II, it experienced a weak currency for a while, with disastrous results. It began its recovery only after the government decided to strengthen the currency. The same happened in Germany.

The same long-term relationships can be found between the real exchange rate and exports in the cases of other highly successful exporters.

This is not to say that countries can increase their exports by revaluing their currencies. It is one thing is when the currency appreciates naturally because exports are growing, and another, quite different, when it does so because the central bank appreciates it artificially through the manipulation of monetary and exchange rates. The appreciation arising from success in exports poses a challenge to governments and private entrepreneurs to shift toward higher-value-added production. The appreciation due to monetary manipulations is unsustainable, and it is the more so the longer it lasts, in such a way that when the adjustment finally comes, it produces large devaluations and crises. Thus, this kind of currency appreciation is an invitation to disaster. Such invitations have been issued very frequently by many developing countries and, as discussed in the chapters on financial crises, fate has accepted the invitation also quite frequently. Since most currency appreciations in developing countries take place because of such manipulations, it is only logical that people should become scared when their currencies appreciate. Yet, as the cases of the most successful exporters show, long-term success is not associated with devaluations.

Nevertheless, people take for granted that, at least in the short term, real devaluations will increase exports over their previous levels in the same country. This may happen, although with varying degrees of success and different lags.

As in Japan, exports in many developing countries have increased for prolonged periods as the real exchange rate appreciated. Figure 3.3 illustrates the point by showing that two of the most successful exporters in the last decade among developing countries, Mexico and China, experienced a negative relationship between the rate of real devaluation and the rate of export growth from January 1996 to June 2004. While the fit of the curve is low in the case of China, the coefficient linking real devaluations with export growth is high (–1.9) and it is significant to the 99 percent level. Of course, as in the case of Japan, currency appreciation was not the cause of the high rate of growth of these countries' exports, which was determined by other factors—among them, in the case of Mexico, its access to the U.S. markets provided by the North American Free Trade Agreement (NAFTA).

Checking the sign of the relationship between real devaluations and export growth in each and every developing country goes well beyond the scope of this book. There are, however, some cases that deserve close attention because they refer to countries where devaluations have been prescribed to counteract declines in their rates of export and economic growth. These prescriptions

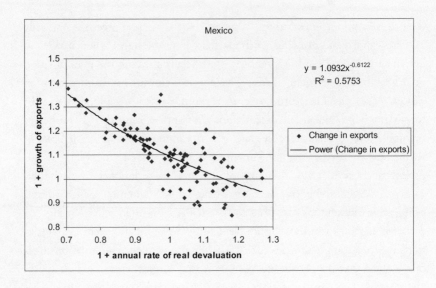

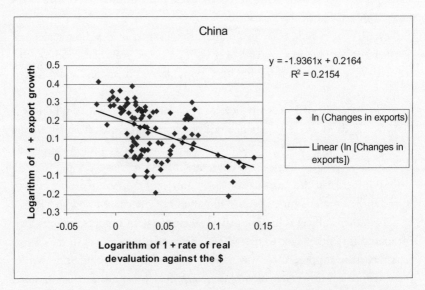

Figure 3.3: Real devaluations and export growth in Mexico and China, January 1996–June 2004. *Note:* The China panel is in natural logarithm form. The coefficient of the real exchange rate has a *t* statistic of −5.2, which makes it significant to the 99 percent level. *Source:* International Financial Statistics of the International Monetary Fund.

were issued in such a widespread fashion that it is commonly thought their cases prove that devaluations are crucial for competitiveness. These cases include Thailand and Argentina before their respective currency and financial crises.

The common perception is that the root of the problems in Thailand was that the country had fixed its exchange rate to the dollar while its exports were increasingly denominated in yen, which at the time were depreciating relative to the dollar. Figure 3.4 seems to support this idea if you look at the immediacy of 1997. There is a brusque downshift in the growth of exports in 1995, a year and a half before the crisis started. The prescribed solution to this problem was to devalue the currency, so as to reduce the economy's labor costs relative to those of the yen area. Yet, if you shift your eyes a little to the right, you will see that six years after the devaluation, Thai exports had not recovered their former pace of growth despite the large devaluations of 1997–1998. The figure includes two trend lines to emphasize the decline experienced around 1995, one estimated with the data from 1975 to 1995 and the second from 1995 on. The difference between the two curves is dramatic. Before 1995, exports were growing at 14 percent per year; after that year, they have been growing at 4 percent. If the problem had been the exchange rate, exports would have picked up to their former rates of growth after the devaluation. Clearly, this was not so. While the weak growth in 1999 could be attributed to the disruptions caused by the crisis itself, the fact that the subsequent recovery has been so slow suggests that there were other problems, more fundamental than the exchange rate, determining the 1995 break in the export growth rate.

Moreover, if the cause of the fall in the export growth rate had been the appreciation relative to the yen, a positive relationship would be expected between *total* exports (i.e., not just the exports to the yen area) and the real exchange rate of the baht relative to the yen (i.e., exports would have diminished with the appreciation of the baht relative to the yen). Figure 3.5 shows that this was not so. From January 1985 to June 1997 the relationship between the real exchange rate against both the dollar and the yen, and exports measured in dollars and yen, was negative. The relationship was negative even from January 1994 to June 1997.

Then, after a period of troubles in which there was no traceable correlation between any real exchange rate and exports, by 2001 the behavior of exports of Thailand settled back in the pattern shown in figure 3.6: Higher exports in both yen and dollars were associated with currency appreciation against the yen.

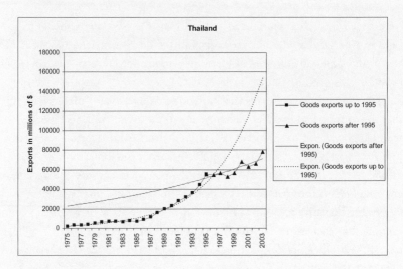

Figure 3.4: Trends in Thai exports, 1975–2003. *Source:* International Financial Statistics.

With regard to this figure, it may be argued that the relationship of real devaluations and export growth became negative after the big 1997–1998 devaluations because these were excessive and the exchange rate was just recovering its sustainable value. Yet, if the idea that the real exchange rate is the main determinant of competitiveness were true, a positive relationship would still be seen between devaluations and exports in Thailand in the period covered in figure 3.6. Exports would be higher when the country devalued more.

The case of Thailand shows that looking at the behavior of exports through the looking glass of the exchange rate exclusively is quite a superficial approach—and one that can be very dangerous for countries given the disturbing effects of large devaluations. Argentina, in the years prior to its 2001–2002 crisis, is another frequently mentioned case in support of the idea that the lack of ability to devalue the currency results in export stagnation. The common thought is that Argentina had to devalue the peso because its exports had collapsed after Brazil devalued its currency in January 1999. This idea is strange for two reasons. First, Argentina's exports, after having declined from $26.4 billion to $23.3 billion in 1999, recovered to $26.3 billion one year later. This can be observed in figure 7.12 in chapter 7. Moreover, Argentina turned its trade deficit into a surplus in 2000, two years after Brazil's devaluation, while devaluing Brazil did so only in 2001. Second, there was no statistically significant relationship between volume of Argentina's exports and the real

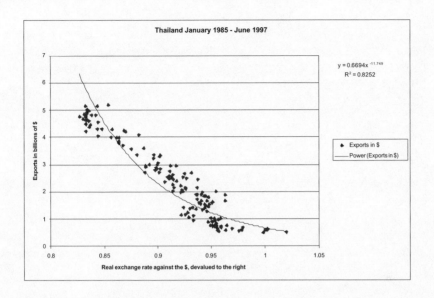

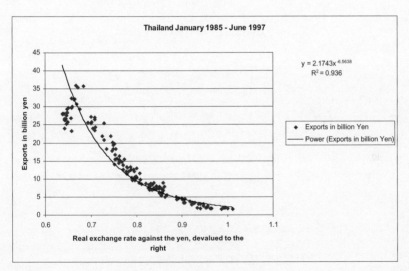

Figure 3.5: Thailand: Real exchange rates relative to dollars and yen and exports in dollars and yen, January 1985–June 1997. *Source:* International Financial Statistics of the International Monetary Fund.

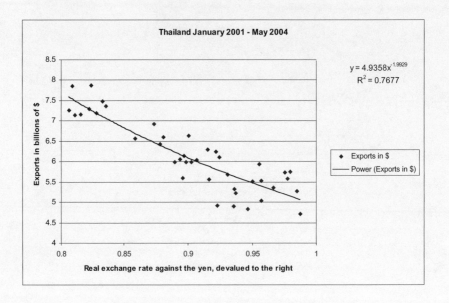

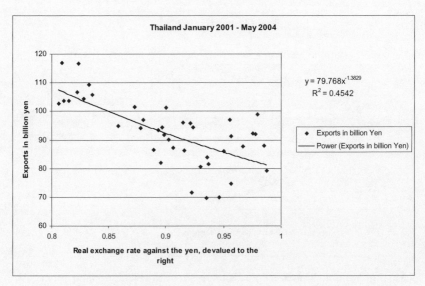

Figure 3.6: Thailand: Real exchange rates relative to dollars and yen and exports in dollars and yen, January 2001–May 2004. *Source:* International Financial Statistics of the International Monetary Fund.

exchange rate against the Real (Brazilian currency) from June 1994 to March 2004. These dates encompass periods before and after the Argentine devaluation of 2001. That is, if there was any relationship, it was too weak to affect the totality of Argentina's exports, even if the real exchange rate varied from 0.5 to 2.5 during the period.[4]

The problems of Argentina have also been attributed to the real exchange rate of the peso relative to the euro. Yet, as with the Real, no statistically significant correlation could be found between the export growth rate and the real exchange rate against the euro from January 1999 to March 2004.

As in the case of monetary independence, discussed in chapter 2, many economists cite Chile as a proof that currency depreciations lead to higher rates of export growth. Superficially, they seem to be right. In fact, the country has pursued a policy of devaluations and has been extremely successful in terms of export growth. Yet, as can be seen in the top panel in figure 3.7, Chile shows a negative relationship between the rates of currency depreciation and export growth for the period covering from January 1990 to March 2005. While the fit of the curve is not high, the coefficient is very high (−1.22) and its $t$ statistic is −9.3, making it significant to the 99 percent level. That is, the numbers show that exports increased when the currency appreciated during the last 183 months. The lower panel suggests an explanation for this behavior by showing a very close fitting between the export growth rate and the changes in the prices of copper, the main commodity exported by Chile. This evidence suggests that the growth rate of Chile's total exports is not a result of policy. It still depends on the international price of copper. Combining the two panels, we can surmise that total exports tend to increase when the price of copper goes up and, when this happens, the currency tends to appreciate in real terms. This interpretation is supported by the fact that, according to the World Bank's World Development Indicators, manufactures represented only 16 percent of the total Chilean exports in 2003.

Remember, these figures do not show that the best policy to increase exports is to appreciate the currency. They do, however show two points: that export performance depends on many factors different from the exchange rate and that these other factors are much more powerful in determining such performance than the exchange rate. This power is evident in the fact that they can propel exports even if the currency is appreciating and deter them even if the currency is depreciating.

Thus, the positive impact of devaluations on exports in comparison with previous exports of the same country should not be taken for granted. How-

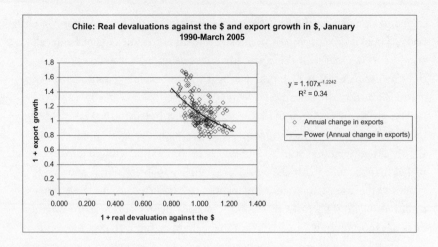

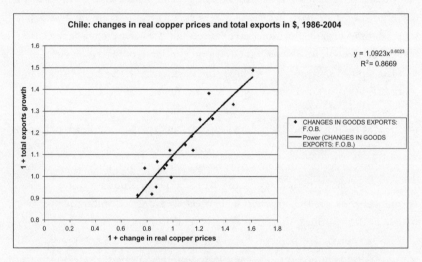

Figure 3.7: Chile: Real devaluations against the dollar and exports growth and changes in the price of copper and exports growth. *Source:* International Financial Statistics of the International Monetary Fund.

ever, even if it is assumed that they had such an impact, the crucial question is whether a policy of devaluations results in higher export growth rates in the long term and across countries. In other words, the question is whether a local currency, and the possibility of devaluing it, would make the country more competitive in the international markets in a lasting way.

Given the strength of the belief in the power of real devaluations to impulse exports, we would expect a strong positive relationship between the two variables. The evidence, however, is not encouraging if all the developing countries are examined together, and it is appalling when they are considered in regional groups.

I ran cross-country regressions for two samples of developing countries with the logarithm of one plus export growth rate as the dependent variable and the logarithm of one plus the devaluation rate as the independent one. One of the samples comprised sixty-three countries for 1992–2002 and the other eighty-one countries for 1997–2002. The relationship turned out to be negative in the two periods, contradicting the idea that devaluations tend to increase exports. The correlation coefficients were very close to each other and statistically significant to the 99 percent level.[5] However, they explain only about 14–18 percent of the variations in export growth across countries. Based on these results, we could say that, while exports tended to increase as the currency appreciated in real terms, the changes in the exchange rate are not a powerful predictor of export performance worldwide.

Yet, the weakness of these results hides important regional differences in regional elasticities, so that when the data is decomposed by regions, the negative relationship between real devaluations and export growth becomes sharper. There is only one region where the relationship is positive: East Asia and the Pacific. All other regions show a negative one.

The negative relationship is stronger in Latin America, the region that has devalued the most. As shown in figure 3.8, the real devaluations of the previous seven years explain 42 percent of the changes in exports in the region—but they do it in the wrong direction. The estimated cross-country elasticity is 0.6, meaning that a country devaluing by 10 percent relative to another is likely to export 6 percent less. Moreover, if one outlier, Brazil, is eliminated from the sample, real devaluations explain 63 percent of the change in exports, and the elasticity increases to 0.88—meaning that a country that devalues by 10 percent relative to another is likely to experience exports 8.8 percent lower. If we multiply this by the percentage explained by the equation, then a real devaluation of 10 percent would reduce exports in the long term by 5.5 percent relative to the countries that did not devalue. The period covered by the figure, seven years, is long enough to internalize lags.

As shown in figure 3.9, the negative relationship was evident also in East Europe and Sub-Saharan Africa. In Central Asia and the Middle East the relationship was also negative, although the number of countries for which

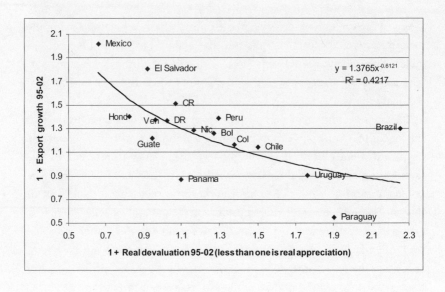

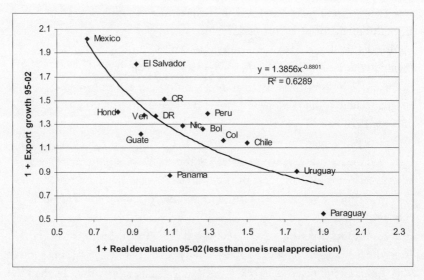

Figure 3.8: Real devaluations and exports growth in Latin America, 1995–2002, with and without Brazil. *Note:* Argentina and Ecuador were excluded from the sample because both changed regimes drastically during the period. Up to 2000, Ecuador devalued at fast rates and then dollarized. Argentina did not devalue until the end of 2001 and then devalued by close to 250 percent. *Source:* International Financial Statistics of the International Monetary Fund.

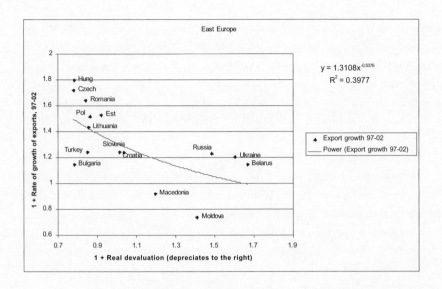

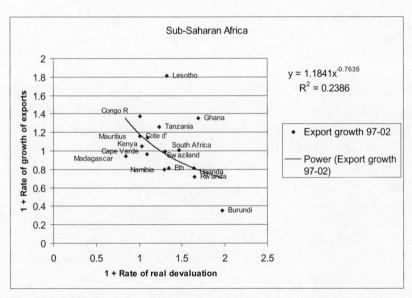

Figure 3.9: Real devaluations and exports growth, East Europe and Sub-Saharan Africa, 1997–2002. *Source:* International Financial Statistics of the International Monetary Fund.

the needed data existed in these regions was to small to produce statistically significant results. The relationship was not significant in the non-Hispanic Caribbean because the region is dominated by currencies pegged to the dollar.

Thus, in most regions, real devaluations tend to be associated with lower export growth rates. That is, opting for a currency regime that allows currency devaluation is not likely to provide a long-term advantage in terms of export growth. Competitiveness and export capacity depend on many other variables, some of which are negatively affected by devaluations.

Before considering some of these variables, we can examine the impact of devaluations against the dollar on the real growth of the economy. After all, financial operations and exporting are only a means to an effect, which is increasing the people's income.

The worldwide relationship between real devaluations and real growth is so tenuous that we can conclude there is no relationship between the two variables in the long term. Yet, there is a clearly negative relationship between nominal devaluations and real growth. I ran a regression using the logarithm of one plus the growth of GDP PPP (purchasing power parity) from 1997 to 2002 as the dependent variable and the logarithm of one plus the nominal devaluation during the same period for seventy-three developing countries. I measured economic growth in terms of dollars of constant PPP in spite of the bias that this indicator tends to have in favor of countries that devalue in real terms, which Dr. Werner von Bankrupt discusses in the epilogue.

The sample excluded outliers devaluing more than 290 percent during the period. The fitness of the regression was low ($R^2$ was 0.21). The coefficient, however, was −0.5 and its t statistic was −4.5, making it significant to the 99 percent level. A sample of fifty-nine developing countries for 1992–2002 gave similar results.

These results suggest that nominal devaluations—regardless of their success in becoming real—are likely to be associated with lower rates of growth. A 10 percent nominal devaluation would result in 1 percent lower real growth. If this is so, and real devaluations are not related to the growth rate of real income, it follows that it is better to keep the same exchange rate in nominal terms.

As in the cases of monetary independence and export growth, many think that Chile is the living evidence of a positive relationship between real devaluations and high real economic growth. In fact, Chile has pursued a policy of real devaluations and has experienced the highest growth rates in income per capita PPP in Latin America. Yet, real currency depreciations in this country have tended to be associated with declines in the income per capita PPP in the following year. A regression of the logarithm of one plus the changes in GDP per capita PPP against the logarithm of one plus the real rate of devaluation one year before produced a negative coefficient of –0.27 with an $R^2$ fitting of 0.44 with data covering 1987 to 2002. The fitting of the curve went up to 0.69 when a dummy variable was introduced to represent 1998, the year when the international effects of the Asian crisis were strongest. Figure 3.10 compares reality with a prediction based on the rate of real devaluation of the previous year and the dummy variable.

Thus, the relationship between the rates of real currency depreciation against the dollar and the rates of growth of GDP per capita PPP at constant prices is clearer in Chile than in the average developing country. However, it goes in the wrong direction.

Why should the relationship between devaluations and exports and economic growth turn out to be the opposite of what is expected by the proponents of devaluations? To answer this question, we have to step out from the narrow models that look at the behavior of exports just in terms of labor costs. The evidence suggests that quite frequently the negative effects that devaluations have in other variables override the supposedly positive effect of reducing the real wage.

As one of the manifestations of this problem, the narrow models focus on reducing the price of one of the factors of production (labor), as the mechanism to spur growth, without paying attention to what happens to the price of the other (capital) when devaluations take place. Ignoring this may be appropriate in countries with international currencies, where, as we have seen, domestic interest rates are not affected by currency depreciations. It is not appropriate, however, in developing countries, where, as we know, these tend to increase with devaluations. This increases the costs of investment and, therefore, reduces the economy's potential for growth in the long term. Of course, it could be argued that the benefits of devaluations can be experienced only in the short term. Yet, the long term is made of short terms. If developing countries adopt a policy of devaluing their currencies even to appreciate them in real terms—as most of them have done for the majority of the last two decades—they would tend to underinvest, with grave consequences for their future.

A second problem is that the continuous use of the exchange rate as a policy variable eventually obscures the role of prices as conveyors of market information. This is another effect that is not present in countries with in-

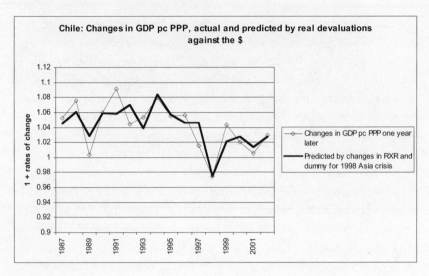

Figure 3.10: Chile: Real depreciation and changes in GDP per capita PPP one year later, 1987–2002. *Source:* International Financial Statistics of the International Monetary Fund for real devaluation/appreciation and World Development Indicators, World Bank, for income per capita PPP.

ternational currencies. In those countries, even large devaluations do not cause drastic shifts in relative prices because they have access to highly diversified economies with rapid capacity of response. There, devaluation mainly shifts the sources of supply of the different goods, privileging the domestic ones, but not increasing the cost of the goods themselves. In developing countries, which lack such diversification, devaluations work their way through most products as they increase the prices of all tradable goods and services, many of which do not have domestic sources of supply. For instance, a devaluation in Europe increases the prices only of the imported machines, not the competing European ones, while in developing countries, it increases the prices of all sophisticated machines and, in fact, of all tradables and all the nontradables with tradable inputs—which is almost all of them. For this reason, relative prices tend to shift violently with nominal devaluations in these countries. If devaluations are frequent, relative prices become quite unstable.

This problem and its effects on investment are frequently underrated. The real world presents a good amount of uncertainties. The situation is worse when you have to predict not just what will happen in the real world but also the reaction of the central banks to such events, particularly because you know that, according to the doctrine prevailing in the developing countries, the response could be dramatic. Such response could take many forms, including episodes of inflation increasing relative to devaluation and the other way around; episodes of fast domestic credit expansion and episodes of even faster credit expansion; and episodes in which the central bank becomes very stringent under an adjustment program of the International Monetary Fund (IMF) after the previous policies have collapsed. In each of these episodes, relative prices will change in unpredictable ways, rendering any plan useless. In business, what you cannot plan, you do not execute.

Central banks are trapped between a rock and a hard place in this issue. If they want to allow economic agents to be able to predict relative prices, their monetary and exchange rate policies must also be predictable. Because of the rational expectations that Dema Gogo learned about in his adventures, however, people adjust in advance to the declared intentions of the central banks, thus blunting the effectiveness of policies. If importers know that the currency will be worth 10 percent less at the end of the importing cycle, they adjust their prices in advance as well. If workers know that their real wage will be eroded by devaluations in the same proportion during a year, they will ask for compensation in advance as well. Such predictability produces a world in which people make their calculations not in terms of prices but in terms of the first differences of these. As long as the central bank pursues this strategy, relative prices become predictable because their rate of change is predictable. People learn to live in the first derivative of prices relative to time. As Dema Gogo understood, however, this is the same as having no devaluation and no inflation, only more complicated.

Having this predictability, even if quite awkward, is positive from the point of view of investors; however, it reduces the effectiveness of central banks. To be effective in their aims, central banks must take unexpected actions when they want to change the course of the economy. As Dr. von Bankrupt advised Dema Gogo through the Devil, they must catch people unguarded. This, however, is the kind of strategy that turns the signals of relative prices most unreliable, logically deterring investment. The impact is worse on the long-term investments that are so needed in the developing countries. This, in fact, is one of the reasons why investors in those countries prefer opportunities that yield high returns in the very immediate future and stay away from investments that could go sour not because of natural market developments but because of the decision of a powerful central banker.

Unexpected actions may also bring about disaster in the short term. As Dema Gogo also discovered, the sliding scale rapidly becomes equivalent to a fixed peg in many dimensions. People soon begin to define stability in terms of the speed of the sliding of the currency and can react wildly when such speed is changed, in the same way that they react to the possibility of devaluation in a fixed exchange rate regime. Thus, changing the slope of the downsliding rule may have disastrous consequences. The adjustment of expectations to the sliding rule as if it were a fixed peg can be exemplified with the case of Mexico in 1994. People speak of the large devaluation of the tequila crisis as if it had taken place in a fixed exchange regime. In fact, Mexico had a sliding exchange rate. What prompted the crisis was the fear that Mexico would devalue more than what people expected. The circumstances were ripe for the crisis because in the previous months, the country had been devaluing at a much slower pace than its inflation rate. That is, Mexico violated the rule of the fixed peg in the first derivative. The final blow was given when the Central Bank of Mexico tried to give an unexpected expansionary shock by printing money at a very fast pace as the elections were approaching. The crisis exploded in the first month of the new government.

In other words, trying to catch the public unguarded is not a good idea. In the long term, it blunts the power of relative prices to allocate resources efficiently. In the short term, it may lead to crises. However, providing predictability by announcing the future rates of devaluation ties the hands of central banks in a way that is similar to fixing the exchange rate, only more complicated.

A third problem in the logic that portrays devaluations as a means to improve competitiveness is that it ultimately assumes that countries should keep on exporting the same things—that is, that the composition of their exports should not change. Few remarks can elicit more indignant denials than this one. If you were to repeat the previous statement, you would be told that nobody, ever, has made such a bizarre assumption. This is true, if we are talking of explicit assumptions; it is not, however, when we look at the implicit ones.

This assumption is easily identified when looking at the prescription that developing countries receive when the prices of their exported products, mostly commodities, fall in the international markets, or when their wages increase in international terms. Such prescription is that they should devalue their currency to restore the profitability of the *existing* activities by reducing the real wages.

This prescription, in fact, assumes that the aim of policy is keeping the existing activities profitable, ignoring the possibility of upgrading or replacing them, so that the new activities could be profitable at the higher wage levels. As we have seen in the examples of Japan and Germany, this, not reducing wages, would be consistent with the long-term development of the country. Weak currency policies tend to discourage this conversion by increasing the costs of the investments needed to carry it out. By continuously reducing the real wage to turn profitable the existing low-value-added export activities, the policy of real devaluations tends to trap the economy within those low-value-added products. Tied to activities that grow only weakly, or in fact decline with time, exports cannot grow healthily in the long run.

It might be argued that there is nothing in a policy of real devaluations that would prevent the diversification of the economy into higher-value-added activities. If the salaries are low for commodity production, they should be low for the higher-value-added activities as well, turning them even more profitable.

This, however, would ignore the fact that devaluations have effects different from lowering the real wage, which include increasing financial costs, reducing the maturity of financial operations, and introducing high volatility in the financial variables. This makes it more difficult to invest in new activities. The following example helps clarify this issue.

Think of yourself as a policymaker in a country exporting garments, a field that is becoming increasingly competitive. As experts in business strategies would advise, you have two options to compete. The first is being the cheapest supplier of your product—you go for volume. The second is to go for value. In this field, that means selling to the high-end markets in boutiques and expensive stores. Competition in this world is not decided by price but by exclusivity of design and prompt reactions to the market trends. Being trendy, these products are perishable, so that boutiques pay prime attention to managing their inventories in real time. Meeting their needs requires sophisticated equipment. The computer systems of the highly competitive producers in this field allow them to produce new designs and put them into production rapidly; to track every piece in the stocks of the boutiques and on their shop floors; to program their production in accordance to the changes in these stocks and deliver it at the right time; and to reduce material waste, a source of losses that could mean dropping out of competition. The computerized equipment needed to run supply in this way is extremely expensive. Moving up the value-added ladder is capital intensive. This capital cannot be substituted with people who cannot do these things as fast and effectively without the expensive computerized machinery.

Thus, you are given the choice as a policymaker. Which strategy would you adopt? You can say that you don't have to make any decision. You may think that if you devalue, you would give an advantage to both kinds of producers. After all, you would be reducing wages for the two of them. Yet, the problem is that those aiming at the high-end market do not really care much for salaries. Most of their costs are in computerized equipment. Therefore, they care about interest rates. Given the way interest rates react to devaluations in developing countries, when you opt for devaluations, you raise the cost of capital in the country and make it more difficult for firms to make the transition to higher value added. Most probably, they will not do it because having to pay much higher interest rates than their competitors will put them out of competition.

There are other reasons why a policy aimed at keeping the existing activities profitable blunts the incentives to move up the value-added ladder. It is always cheaper to keep on producing the same thing than trying new ventures. This is particularly true in terms of the knowledge required to produce and distribute, which producers have already accumulated in the existing products. Moving to other products requires acquiring new knowledge, which in reality always means high initial costs in terms of failures. Why move into these problems if high profits can be made in very simple commodity production? Commodity producers will always prefer government protection for the existing activities than moving into risky new products, and devaluations are a form of government protection.

Moreover, on the side of labor, the lower the salary you pay, the lower the possibilities that the workers would ever get the education they need to become more productive and able to add value to more sophisticated production. If your policy is to deliberately reduce the real wage, you trap them into this low-level equilibrium.

Thus, if you are a policymaker, you see that there is a hidden decision about the composition of exports in the devaluation prescriptions. Given the problems of domestic currencies in the developing countries, your strategy can be aimed at eliciting production based on depressed wages or on low interest rates, but not on the two together. You have to make a choice.

Is it then an exaggeration to say that the policy of continuous devaluations tends to trap countries in low-value-added activities?

The costs of tying policy to the survival of existing products are always high. They are even higher when, as today, the world is experiencing a drastic shift in the composition of production and consumption. The last two or three decades of the twentieth century watched the gradual emergence of a technological revolution based on the combination of computers and telecommunications, and the associated globalization of chains of production. The essence of this technological revolution is the connection in real time that it establishes between minds around the globe, allowing for the coordination of complex tasks at a distance. This capacity is already having momentous effects on the design of products, production methods, marketing, and financing.

One of the effects of this revolution is that, by multiplying the power of the mind, the marriage of computers and telecommunications is converting knowledge and the ability to coordinate complex tasks at a distance into the main source of wealth. As this happens, the prices of goods that embed knowledge are increasing relative to those that do not require it for their production. The other side of this coin is that the prices of the goods with less knowledge imbedded, non-oil commodities, have fallen dramatically in the last twenty-five years, well beyond the usual cycles of these products. Figure 3.11 shows the path of the real prices of the product with the worst fall (coffee) and that of the product with the least pronounced fall (fish meal), as well as that of the average. All the other thirty non-oil commodities reported in the International Financial Statistics of the IMF are between those two. The magnitude of the fall is very large. In 2003, the price of coffee was 25 percent of the price it had in 1961; that of fish meal, 75 percent; that of the average of all thirty-four commodities, 46 percent. Of course, the fall was much larger if we take the boom levels of the 1970s as the basis for the comparison. With such fall in prices, it is only logical that countries aiming at turning these products profitable through devaluations would experience low export growth rates in dollar terms and in general economic activity. Through this effect, devaluations trap developing countries into a low-level equilibrium.

Is it true that countries that devalue the most in real terms tend to remain trapped in commodities exports? Figure 3.12 shows that over the long term the composition of Latin American exports varied in a way that was consistent with this hypothesis. The change in the share of manufactures in total exports was negatively related to the real depreciation of the local currency over the 1965–2003 period. The elasticity linking the two rates of change was –0.61 and it was significant at the 95 percent level.

How is the future of countries dependent on non-oil commodity prices? Is it bad to remain dependent on commodities? One might think that the fall in the real prices of these products could be reversed in the future as a result

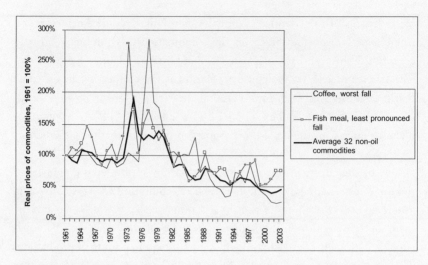

Figure 3.11: Real prices of thirty-two non-oil commodities, 1961–2003. *Source:* International Financial Statistics of the International Monetary Fund.

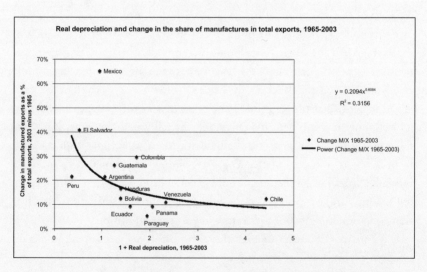

Figure 3.12: Latin America: Real depreciation and changes in the share of manufactures in exports, 1965–2003. *Note:* The sample excluded Brazil, Nicaragua, and Uruguay because of missing data. Costa Rica was excluded because the share of manufacturing in total exports largely depends on the production of one single enterprise, Intel, which received incentives not available to other producers. Panama depreciated in real terms because its inflation was much lower than that of the United States over the period covered by the figure. *Source:* Manufacturing share in total exports from World Development Indicators, World Bank. Exchange rates from the International Financial Statistics of the International Monetary Fund.

of the increase in the world's income and the specialization of increasing numbers of countries in the knowledge-intensive products. In fact, there was an upswing in the prices of commodities in 2003–2004, generally attributed to China's demand. As can be seen in figure 3.11, however, this increase still has to go a long way to reach the levels of the real non-oil commodity prices of the 1960s, not to speak of those of the 1970s.

In any case, there are four problems with basing a strategy of development on the rosy expectation that the real prices of non-oil commodities will eventually experience a historical boom. First, a country cannot base its growth strategy on the expectation of eventual booms. Second, the production of commodities will always be subject to the competition of producers with the lowest salaries in the world. Third, the prices of commodities tend to be highly volatile. Fourth, the production of commodities is also subject to technological progress, which would tend to reduce their prices by reducing their costs of production in technologically advanced countries. That is, the production of commodities can also become a knowledge-intensive activity, and this is becoming a reality in some areas. Monetary and exchange rate policies aimed at keeping the current production profitable protect not just the products but also the existing method of production, so that even if such production becomes profitable with higher wages in other economies, the countries pursuing them would also miss this advance.

Moreover, the rapid growth of China is raising the bar in this competition continuously. As China moves up in the ladder of production, more products come to be subject to the massive competition of a country with very low wages at international prices. The only possibility that the other developing countries have to keep their incomes from falling is entering the route of more specialized products with higher value added. This requires structural changes that will not take place if countries continue to protect the current low-value-added products and production methods.

The reasoning supporting devaluation as a means to revive an ailing economy gives top importance to avoiding unemployment. Yet, the underlying logic has the same flaws as when applied to the promotion of exports. Devaluation elicits two opposing reactions from the economy: By lowering wages, employment may be increased in the short term, but at the same time, by increasing interest rates, the very activity that would create employment in the long term is discouraged. Immediate employment creation is traded for long-term expansion of productive capacity. It was probably for this reason that Keynes did not recommend reducing the real wage as a way to overcome the Great Depression. Instead, he thought of reducing the real rate of interest, which would increase employment through both new investment and utilization of existing capacity. This course of action does not generate reactions working at cross-purposes, as devaluation does.

The necessary reduction in the real wage points at yet another problem of devaluations: the asymmetry of the burden of the monetary adjustment among different groups in society. Since the impact of real devaluations on the revitalization of exports depends on a redistribution of income between the owners of capital and the workers, wage earners are the most vulnerable people among those who are affected negatively by devaluation. Other sectors are also affected negatively, prominent among them the people holding financial instruments denominated in local currency. However, those have natural defenses; the rates of interest go up to compensate for the devaluation. If savers are not satisfied, they can export their savings. The owners of capital of firms working on nontradable activities may be negatively affected, because the prices of their products decline relative to those of the producers of tradables. Yet, the cost of their nontradable inputs goes down as well. Also, since the price of their products declines relative to those on tradables, their demand expands.

These defenses are not available for the workers. While migration is possible, its costs are extremely high, so that only a small portion of the population has this option open. Most of the workers are tied to their place of residence and have to take the salaries paid there. Thus, the ultimate bearer of the reduction in the prices of nontradables is the wage. In compensation, devaluation is supposed to increase the demand for workers precisely because it reduces the relative cost of wages. The only defense available to workers in these circumstances is exerting political pressures to have their salaries increased. Thus, the policy of real devaluations poses a difficult decision to governments. To ensure that the policy would work, they have to engineer a redistribution of income from the poor to the rich.

I further discuss this point in chapter 9. For purposes here, I quote an article published in *The Economist* on July 21, 2005. This article reported that by 2005, the real wages in service jobs in Argentina were a quarter below their pre-crisis levels and that the share of wages in GDP had fallen by 15 percent when compared to the years before the 2001 devaluation. On the other hand, the wealth in local currency of the Argentines that took their savings abroad on time has increased so dramatically that they have generated a housing boom. The houses, however, are out of the reach of the workers. Houses are priced in dollars.[6]

This redistribution of wealth has nothing to do with economic efficiency and, of course, it does not lead to it. It is just the inevitable effect of devaluation in a country where some citizens exported their savings while others did not. While the case of Argentina is remarkable for the size of the devaluation, this effect is present in all countries with weak currencies. The natural incentive that these create for savers is to denominate their savings in dollars, domestically or abroad, and enjoy the capital gains that would flow to them every time the currency is devalued in real terms. This incentive is not conducive to growth in either exports or GDP in general. It is just the manifestation of the reversed liquidity trap—which sometimes is just endemic with low intensity while at other times becomes disastrously acute.

In summary, devaluations have contradictory effects on the growth of exports and the economy in developing countries. They reduce the costs of tradables producers by reducing the real wages; yet, at the same time, they increase those costs through their effects in the rate of interest, the maturity of the loans, and many other variables crucial for an efficient economic performance. Their net impact cannot be determined theoretically. It depends on which of these effects are stronger. The evidence shows that in most cases, most of the time, the negative effects are stronger—to the extent that the sign of the relationship implied by the statement "devaluations increase the competitiveness of countries" is reversed. It should read, "the facts suggest that devaluations tend to reduce the competitiveness of countries."

# Chapter 4 The Costs of Stability

We saw in chapter 3 that the regime of floating domestic currencies, which in developing countries has meant a regime of continuous devaluations for most of the time, has failed to produce what it promised in terms of high export growth rates and economic activity in response to devaluations. There are many other variables that intervene in the determination of competitiveness. They are so strong that the positive relationship could not be found between real devaluations and the growth of exports and economic activity that common opinions would lead us to expect. Moreover, in many cases, we found that the relationship was of the opposite sign, suggesting that the negative effects of devaluations in these other factors override the supposedly positive impact of real wage reductions on growth rates. These disappointments add to the ones previously discussed in terms of attaining monetary independence from the rest of the world. The fact that many of those disappointments were caused by the bad management of the domestic currencies does not detract from the fact that they have resulted in patterns of behavior that differ markedly from those prevailing in developed countries, gravely reducing the ability of the monetary authorities to take advantage of the freedoms associated with having a local currency.

There are other disillusionments associated with local currencies. Even if theory never promised it, many people take for granted that monetary and exchange rate policies can substitute for fiscal policies as an instrument of aggregate demand management.[1] This is plainly not so. Most economists, when confronted with the direct question, will answer that, of course, each of these instruments addresses different dimensions of economic behavior and therefore cannot substitute for each other. Nevertheless, they continue to say that the combination of monetary and exchange rate policies provides an easier and more flexible mechanism to manage demand than fiscal policy. They argue that expanding or reducing the growth rate of monetary creation and devaluing the currency require only administrative decisions, which can be made at any moment, while fiscal adjustment is a painful process that usually involves legislative action and long lags. This is actually one of the main arguments branded to reject dollarization because dollarized countries cannot apply monetary policies. I have become used to people saying, "El Salvador now especially has to watch its fiscal deficit, because it is a dollarized country," implying, sometimes saying explicitly, that keeping fiscal deficit reasonable is more important in a dollarized than in a non-dollarized economy. The fact is that keeping in place a prudent fiscal policy is as important in a non-dollarized as in a dollarized economy because exchange rate policies cannot compensate for a loose fiscal situation, and monetary policies can do it only within certain limits and at outrageously high costs. In fact, as we will discuss in this chapter, monetary and exchange rate policies may gravely increase the costs of managing fiscal problems, introducing nonlinearities that multiply the possibilities of disaster.

The crucial importance of fiscal policy in the determination of demand is obvious. When a government runs a fiscal deficit, the purchasing power it injects to the economy through its expenditures is higher than that which it withdraws through taxation. People spend this purchasing power in consumption or investment, increasing the overall nominal domestic demand in the economy. If the economy is close to full employment, or if the composition of the new demand is different from that of domestic production, the excess purchasing power spills over the balance of payments and the country runs a current account deficit, experiences an increase in the rate of inflation, or both. Normally, the rate of inflation will not increase and the exchange rate will stay put as long as the current account deficit is financed with capital inflows. When the capital inflows stop, however, the current account deficit becomes unsustainable and the currency depreciates, turning the purchase of foreign exchange more expensive than before, thus taming the appetite for imported goods and foreign financial instruments. This effect is the source of the idea that exchange rate policies can stabilize a country suffering from excessive domestic demand.

Yet, if the fiscal deficit is not reduced, the economy remains unstable after the devaluation. With the fiscal deficit running, nominal domestic demand continues to grow. With the leakage to the balance of payments closed by the external lenders, excess demand then straightforwardly results in inflation. Since all economies have a certain propensity to import (no country is self-sufficient), the pressure to import is not diminished, and, with a limited supply of foreign exchange, the currency rapidly devalues. The lack of imported inputs negatively affects domestic production and recession ensues, not for lack of demand but for lack of imported supplies.

Stabilizing such an economy and restoring its ability to grow requires reducing the fiscal deficit or turning it into a surplus, independently of the exchange rate regime. Equally, devaluations cannot compensate for the decline in income caused by negative external shocks, such as negative changes in the terms of trade—that is, when the prices of exports fall relative to those of imports. The adjustment has to be fiscal in this case because the problem created by a negative external shock is that the income of the country has gone down and the population, including the government, must adjust their expenditures to the new, lower level of income. If the country keeps the same rate of fiscal expenditures, a fiscal deficit will appear as the fiscal revenues decline, and this fiscal deficit will feed into higher rates of inflation or wider deficits in the balance of payments. A higher balance of payments deficit can be managed if the shock is temporary. If the shock is permanent, however, it is necessary to cut expenditures or increase the fiscal revenues. It is clear, then, that the possibility of devaluing the currency does not free economies from the need to act fiscally when an adjustment of nominal domestic demand is required.

Still, central banks can compensate for a loose fiscal policy by running a restrictive monetary policy that would withdraw purchasing power from the population while the fiscal deficit is injecting it. Central banks can do this in two main ways, which are collectively called monetary *sterilization*. The first one is to issue securities and sell them to the banks. The second is to increase the legal reserve requirement, which is forcing banks to deposit with it higher portions of their deposits from the population. In both cases, the money captured by the central bank disappears from circulation, thus reducing the nominal purchasing power of the population in the domestic currency. The second method, however, additionally reduces the ability of the banking system to multiply money, so that its effect is more drastic. In any case, these mechanisms allow central banks to withdraw the excessive acquisitive power created by its sister government institution, the Ministry of Finance. In the process, the central bank prevents inflation and devaluation because it is not injecting additional money in net terms.

This, of course, creates a contradiction between the fiscal and the monetary policies. The contradiction is more glaring in countries where, as it is most common, the central bank finances a substantial part or the entirety of the fiscal deficits. The advantage of this contradiction is that it allows the central bank to change the composition of credit. It can first grant credit to the government and then sterilize money that would have been used to finance the private sector. Sterilization has another advantage; since the operation of giving and taking is carried out in two different steps, its objective is not transparent to the public.

While sterilization can effectively keep the rates of inflation low when the fiscal policies are inflationary, its costs can easily become staggering. It masks the subjacent macroeconomic imbalances with an appearance of low inflation, but it does not remove the imbalances or the negative effects they have in the economy. One of these effects is, of course, that sterilization crowds out the private sector from the credit markets. This is precisely the intention: to redirect the deposits in the banking system to finance the government to avoid the inflationary effects of central bank credit.

As shown in table 4.1, with the exception of Sub-Saharan Africa, where credit is almost twice as much as deposits because of the large inflow of external credit granted by donors, credit is substantially lower than deposits in all developing regions. The difference is mostly given by sterilization. The impact of the sterilization rates used in the developing countries on the financial intermediation to the private sector is substantial, to the point of nullifying the advantages that some countries have over others in terms of attracting resources from the public. The largest sterilization rate is found in South Asia, where the inflation rates tend to be low even if their fiscal deficits are not. As it is apparent in the table, the ratio of credit to the private sector to gross domestic product (GDP) in that region is roughly the same as in

Table 4.1: M2 and Credit to the Private Sector in 2001

| Region | M2 % of GDP in 2001 | Credit % of M2 in 2001 | Credit % of GDP |
|---|---|---|---|
| East Asia and Pacific | 130.2 | 84.4 | 110.0 |
| Europe and Central Asia | 34.7 | 60.6 | 21.0 |
| Latin America and the Caribbean | 27.2 | 88.4 | 24.0 |
| Middle East and North Africa | 59.0 | 79.7 | 47.0 |
| Sub-Saharan Africa | 35.8 | 181.7 | 65.0 |
| South Asia | 52.0 | 55.8 | 29.0 |

*Source:* World Development Indicators, World Bank.

Latin America, despite the fact that its ratio of deposits plus currency in circulation (M2) to GDP is almost twice as large. The average country in East Europe and Central Asia (the formerly communist countries) allocates less credit to the private sector than Latin America as a percent of GDP, even if they mobilize substantially more resources from the markets. Roughly 40–45 percent of the funds mobilized by the banking systems of East Europe and Central and South Asia go to finance the government.[2]

Thus, while sterilization keeps inflation rates low, it represses financial intermediation to the private sector as much as high inflation does. The economic complications and costs of sterilization vary with the interest rates that central banks pay to the banks on their deposits. Central banks can minimize the disruption by paying market lending interest rates for the sterilized funds, adjusted by risks and administrative costs. If central banks do so, banks buy the securities or deposit their funds in the central bank as a substitute for lending to the private sector. Since the government's demand for funds is additional to that existing from the private sector, the banks have an incentive to increase their deposit interest rates to get more deposits. This, in turn, causes an increase in the lending rate. However, since the banks are adequately compensated for their deposits with the central bank, the spread between the deposit and lending rates remains roughly unchanged. The problem with this solution is that the central bank incurs financial costs, which increase with the amount sterilized. This causes cash losses to the central bank, which can cover them in two ways. One is to get a transfer from the Ministry of Finance, which, in the situation we are describing, it is in no position to do. The other is to create money to cover them, which throws the central bank into a vicious circle, because it has to sterilize the money created to pay the interests caused by sterilization. This increases its financial costs again, which then must be covered with further monetary creation. The problem gets further complicated because the higher interest rates also increase the financial costs of the government on the instruments it sells in the market, thus increasing the fiscal deficit.

Alternatively, central banks can also pay lower rates than the market or no interests at all. They can do that by creating legal reserve requirements at zero interest rates or, which is equivalent, by forcing banks to buy its securities at low interest rates. In this case, the banks do not have an incentive to receive more deposits from the public, so the deposit rate remains more or less at the same level. The spread between the deposit and the lending rates, however, increases because now the banks have to recoup the costs of their deposits with a lower amount of lending. The lending rate increases over the deposit rate. Thus, the private sector is taxed through the spread between the deposit and the lending rates.

This method seems to be ideal if you think that interest rates are not important. Yet, it generates weird nonlinearities in the economy that can effectively trap the economy into a low-level equilibrium of output and growth. The high economic costs of managing domestic demand with this method can be illustrated with the case of Brazil, a country that has been frequently praised because it has been able to keep inflation low while carrying out substantial devaluations. Furthermore, in spite of these devaluations, there is no visible spontaneous dollarization in the country. Apparently, Brazil has attained the dream of developing countries: true monetary independence.

Brazil has struggled with its currency for a long time. During the 1980s and early 1990s, it experienced extremely high rates of inflation and devaluation that kept on going even as the country changed its currency twice. The government was able to bring down inflation in 1994, when it created the Real and adopted a monetary regime that was almost like a currency board. In a currency board regime, the central bank commits itself to back its monetary liabilities (called reserve money or monetary base) with reserves in foreign exchange. This means that it surrenders its right to create money except when selling it in exchange for foreign currency at a fixed exchange rate. Brazil, however, left the door open to move the exchange rate by small amounts. The idea was to make some adjustments, so that the exchange rate against the U.S. dollar, which at a certain point was at 0.85 reais for the dollar, would finally converge to one to one.

The problem was that inflation remained high above the devaluation rate in the initial year of the new regime, and the currency rapidly appreciated in real terms. The government tried to compensate for this by increasing the rate of nominal devaluation while the inflation rate kept on falling. This stabilized the real exchange rate and introduced a mild tendency to real depreciation in 1997–1998. By the end of 1998, while the nominal exchange rate had gone to 1.7 per dollar (overshooting the target by 70 percent), the real exchange rate was still 23 percent lower (appreciated) than in January 1994. That is, Brazil was devaluing its currency in nominal terms while appreciating it in real terms.

In January 1999, the country abandoned the so-called currency board and allowed the Real to float in the midst of a currency crisis prompted by a drastic reduction in international financing. The currency depreciated quickly until September 2002, when the government turned to appreciate it sharply in nominal and real terms. From March 2003 to March 2004, the Real fluctuated within a very narrow band in real terms. The result of all these movements was one of the classical cycles in which a phase of inflation higher than devaluation gave way to a phase in which devaluation was higher than inflation, resulting in a real devaluation of approximately 40 percent relative to January 1994 during the decade.

The ultimate source of the imbalance that afflicted the country up to 1998 was an excessive expansion of credit to the government. The fast expansion of this credit is clear in figure 4.1, which shows the share of the credit to the government in the total credit of the entire banking system (the sum of the commercial banks and the central bank), as well as the size of this credit relative to the size of M2 (the monetary liabilities of the banking system). As shown in the figure, the total credit of the consolidated banking system to the government increased throughout the currency board period, from about 10 percent of the total in early 1996 to almost 40 percent in late 1998. The monetary creation resultant from this expansion was such that the ratio of total credit (including credit to the government) to M2 went from an already high 140 percent to 170 percent. It was in this moment, at the end of 1998, that the government abandoned the currency board and started its policy of big devaluations.

Devaluation did not address the fundamental problem, however. The figure shows that for a period lasting from the first big devaluation to the end of 2001, credit to the government declined as a manifestation of a more stringent fiscal policy. Yet, the government was not consistent in this new policy. After this lull, credit to the government started to grow again at approximately the

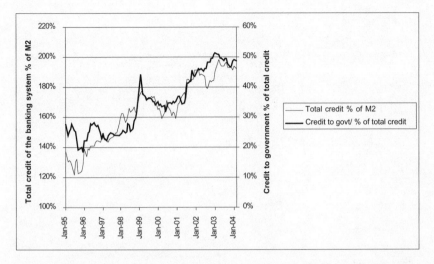

Figure 4.1: Brazil: Credit to government percentage of total credit of the banking system and total credit percentage of the total monetary liabilities of the banking system (M2). *Source:* International Financial Statistics, International Monetary Fund.

same rate as before, so that by early 2004, it was already 50 percent of total credit, while total credit was 200 percent of the total liabilities of the banking system.

It is amazing that this rapid credit creation did not result in higher inflation rates. Prior to late 1998, the government kept inflation low in spite of the credit expansion by reducing the rate of devaluation. According to the same logic, the inflation rate should have increased when the government shifted to a policy of fast devaluation. However, while the rate of devaluation moved very closely with the rate of expansion of the credit to the government, the rate of inflation remained quite stable around an average of 8 percent.

The disconnection between inflation and devaluation would seem to suggest that Brazil is the vivid example of the benefits that common wisdom expects from local currencies. The country conducts its own monetary policy, lets the exchange rate adjust for any inconsistency with the rest of the world—sometimes with devaluations, other times with appreciation—and keeps inflation under control. Brazil seems to have achieved the dream of developing countries: true monetary independence.

Reality is not so rosy, however. The apparent stability is based on huge amounts of sterilization, so large that they distort the entire economy. Figure 4.2 shows that throughout the entire cycle, the central bank withdrew from

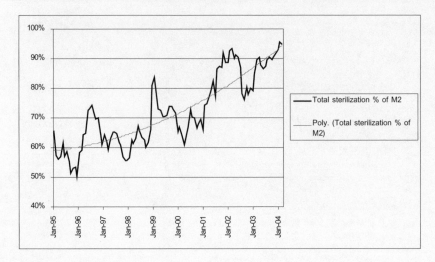

Figure 4.2: Brazil: Sterilization as a percentage of M2. *Source:* International Financial Statistics, International Monetary Fund.

circulation increasing shares of the money it created when giving credit to the government. In 1998, when the crisis hit, the amount withdrawn was around 80 percent of the remaining M2. By early 2004, it was more than 95 percent. The central bank did this by forcing the banks to deposit with it increasing portions of their deposits from the public, and by selling increasing amounts of securities to the banks. The amount sterilized reached about 65 percent of the total deposits of the banks at one time, and was about 50 percent of them at the beginning of 2004. In this way, the central bank quickly created money to finance the government with one hand but simultaneously took it away from the private sector with the other hand.

In the case of Brazil, the central bank does not pay interest rates on the deposits it holds from the banks. The impact of this policy on the financial costs of the banks is massive. This is because the banks must cover the costs of their entire deposits with just the portion of them that they can lend. For example, if the deposit rate of interest were 19 percent (as it was on average in 2000–2004) and the legal reserve requirement 62 percent, the financial cost of the funds that the banks could lend would be 50 percent, so that for this reason alone, the spread must be at least 28 percent. Add 7 percent to cover the banks' expenses and you get 35 percent, which is more or less the spread between the deposit and the lending rates in Brazil.[3]

Creating such a large wedge between the deposit and the lending rates has another effect. The interest rates that the government pays on its treasury bills are linked to the deposit rates and are practically identical to them. Thus, while on average the private sector paid 61 percent interest rates on its loans from January 2000 to March 2004, the government paid 19 percent.

In this way, the private sector pays very high rates of interest to nullify the impact of devaluations on the inflation rate and to keep the financial costs of the government relatively low. The spread is so large that when multiplied by the total banking system credit to the private sector it represents 10.8 percent of GDP. The equivalent figure, adjusted for the ratio of credit to GDP, is 0.85 percent and 0.89 percent of GDP in the United States and El Salvador, respectively.[4] We can assume that this is a reasonable cost of intermediation. When we deduct it from the spread in Brazil, the difference is about 9.9 percent of GDP. The private sector passes part of this burden on to the government through deductions from the corporate income tax, which has a maximum rate of 15 percent. When adjusted for this, we have a figure of 8.4 percent of GDP. The Brazilian private sector pays this *annual* cost for the benefit of severing the linkage between the rates of devaluation and inflation.

Two comparisons can be made to put this amount in perspective. One is that the intermediation cost in Brazil, net of taxes and of a reasonable margin of financial intermediation, represents 56 percent of the average of the total tax revenues of Latin American countries as a percent of GDP. The other is that this cost is about 17 percent of the size of the government's external debt in 1998, when the big devaluations began. This means that if the government had used those resources to repay the external debt instead of to pay for the privilege of devaluing without increasing inflation, it could have repaid the entire amount in six years. Instead, the burden of the debt increased by 60 percent from 1998 to 2003, as devaluations increased the reais value of the dollar-denominated debts.

In addition to increasing the burden of the external debt, devaluations also negatively affected the domestic interest rates. The top panel of figure 4.3 shows how the dollar-equivalent rates of interests (i.e., the domestic rates deflated by the rate of devaluation of the currency) are related to the rate of devaluation in the same way as in the developed countries: Lowering these rates relative to those prevailing in the United States results in a depreciation of the currency.[5] However, the second panel in the figure shows that the relationship between the *real* rate of interest and the rate of *nominal* devaluation is positive in most ranges of devaluation, meaning that *the real rate of interest increases when the rate of devaluation is increased*, and decreases when

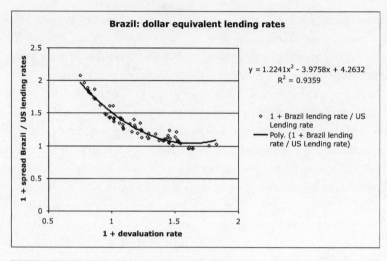

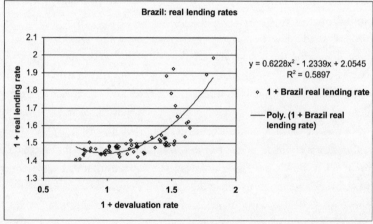

Figure 4.3: Rate of devaluation of the Brazilian reais against the U.S. dollar, January 1999 to April 2004. *Source:* International Financial Statistics of the International Monetary Fund.

devaluation slows down. As discussed in previous chapters, this tends to happen in developing countries, and it is very disturbing. If the low inflation rates seemed to suggest that Brazil is monetarily independent, the behavior of the real interest rate denies such conclusion.

Moreover, it can be observed that the relationship between the real lending rate and the rate of devaluation shows two strongly nonlinear effects. One is that during the period of analysis, the real rate of interest increased at a pace that became faster as the rate of devaluation increased. The other is that while the same rate decreased when the rate of devaluation declined, it increased again when the currency *appreciated* (values lower than one in the horizontal axis)—most probably because devaluation expectations increased as the currency appreciated in ways that the population saw as not sustainable.

Thus, if we assume that the recent past is a guide for future behavior, it can be concluded that managing the interest rates is Brazil is a very complex business. To reduce the dollar equivalent rate of interest, the rate of devaluation should be increased. This, however, will also increase the real rate of interest. Conversely, to reduce the real interest rate, the rate of devaluation should be reduced, which of course requires increasing the dollar equivalent rate of interest. Yet, if you go too far in reducing the rate of devaluation and start revaluing the currency, the real interest rate will not decrease, but instead it will increase, possibly due to increased devaluation expectations. Ironically for those who believe that central banks can reduce interest rates by manipulating the exchange rate, during this period the real interest rate reached its minimum precisely at one, which means neither devaluation nor appreciation.

Like Gogo, you will ask yourself what you are gaining by having a currency if the real interest rates are at their lowest when you do nothing. The classical answer to this question is that you gain the ability to create a wedge between the rate of devaluation and that of inflation. This answer ignores the fact that there might be a cost associated with having such ability. Such cost can be staggering. At its lowest, with zero appreciation or devaluation, the real lending rate in Brazil was 44 percent, while the nominal rate was 56 percent (or 52 percentage points over the lending rates in the United States).[6] On average, the *real* interest rate was 47 percent between January 1999 and April 2004. That is, if you took a loan of one hundred reais to buy a house valued at one hundred reais, by the end of two years you would have paid *in interest* the equivalent of another house.

The enormous premium of the reais lending rates over the international dollar rates, of course, includes the country risks not associated with the currency. There is no way to estimate these other risks in Brazil because the country does not permit foreign currency deposits. However, we can make a plausible guess. One would assume that they should not be higher than, say, those of El Salvador. Measuring the noncurrency risk is easier in El Salvador because the country is dollarized, so that the difference between its rates of interest and those of the United States measures the pure country risk—that is, excluding the currency risk.[7] Since dollarization in January 2001, the lending rate in El Salvador has been 2 percentage points higher than in the United

States. If this figure is used for Brazil, it can be estimated by difference that the currency risk in that country is about 50 percentage points. This is a very high cost to pay for the privilege of having a local currency.

Political pressures to reduce the lending interest rates are strong in Brazil. Doing so, however, is very difficult because the problem is mainly with the spread between the two rates (i.e., the difference between the lending and deposit rates), which averaged an astonishing 35 percentage points during the period. The spread is so high that it accounts for most of the real lending rate, which averaged 47 percent. While the real lending rate is incredibly high, the deposit rate, at about 12 percent, is within the range of most developing countries. Given this large spread, and barring the case of negative nominal deposit rates, the nominal lending rate could not be lower than its current levels. Thus, reducing the real lending rates necessarily implies reducing the spreads. Doing so, however, is very difficult because, as we have seen, the spread is precisely the main instrument that the central bank uses to keep the inflation rate low while devaluing the currency quickly.

In the context of these high spreads, we can begin to analyze the benefits that the private sector can obtain from another praised feature of the Brazilian system: the fact that there is no spontaneous dollarization in the country, at least not in the sense of the denomination of bank accounts in dollar terms. Many people portray this as a sign of the monetary independence of the country and a demonstration of rationality that protects private borrowers from the large losses they would suffer under the country's rapid devaluation rates. Many think that the Brazilian borrowers are happy because of this, and this may be correct. Yet, three facts should be considered before passing judgment. First, the government does not allow dollar deposits in the country, so that even if the Brazilians wanted to have dollar deposits and loans, they could not get them. Second, deposits in Brazil are low by international standards when measured against the country's GDP. They fluctuate around 20 percent of GDP, while in El Salvador they are around 40 percent in spite of the enormous difference in real deposit interest rates (12 percent in Brazil and 1 percent in El Salvador). The third fact is surprising: The interest rates that the private sector pays on its local currency debts are so high that they surpass what they would have paid if they had borrowed in dollars, even with the high devaluation rates of Brazil.

To demonstrate this point, we can simulate a case in which two brothers living in Brazil decide to borrow the equivalent of one hundred reais in January 1999—one in dollars from a bank in the United States and the other in reais from a bank in Brazil. They refinance their debts every month at the rate of interest prevailing in the respective market at that moment. At the end, they compare who owes more reais. Of course, the principal of the debt of the brother owing dollars would increase with devaluation, giving him a natural disadvantage in a country that devalued its currency by 143 percent and experienced an inflation of only 56 percent in the ensuing years. Still, interest rates in Brazil are so high that while the brother who borrowed in dollars would owe 330 reais at the end of March 2004, the one who borrowed in reais would owe 1,300 reais.

The comparison should not conceal the fact that even the brother who borrowed in dollars would have paid a stiff rate of interest in reais terms, averaging 25.5 percent per year. This looks low only in comparison with the average annual rate paid by the brother borrowing in reais, 62.5 percent. To measure the magnitude of the rates paid in dollar terms in Brazil, we can compare the real debts (i.e., adjusted for inflation) accumulated by the brother who borrowed in dollars with that of their cousin who lives in a dollarized developing country, El Salvador, over the same period. While the Salvadoran cousin would have accumulated a balance 38 percent higher than his initial borrowing, the Brazilian cousin's balance would be 120 percent higher.

Because of the large spread, the cost of the borrowers is not the benefit of the depositors. As we saw above, a continuously refinanced debt contracted in reais would accumulate higher balances than a debt of the same reais magnitude borrowed in dollars in the United States. We would expect that the same would happen with deposits—that is, that the balances of a deposit denominated in reais would accumulate higher balances than one deposited in dollars in the United States. This, however, would not be true. For most of the period, the balance in reais of the brother who deposited the equivalent of one hundred reais in a U.S. bank would have been higher than the balance in the same currency of the brother who deposited the same amount of reais in a Brazilian bank. By September 2002, the first would have accumulated 378 reais while the second would have only 196. The difference would have narrowed only after the government started to appreciate the currency in September 2002. Nevertheless, by March 2004, the brother with deposits in dollars would have accumulated 288 reais while the one who deposited in reais would have 261. That is, the private sector pays higher rates in its credits but receives lower rates in its deposits than in the United States. What Brazil has is a double-edged sword.

These facts put the prohibition of dollar deposits and loans in Brazil in a different perspective. There is a clear incentive for the government to prohibit dollar deposits and loans. If they could, Brazilians would move to dollars because, even at the country's high rates of devaluation, it is much cheaper to borrow in dollars than to pay the high intermediation charges prevailing in the country. At the same time, depositors would earn more if they made deposits in dollars, too. Thus, the prohibition traps the Brazilian private sector into the high-spread system that allows the government to devalue the currency without increasing the inflation rate and to simultaneously keep its own financial costs low. If the government allowed dollar deposits, it would have to find another way to finance its deficits and keep the rate of inflation low.

Maybe the government really does not need any complex mechanism to finance its deficit because the deficit itself is just another consequence of the nonlinearities of the monetary system. It would not exist if these nonlinearities disappeared. I show this in table 4.2, which covers the period when the new policy of devaluations was adopted. The first three rows of the table show the government's primary balance (the difference between revenues and expenditures before interest payments are taken into consideration), the interest payments, and the fiscal surpluses and deficits, all of them as a percent of GDP. The last row shows the implicit real rate of interest (the ratio of the interests actually paid to the average debt). The right side of the table shows what the interest payments and the fiscal balance would have been if the government of Brazil had paid the real rates paid by the government of El Salvador in the same years. (El Salvador had not dollarized its economy at the time but had a fixed exchange rate and a law that prohibited the central bank to finance the government.) As you can see in the table, the fiscal deficit would have become much smaller in 1998 and it would have turned into substantial surpluses in the ensuing years if the government had paid those rates. The projected surpluses would have allowed the government to increase its social expenditure while keeping reasonably small deficits, one of the main objectives that remain unattainable under the present system. This is another cost added to the economy by the way that the stability of the currency is maintained.

Looking at these figures, one gets the impression that the instability in Brazil is largely attributable to the increasing complexity of the monetary quagmire that the government has created to keep its currency stable. If the interest rates that the government pays were close to the international levels, the fiscal deficits would disappear. Since they are so high, the government has a deficit. Then, the deficits lead to the need to print money to finance the

Table 4.2: Fiscal Deficits and the Financial Cost of the Government

|  | With actual real interest rates (%) | | | With El Salvador's real interest rates (%) | | |
|---|---|---|---|---|---|---|
|  | 1998 | 1999 | 2000 | 1998 | 1999 | 2000 |
| Primary balance | 0.00 | 3.10 | 3.50 | 0.00 | 3.10 | 3.50 |
| Interest payments | 7.30 | 7.90 | 4.40 | 1.46 | 2.54 | 2.04 |
| Fiscal surplus or deficit (−) | −7.30 | −4.80 | −0.80 | −1.46 | 0.56 | 1.46 |
| Fiscal turnaround |  |  |  | 5.8 | 5.4 | 2.3 |
| Implicit real |  | 18.90 |  |  |  |  |
| Interest rate | 21.00 |  | 8.90 | 4.20 | 6.07 | 4.14 |

*Note:* The fiscal balances have been adjusted to eliminate the impact of privatizations and arrears recognition. *Source:* Evan Tanner and Alberto Ramos, *Fiscal Sustainability and Monetary versus Fiscal Dominance: Evidence from Brazil, 1991–2000*, IMF Working Paper WP/02/5, IMF Institute and Western Hemisphere Department, Washington DC, 2002, Table 2.

government, and money printing creates the need to devalue the currency. Currency devaluation then increases the real rates of interest, which raise the fiscal deficit. In the midst of this process, the central bank creates the wedge between the rates the government and the private sector pay to reduce the impact of the monetary creation on inflation. This vicious circle would be ended simply by reducing the real interest rates to the levels prevailing in a small country that did not use its central bank to finance the government. None of the extremely complex operations that mar the system would be necessary.

You may notice that the magnitude of the Brazilian deficits is not so large as to justify the protracted instability of the country. Moreover, at 48 percent of GDP, the debt of the government in 1998 was not large enough to create the external debt scare that started the new policy of large devaluations. The real appreciation of the currency that the country accumulated from 1994 to 1998 (23 percent) did not justify the 78 percent devaluation that the government applied from December 1998 to April 2004, much less the 170 percent devaluation that it applied from the first date to September 2002. These small causes led to the large instability of those years only because the local currency magnified them. Brazil went down that slope that terrified Dema Gogo, where you have to speed up to remain in the same place and where small causes have very large effects. What initially is just a problem of government financing suddenly requires dramatic actions by the central bank, in magnitudes that start relatively small but eventually become very big. This relationship between small causes and big effects is one of the definitions of nonlinear phenomena, which is what the possibility of devaluation creates in a country with a weak currency.

Ironically for a country that supposedly attained monetary independence, many have noted that one external variable, the extreme variability of the country's international capital flows, is one of the main reasons why the relatively low fiscal deficits produce wide fluctuations in the economy, causing the catastrophic movements in the exchange rate and all the associated monetary and financial instability. That is, the blame for Brazil's instability is put squarely on the international capital markets. Yet, as I show below, the extreme variability of these flows seems to be a consequence of the nonlinear behavior of the domestic monetary system.

The country's access to international capital markets is so volatile that many people regard its negative turns as "external shocks." Figure 4.4 compares the spreads of the Brazilian bonds over the yields of the U.S. Treasury bonds with the spreads of other countries during one of the difficult periods for Brazil. The fact that on average Latin America experienced a substantial increase in the spread of its bonds during the same period makes it believable that the Brazilian woes of the time were "external." Yet, the bottom of the figure shows the spreads of three other Latin American countries—Mexico, Panama, and El Salvador—which certainly increased, but by much less. Two of these are dollarized while Mexico is not. All of them, however, enjoy monetary stability.

The scale of the graph dwarfs the spread differences in ranges close to normality. At its lowest, by the end of 2003, the spread of the Brazilian bonds was 6.6 percentage points, while that of dollarized El Salvador was 3 percentage points. By that time, Brazil's spread had come down from its peak at 23 percentage points one year before, while that of El Salvador had also come down, but only from 3.75. Given that the external debt of Brazil is around 75 percent of GDP, the difference in spread relative to El Salvador is equivalent to 2.5 percent of GDP. Brazil could spend this money in social services as part of the fiscal improvement we discussed regarding figure 4.4.

Many people think that the dramatic increase in the spread experienced by Brazil in that period was natural because the country faced crucial presidential elections, which presented the possibility that a far leftist, who could choose to not abide by market rules, would become the president. Yet, the same happened in El Salvador, and the spread did not increase significantly. In fact,

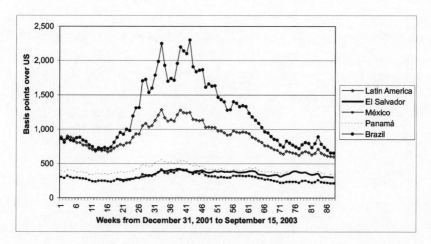

Figure 4.4: Spreads of government bonds over the U.S. Treasury bonds in the international markets, 2002–2003. *Source:* JP Morgan.

the spread was falling at the end of the period shown in figure 4.4, even if this uncertainty remained in place (the elections were in March 2004). At the time, the polls, which the subsequent events proved widely wrong, predicted that the extreme leftist had a good chance of becoming president. Nevertheless, the response in the international markets was radically different. In the case of Brazil, this shows a nonlinear nature that is the mirror image of the nonlinear character of its domestic monetary events. Of course, keeping the economy in equilibrium is very hard in Brazil, and the possibility of having less than top economists managing it scared the market.

Why did Brazil borrow at those extremely high rates? It could not afford not to. Figure 4.5 shows how the level of reserves of the central bank moved in synchrony with the capital flows. This does not have to happen because a country can also gain reserves by closing the current account deficit in the balance of payments. This should not be a problem in Brazil, because one of the supposed advantages of local currencies is that the current account deficit can be closed quickly by devaluing them. Figure 4.5, however, also shows that for three years, the large devaluations that started in 1999 did little to arrest the deficit in this account. This happened for two reasons, both of them related to the monetary instability of the country.

First, as we already have seen, the government continued to run fiscal

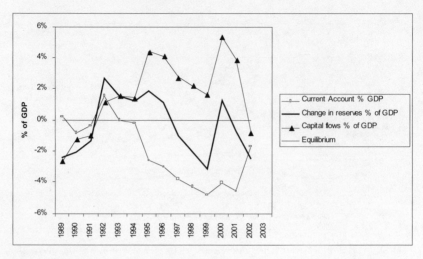

Figure 4.5: Balance of payments and capital flows. *Source:* International Financial Statistics, International Monetary Fund.

deficits, largely caused by its excessive financial costs, which did not come from excessive debt but from excessive interest rates. Second, devaluations increase the size of the current account deficit relative to the size of the economy because it is denominated in dollars while GDP is denominated in reais. The magnitude of this effect can be quite substantial. For example, if you have a deficit of $40 million and your GDP is $1 billion, your deficit is equivalent to 4 percent of GDP. Devalue your currency by 48 percent, as Brazil did in 1999, and this deficit becomes 6 percent of GDP. Thus, monetary instability created the fiscal deficits leading to and then increasing the size of current account deficits as a percent of GDP.

As long as you remain in this vicious circle, the only way you have to dampen the vibration of the system is getting capital inflows from abroad. If they come in, you gain reserves, your need to print money is assuaged, and everything improves. If they do not come in, you become willing to pay the high rates that Brazil pays in the international markets for the dollar loans.

In other words, the power to print money, rather than freeing Brazil from the conditions prevailing in the international markets, has turned the country excessively dependent on capital inflows coming from those markets. This is true not just in terms of financial variables but also in those of real growth of production. Figure 4.6 shows how the growth rate of real GDP varied with the changes in the capital inflows of the country in 1995–2002.

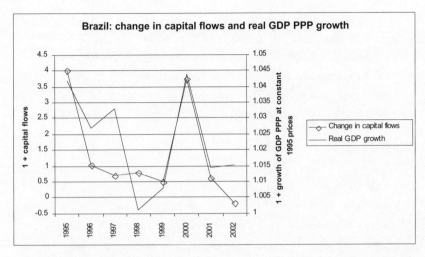

Figure 4.6: Rates of change of nominal capital flows and rate of growth of real GDP in dollars PPP, 1995–2002. *Source:* International Financial Statistics, International Monetary Fund for capital flows and World Development Indicators, World Bank, for GDP PPP.

In the case of Brazil, the dollars coming from abroad have the same powers that conventional theory attributes to the domestic currency. The monetary rule in Brazil would seem to be that if the economy is weakening, the Central Bank of Brazil should print dollars. Short of doing that for obvious reasons, it should avoid printing domestic currency because that only muddies the waters, increasing the interest rates and the fiscal deficits, imposing enormous implicit taxes on the users of the financial system, generating nonlinear vibrations that affect the entire economy and, more than anything, losing dollars and increasing their price. Through this, it increases the price of growth. Lurking beneath these facts we can see the old liquidity trap of Keynes, applied in reverse because the relevant currency to stimulate growth in Brazil is really the dollar, not the reais.

The nonlinear effects of having a domestic currency are not as pronounced in countries where, as in Mexico, the system is near its equilibrium. It is when the system strays from such equilibrium, as in the case of Brazil currently, and in Mexico a decade ago, that the events become highly nonlinear. They do so because, even in a country like Brazil, without dollar accounts and with low inflation relative to its rate of devaluation, two measures of value collide, so that each economic variable fluctuates in different ways depending on what measure of value is applied to gauge them.

In summary, this brief analysis shows that the costs of keeping Brazil's monetary independence, in the sense of severing the linkage between devaluation and inflation, are staggering. Rather than freeing the country from the external environment, the monetary system has trapped it in a vicious circle of dependence on international capital flows.

Moreover, it is clear that having a local currency has not helped Brazil to smooth out the fluctuations of its economy. On the contrary, the economy is highly volatile.

What about exports? While it would be ideal to compare export growth with real devaluations for at least a decade, the data before 1995 distorts the results because at the time the country was in the midst of a crisis. In 1994, the rate of devaluation was 608 percent and the rate of inflation 2,077 percent. From 1990 to 1993, devaluation averaged 1,376 percent and inflation 1,565 percent per year. Brazil overcame the crisis only in 1995, when the devaluation rate fell to 14 percent and the inflation rate to 66 percent. In a calmer period, from 1995 to 2003, there was a positive relationship between export growth and the real devaluations of one year before. The data series is short and the relationship is not strong. The movements in the real exchange rate explain only 28 percent of the changes in exports and the elasticity of exports to the exchange rate was only 0.20 (exports grew by 2 percent when the currency devalued by 10 percent within that 28 percent). If the outliers are eliminated, the positive relationship disappears. Yet, it exists. Thus, it seems that, in spite of all the problems in the financial system, Brazil gained from its ability to devalue its currency in terms of expanding its exports.

When analyzing the performance of a monetary regime, however, we have to compare it with the performance of a country with a different regime during the same period. The comparator can be El Salvador, which, even if not yet dollarized, did not devalue after 1992. Still, El Salvador, with zero devaluation, outperformed Brazil by an ample margin. As reported by the World Bank's World Development Indicators, in 2004 its exports amounted to 418 percent of their value in 1992, while those of Brazil were 314 percent.

A final argument in favor of a local currency is that it spurs growth. Figure 4.7 compares the growth of the two economies since 1995. The gross domestic product (GDP) of the two countries is measured in international dollars with purchasing power parity (PPP) at constant 1995 prices. As explained by Dr. Werner von Bankrupt in the epilogue, this measure tends to favor countries that carry out large real devaluations. Also, the Salvadoran GDP is likely to be substantially underestimated due to domestic measurement problems. Still,

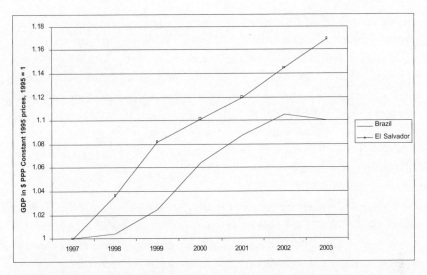

Figure 4.7: GDP in dollars PPP at constant 1995 prices, Brazil and El Salvador. *Source:* World Development Indicators, World Bank.

the figure shows that the Salvadoran economy grew faster and with much less volatility than the Brazilian one. This happened even if the Salvadoran economy suffered dramatic external shocks that included devastating hurricanes and earthquakes, a catastrophic fall in the international prices of all its agricultural products, and large increases in the prices of oil (different from Brazil, El Salvador does not have oil).

As I advised in the introduction, we should not fall into the usual trap of attributing the entire economic performance of a country to its exchange rate regime. Long-term exports performance and competitiveness depend mainly on many other variables. The same happens with the long-term economic growth rate. Nevertheless, I made the comparison to show that reality does not support what people normally assume about the effects of devaluations in the economic performance of a country.

Having said that, we cannot but suspect that Brazil's extreme volatility must have an effect on its rate of growth. While we cannot measure the potential of the Brazilian economy, it is certain that being such a huge country with plentiful natural resources and a very sophisticated elite, such potential exceeds by a wide margin its actual performance. Measuring the cost of the high volatility, the difficulty of making plans, the lack of long-term financing, and other consequences of the so-called monetary independence is well beyond the scope of this book. Yet, it is clear that, while the huge financial costs paid by the private sector to keep inflation low go into the calculation of GDP, they are senseless economically. Strictly, they should not be included, so that GDP would be smaller. Many would argue that these costs bring about a substantial benefit, the relatively low inflation rates of the country, but we must remember that this cost is necessary only because monetary independence created the deficits through high interest rates. In fact, the potential of the Brazilian economy must be enormous because it still grows in spite of having so many monetary and financial obstacles—all of them created by the manipulation of money.

As discussed earlier, the theory of floating rates would say that, for all these problems, Brazil should be enjoying some very important benefits because it has a flexible domestic currency. The ability to print its own money should make it resilient to external shocks; independent from international finance; able to spur export growth at will; and allow it to keep a steady balance of inflation, devaluation, and growth. Our analysis, however, shows that this is not the case.

Other people have noticed. In its April 2003 rating, Moody's Investment Service lists as Brazil's credit challenges its significant overall vulnerability to domestic and external shocks; the volatile access to international capital markets; the large and growing external debt; the limited export growth and relatively large foreign currency debt; and the need to balance inflation, growth, and currency stability. The list appears to be that of a country that does not have its own currency because it contradicts all the common ideas about the advantages of having such a currency, which I compare with Moody's opinion in table 4.3.

It is important to notice that the external shocks referred to in Moody's report were different from the normal definition of that term. Normally included under that term are exogenous disasters, such as hurricanes, earthquakes, catastrophic falls in the international prices of products that provide their income to substantial portions of the population, or, for non–oil-producing countries, catastrophic increases in the price of that product. Moody's is referring to shocks generated by the Brazilian monetary system itself. As its document clarifies in its second page, the external shocks are the "reversals of capital flows and sudden changes in investors' confidence." Many people think that such changes are the result of the unpredictable vagaries of international markets and, therefore, they classify them as external shocks. There is no doubt that there is something to this; yet, the Brazilian system

Table 4.3: Features that the Brazilian System Should Have, According to Common Belief and Moody's List of the Country's Challenges

| Features | Theoretical Prediction | Moody's Opinion |
|---|---|---|
| Resilience to external shocks | High | Significant overall vulnerability to both external and domestic shocks |
| Access to capital markets | High independence from external financing because it can create its own money | Volatile access to international markets and large and growing external debt |
| Ability to spur export growth | High because it can encourage them through devaluations | Limited export growth |
| Ability to balance inflation, devaluation, and economic growth | High because of monetary independence | It needs to attain such balance |

*Source:* Moody's Investor Services rating of Brazil, April 2003.

magnifies the extent of the changes, so that what would be a gentle wave for others becomes a tsunami in Brazil.

The example of Brazil shows how a weak local currency creates highly nonlinear movements in monetary and financial variables when the economy strays away from equilibrium. Many proponents of local currencies may grant that this is true, but then counter that this does not invalidate the usefulness of local currencies because they behave well when close to equilibrium, which is where you should be in any case.

We have seen that the dual measures of value create serious problems even when developing economies are close to equilibrium, including the lack of long-term credit, the higher interest rates, and, as discussed in chapter 5, the lack of integration with financial globalization. Yet, for the moment, we may accept the argument that these problems are less important than those faced by Brazil.

Stating that the problems of local currencies become bad only when the system is away from equilibrium destroys one of the main arguments presented to assert the superiority of these currencies: that they give countries resilience against drastic external shocks. If the experiences of Brazil and many other countries I analyze in part 2 are worth a thought against established doctrine, it seems that the power to print money not only leads to crises but also is quite damaging when used to resolve them. Printing money in developing countries is at best a fair-weather friend; at worst, it is a perfidious one because it can magnify a relatively small disturbance—like Brazil's fiscal deficits that would disappear with lower interest rates—into a serious monetary problem.

## Chapter 5 Missing Financial Globalization

One of the most damaging effects of the instability of local currencies in developing countries is that it distorts the perspective of economic policy. The stabilization of the local currency becomes the overriding objective of the government. Given the repeated failures in attaining such objective, adjusting to unstable monetary conditions becomes the top priority item in the agenda of both the public and private sectors. A substantial portion of people's energy goes into continuously adjusting to high and variable rates of inflation and devaluation rather than into economic development. The study and practice of economics collapses to the obscure art of devising devilish schemes that would keep the economy from falling over the edge. Economics students dream of becoming governors of central banks or ministers of finance to attain with a bold measure what people take for granted in other countries: economic stability. Most damagingly, as in Brazil, the overruling necessity to stabilize the local currency leads to a willingness to distort the entire economy for the sake of attaining this objective. That is, the sway of the theories and the institutions involved in the current regime of weak floating currencies in the developing countries is so strong and resilient that when some inconsistency with reality appears, the natural reaction is to protect the local currency, bending everything else around this objective, so that the model is proved right.

In this fashion, for example, if short-term capital flows disrupt the harmony of currency floating, then they should be prohibited. If keeping the stability of the local currency requires raising interest rates to unreasonable levels, so be it. After all, the high interest rates can be easily attributed to the lack of local capital characteristic of developing countries. If the fiscal deficits arise because of the high interest rates, then the entire economy should be distorted to make them sustainable and forget that the resources thus wasted could be used to invest in education and health. If this also means that long-term credit will not exist, that is acceptable. If external financing is becoming a problem because of continuous devaluations, the private sector should not be allowed to borrow abroad, even if this isolates it from the benefits of financial globalization. If people want a stable currency to save, reduce their transaction costs, and carry out international operations, this is merely an evidence of their naïve view of something that only specialists can understand: the value of a weak currency. If they, in a rash gesture of ingratitude, want to abandon the local currency for the dollar in their domestic contracts, and worse still, in their deposits, the government must immediately and decisively prevent them from doing it. If currency mismatching develops, it is the international, tradable currency that should go, not the weak, nontradable domestic one. Nobody but the government should have a say in monetary matters and nobody else should have access to that evil substance, dollars. Then, after having done all this, price stability can be attained, but at a huge cost that includes generating instability in many other crucial variables that affect the growth of the economy.

In this chapter, I focus on one of the dimensions of the sacrifices made for the sake of defending the existence of a local currency: access to the globalized financial system. Unless stated otherwise, the source of the data in this chapter is the Global Development Finance database, published on the World Wide Web by the World Bank.

Developing countries, having transferred their standards of value abroad, are more integrated to *monetary* globalization than the developed ones. Their domestic rates of interest react to those prevailing in the international markets in an immediate and clear way. In contrast, with very few exceptions, these countries are missing the *financial* side of globalization. They remain as financially isolated as ever.

This is a pity because developing countries would benefit the most from financial globalization. Typically, their domestic financial systems are quite small and unable to meet the countries' credit needs; their interest rates and the spreads between the lending and deposit ones are too high; the range of services that their systems provide is very narrow; and, given the volatility of the modern world, they are in desperate need of derivatives and other sophisticated financial instruments to manage their risks. Very frequently, they fall into devastating crises because they lack short-term financing. The integration to the globalized financial markets would resolve these problems.

Unfortunately, a permanent integration with the international financial markets must be rejected if the aim of policy is defending the local currency. From this perspective, international financiers are seen with deep ambivalence, sometimes as sources of funds badly needed for investment or stabilization and sometimes as dangerous carriers of currency rigidity. The changes in these perceptions go with the endemic cycle of the local currencies. We can identify three phases in this cycle.

In the moment just after a currency crisis has happened, inflows of foreign currency are badly needed to convince the population that a new exchange rate is sustainable. Foreign investors are wooed to lend to the country. The International Monetary Fund (IMF) sets the example by providing the country with foreign currency loans. Short-term loans, essential for trade, are much welcomed. The second phase comes when the country has recovered from the crisis and needs capital inflows from abroad to finance investment and growth. At that time, obtaining credit from abroad is seen as the sign of accomplishment. The third phase comes when the local currency becomes troubled again and the immediate prescription is devaluation. At that moment, the previous success in attracting capital from abroad is seen as a grave mistake. By this time, the foreign lenders have become villains. With substantial obligations denominated in foreign currencies, countries develop what is referred to in the literature, somewhat derisively, as the "fear of floating," which is the reluctance of governments to face the financial crisis that would be prompted by devaluation. In this situation, the experts and the international institutions push for devaluation and the governments resist. The culprit of this situation is the interconnection with the international markets.

In these circumstances, the fear of floating must be overcome. While this fear is related to all foreign currency liabilities, those who want to remove it focus on what they see as the most illegitimate of them all: the foreign currency accounts in the banking system. The recommendation is then that the government should pesify (convert into domestic currency) the domestic foreign currency obligations and then proceed immediately with a devaluation, which confiscates the funds of the savers in foreign currency. This would pay for the monetary disaster that the lack of trust in the local currency has caused. This, for example, was the case in Argentina in the early 2000s.

Of course, the credibility of the government, which had allowed the buildup of domestic obligations in previous phases, would be seriously compromised. However, this does not matter if the loss of credibility (the basic condition to get access to all financial operations) removes the fear of floating. The credibility loss, which may take decades to overcome, plus the high interest rates, the scarcity of funds for investment, the lack of financial services, and the absence of mechanisms to manage risks, as well as other costs to the economy, must be sacrificed for the sake of attaining the most important objective of economic policy: stability *with* a local currency. The patient could almost die in the process, but the local currency, the system of flotation to which it is attached, and the establishment that controls it would be saved.

The casual way that foreign currency deposits are treated in this kind of literature—as contracts that governments can force private partners to dissolve—is part of the cavalier approach to the integration of developing countries to the global markets. It also reveals an unpardonable disregard for the rights of the citizens of the developing countries. The economists who write offhand that such contracts should be broken by government command surely would not do it if they had their pensions and savings invested in those accounts. They would question the legitimacy of such a gross intervention of the government against the freedom of consensual contracts among private parties. Amazingly, many of these economists turn around and write papers saying that the problem in developing countries is that contracts are not respected. They do not see the contradiction because, for them, financial operations in foreign currencies are illegitimate in a higher order of magnitude than that of contract defaults: Their presence reveals the weaknesses of the local currencies and the failures of the international system that supports them. For this sin, people who deposited in dollars must be punished.

Short-term capital flows are second only to foreign currency accounts in domestic banking systems as a target for those who want to remove the fear of floating. Few economists would openly say that countries should pesify those obligations as well because the lenders are not within the jurisdiction of the pesifying government and can contest the decision in foreign courts. They can get the country's foreign assets foreclosed and exert other kinds of pressures, such as curtailing all short-term credit to the country, an action that can have devastating effects on trade. Thus, ideally, the removal of fear of floating must be approached from a preventive angle in this area.

The preventive idea is that countries should not permit the inflow of short-term loans *to the private sector*. In this vein, many economists, some of them very famous, who would never propose that short-term credit should be banned across borders in developed countries, argue that they should be prohibited in the developing ones. That is, countries should discriminate between foreign direct investment and long-term financial capital inflows, which should be allowed to enter the economies, and short-term financial capital flows, which should not be allowed in because they are inherently unstable.

The advocates of this idea would seem to have the evidence on their side. All crises in developing countries have shown a common pattern of boom and bust. In the first phase of this cycle, the prices of certain assets go up relative to other assets and to current production. In the second phase, the boom ends and all prices revert to their previous levels. Typically, enormous amounts of short-term capital flow into the country during the first phase, leading to a real appreciation of the currency. The outflows cause the opposite effect, leading to sharp devaluations and currency crises. This coincidence between capital inflows and outflows with the two phases of the boom cycle has prompted the idea that these flows are the causes of the crises.

The argument for establishing short-term capital controls has several flaws, however. First, the short-term capital inflows that propel the booms leading to such crises do not go into countries at random. They go to countries offering opportunities to earn short-term speculative profits generated by real and financial distortions, and, once inside those countries, the incoming capital goes to finance the areas most distorted by the speculative incentives.

Second, in all cases, the local governments created the distortions that led to the inflows and then to the outflows. Putting them in control of the flows is assigning the wolf to take care of the sheep. The case of Chile in the years preceding its crisis of the early 1980s illustrates this point. The buildup to the crisis took place while the government had in position controls on short-term capital flows. When the local banks began to show signs of serious illiquidity problems, the government faced the choice of confronting the crisis immediately or delaying it by getting additional financing; it decided on the second option. Taking advantage of the international bank's ignorance of the true situation of the Chilean banks, the government removed the capital controls and allowed the banks to borrow abroad. The additional liquidity only helped banks to continue financing the debtors that were already trapped by the bust, thus worsening the banks' insolvency problems and the size of the crisis when it finally exploded. The Chilean case could be seen as adding to the argument that the governments should bar short-term capital flows. The point is, however, that it was precisely the government that eliminated the controls at the worst possible moment. This was not an isolated case. Governments tend to borrow heavily in the short-term markets when hopelessly trying to forestall an incoming solvency crisis. As shown by the Chilean case, governments can lift prohibitions that they have set when pressed by liquidity problems.

Third, the argument to ban short-term capital flows as the culprits of financial crises is based on a faulty assumption. It assumes that the capital that flowed out when the crises exploded was the same that came in during the upswing that preceded the collapse and that the locals sat passively while the boom and bust were going on. In reality, all liquid capital tends to leave during crises, and there is nothing to guarantee that a piece of capital that entered, say, yesterday, for a period of thirty days, would be more liquid than one that entered the country two years ago, for a period of two years. The financial system generates liquidity every day, as thousands or millions of loans of different maturities mature. Moreover, the deposits in the banks are legally liquid at any time and they are the source of a large portion of the capital outflows. That is why withdrawals from the banks are associated with losses of international reserves. A ban on short-term capital flows would not prevent this other liquidity to escape from the system. The capital that flowed out during crises would have done so anyway even in the presence of short-term capital controls, because such controls would not have been applicable to most of the money flowing out.

The tequila crisis illustrates this point very clearly. In its aftermath, the blame for the run on the currency was put squarely on the international holders of tesobonos (bonds denominated in dollars). While tracking the identity of the people who took the money out of Mexico was not really relevant, its findings showed beyond any doubt that it had been local investors who had started the stampede.

Fourth, in a stable monetary environment, short-term credits are stabilizing. This is as true for companies and individuals as for countries. Can you imagine a world without short-term credit? The smallest problem of illiquidity, which might appear even among the most solvent of the debtors, would mean bankruptcy or enormously high losses for them, and valuable assets would have to be sold urgently at very low prices to meet a deadline. Short-term capital flows are indeed the mechanism that the economy has to prevent short-term liquidity problems from becoming serious problems of insolvency. In full agreement with this, the IMF, which presides over the local currency systems, is a short-term lender. It works precisely on the idea that short-term capital flows can help stabilize the domestic and the international systems.

Short-term capital flows do not work in this way in developing countries because of the instability of the local currencies. The conflicts created by these flows are not inherent in the economies of the developing countries but in their local currencies.

People who see the freedom of capital movements as the cause of financial crises also forget that this was the idea among developed countries during the crises that preceded the end of the Bretton Woods arrangement. In those times, the currency crises in *developed* countries were also associated with huge flows of short-term capital. Gradually, these countries understood that the source of instability was not the freedom of capital movements but the artificial differences in the short-term yields of financial instruments in different countries, and that these differences arose from government interventions in the local financial and monetary systems. The crucial insight leading to the solution of the problem was that to keep currencies and financial variables stable they did not need to control international capital flows; instead, they had to let markets set the rate of interest within the international context and pursue prudent macroeconomic policies that would guarantee the strength of the currency. The same insight could be applied today to the destabilizing flows of short-term capital that have accompanied the recent crises in developing countries. The problem is in the distortions in the domestic markets, not in the capital flows that react to them.

The instability of flows is not limited to the short end of financing. Long-term operations are also volatile. Figure 5.1 shows the net flows (total disbursements minus total service) of long-term credit to developing countries. As discussed with regard to Brazil, the volatility of these flows is largely determined by the unstable condition of the local currencies. Two peaks are apparent in these flows—one in 1980 and the next in 1998. The declines that followed those peaks coincide with the Latin American and the Asian crises, respectively.

This volatility is the inevitable result of the idea that it is worth sacrificing

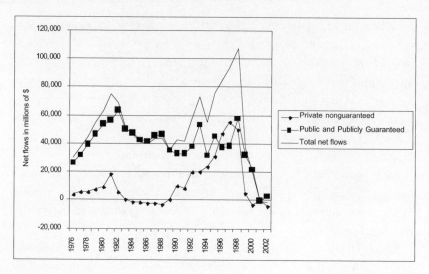

Figure 5.1: Net flows to public and private sectors, all developing countries. *Source:* World Bank's Global Development Finance Statistics

the credit integrity of developing countries for the sake of gaining a mirage, the short-term advantages offered by the manipulation of the currency, which, in any case, fail to materialize.

Real devaluations worsen volatility in yet another way. As Dema Gogo learned in his monetary adventures, real devaluations increase the burden of the external debt (which is denominated in foreign currencies) on the country's GDP (which is denominated in the devalued domestic currency). When devaluations are drastic, as they are when there is a currency crisis, this increase is significant so that, in many cases, the burden of the debt becomes unmanageable. At this point in the cycle, the group of villains is extended to comprise not just the international providers of short-term funds but also those of long-term loans and bonds. The prescription that they should share in the losses of the country—take "a haircut," as it is said—becomes legitimate. In this way, for example, the burden of the external debt of Argentina leaped from 59 percent to 157 percent of the country's gross national income (GNI) as a result of the devaluation of the peso. This, in turn, justified the largest default in the history of developing countries, which wiped out the savings of many international investors, including a large group of Italian pensioners. Nobody should be surprised that the flows of international capital are so volatile.

The interaction between the foreign creditors and the weak borrowers then becomes a vicious circle. The declining net flows caused by the weakness of the currencies become a reason to devalue further, increasing the burden of the developing countries' external debt, which in turn scares the lenders even more. The possibility of having more stable capital flows, however, is sacrificed for the sake of the freedom to manipulate the local currencies.

Developing countries are also missing the trend to disintermediation that has characterized the international markets in the last few decades. New financial mechanisms have emerged all over the world, dramatically reducing the share of banks in total financial transactions. Capital markets have grown faster than banks in most developed countries, including countries like Germany, which had relied for more than one hundred years on a model based on strong universal banks. Also, the result has been a dramatic drop in the cost of capital and financial transactions. Moreover, developing countries have been left behind in two other crucial developments: the derivative markets and the wide range of financial services now offered globally.

As a manifestation of this lack of integration, the financing of developing countries changed very little over the last thirty years. This is clear from several indicators. For instance, the share of the private sources of international credit out of the total credit to these countries, at 57 percent in 2002, was about the same as in 1976. This happened in a period that witnessed an unprecedented expansion of private international credit among developed countries.

Moreover, the segment of the domestic economies that is less integrated into the international financial markets is the private sector. About 75 percent of the credit from private sources goes to governments. By the end of 2002, the share of the private sector in that credit was only 5 percent higher than in 1976.

The evidence also shows that the picture has not changed much from the late 1970s in another dimension: commercial banks and official creditors remain the main providers of credit to these countries. The combined share of commercial banks and multilaterals (the World Bank, the Inter-American Development Bank, the Asian Development Bank, and similar institutions) went through a cycle of up and down during the 1980s and 1990s and ended up at a level very similar to what it had been in 1976 (48 percent against 53 percent, respectively). Surprisingly for many, the share of the multilaterals increased by almost 10 percent, while that of commercial banks went down by a slightly higher magnitude. That is, developing countries are substantially more dependent on credit from multilateral institutions than they were in 1976. They are going backward.

The private sector in developing countries has also missed the development of the bond markets. Bond financing has been concentrated on credits to the public sector. Commercial banks, at over 80 percent of total credit to the private sector, remain the main providers of resources to private companies.

There are substantial differences in international private sector financing across developing countries, with a lion's share going to ten big borrowers. In 2002, the balance of private, nonguaranteed external debt represented about 45 percent of the total external debt of those countries, while in the rest it accounts for only 13 percent.

Yet, traditional creditors remain crucial even for the big borrowers. The share of commercial banks in their borrowing fell from 60 percent to 40 percent during the period. They, however, lost as much terrain (10 percent) to bonds as to the most traditional of all vehicles, the multilaterals. Moreover, bonds became more important in the smaller borrowers than in the bigger ones—mainly because public sector borrowing is more important in those countries and bonds are used primarily by public debtors. It is also important to note that fifty-three countries did not receive any private, nonguaranteed financing in 1996–2002.

Developing countries could use foreign capital markets; in fact, this is already happening. Many firms from developing countries now float equity and debt in New York, and some groups of neighboring countries have created regional markets. These attempts, however, are very limited and have no noticeable impact on the financial development of these countries. The foreign exchange risk is always present.

Globalization also opens the opportunity to provide financial services from abroad, including not just deposit taking and lending but also other, more sophisticated products. Such possibility is particularly attractive for developing countries, which cannot attain the minimum size required for developing these products. Yet, those services are always tied to markets and instruments denominated in international currencies.

In summary, while there are some signs of an increasing globalization of financing to the developing countries, most developing countries are still isolated from the process. The share of the official creditors has increased in the total financing of those countries, including the big borrowers. Within the official creditors, the share of the multilaterals has also increased. In addition, while bonds have increased their participation substantially, they have done so primarily in the financing of the public sector. The ups and downs have been so marked that it is impossible to detect a clear trend. This makes sense because there is no reason why foreign creditors should be expected to take risks that the domestic intermediaries do not want to take.

Some authors have suggested that developing countries could resolve the problems caused by the weakness of their currencies by developing hedging instruments. Yet, to succeed, hedging instruments would have to resolve several problems, among them:

- Symmetrical risks, so that the variable you are hedging on could go one way or the other. This is so because to hedge, someone must be taking the opposite position of yours. In developing countries, the risk of depreciation is much higher than that of appreciation—the latter being almost inexistent. In these circumstances, nobody bets for the appreciation. The current appreciation of most of the currencies of developing countries does not eliminate this problem because it is due to a boom in commodity prices, which could be easily reversed.
- A very deep financial market—something that does not exist in the developing world.
- There is a moral hazard in developing markets because one of the main potential users of hedging—the government—also has the power to devalue or not devalue. This does not happen in developed markets, or, in those cases where it may (there are some governments in developed countries that float debt in a foreign currency), the market believes that the risk is negligible that the government would take action to devalue or appreciate the currency for this reason.

That is, hedging instruments cannot work properly in countries with currencies that do not enjoy international acceptance.

Some governments have tried to resolve the problem of the lack of a counterpart by taking the other side in what they call hedging operations. In these operations, the central bank guarantees the conversion of the proceeds of loans from abroad at a defined exchange rate. This, however, ties the reserves of the central bank, so that the risks of this become correlated with the risks of the banking system. In other words, the overall risks of the country are not reduced, only redistributed among sectors—and in a perverse way, because the "hedging" reduces the financial capacity of the central bank when it is needed the most.

It is important to notice that the problems I discussed in this chapter are unlikely to be resolved in countries with local currencies. Even if countries adopt strong currency policies, building up the credibility of their currencies would take a long time, during which they would still be vulnerable to currency crises. Moreover, the economies of most of these countries are too weak to develop domestic financial services and instruments that would be comparable to those available in the international markets. As they have been in the past, local currencies are likely to remain as sources of a damaging isolation. They are also sources of financial crises, which is the subject of part 2.

Part Two  **The Reversed Liquidity Trap and Financial Crises**

# Chapter 6 The Financial Risks
# of Monetary Regimes

The conviction that countries must have their own currencies and the power to devalue them has another dimension, in addition to those discussed in part 1. It is their supposed usefulness in case of a financial crisis.

The idea that local currencies are most useful during financial crises is based on three main arguments: First, devaluation has become unavoidable in all financial crises in developing countries. If the currency cannot be devalued, something unimaginable could happen. Second, without a local currency, the central bank cannot print the money that is needed to satisfy the run on deposits. Third, by increasing exports and the economic growth rate, devaluations create the conditions for a fast recovery of the solvency of the countries in crisis.

In this part of the book, I argue that these arguments are fallacious for several reasons. First, it is certainly true that devaluations were unavoidable in all cases of financial crises. However, this is because, as already discussed, people in the developing countries run toward their standard of value when in critical situations, and this standard is the foreign currency. This is why a currency run has preceded the runs on the banks in all crises. The latter, in reality, is a result of the former, so that the bank runs would not have taken place without the currency run. This, a situation that does not exist in dollarized economies, is what forces the devaluations. Moreover, while the preference for the foreign currency is always present (as shown by spontaneous dollarization), crises do not start in the vacuum. All financial crises have started because in the immediate past, the central bank created substantial macroeconomic imbalances through the manipulation of the local currency. That is, central banks first make devaluation unavoidable and then have no other choice but to carry it out. This cannot happen in a dollarized economy because the government cannot manipulate the currency. Actually, rather than being an advantage, the existence of a local currency creates a major disadvantage in this respect. By their sheer existence, these currencies create the possibility of devaluation, generating fears that then affect economic behavior. They eventually lead to the currency panics that elicit the runs on banks and gravely complicate the situation.

Regarding the second argument, reality shows that the power of central banks to act as lenders of last resort in developing countries is mythical. Because of the reversed liquidity trap caused by the runs on the currency, the central banks need as many dollars as a dollarized economy to defend the financial system. In fact, they need more, because dollarized economies do not have to defend the currency.

With regard to the argument that devaluations make possible a fast economic recovery, experience shows that they complicate the solution of crises in many different ways and introduce serious complications in the subsequent recovery. For example, they increase the burden of the external debt precisely when the economy is more vulnerable, so that even if the economy recovers, it has to allocate more resources to the service of such debt. They also result in surges of interest rates and in a general turmoil of relative prices that confuses the signals provided by the economy for the allocation of resources.

I discuss each of these arguments in the following chapters. In the last chapter, I show how a dollarized economy, Panama, has never fallen into a catastrophic crisis, such as those affecting countries with their own currencies, despite the fact that the country has fallen into macroeconomic problems as grave or graver than theirs.

Certainly, dollarized countries may have financial crises, but their crises would not be complicated by the currency runs. This makes it much simpler to resolve them, as the case of Panama clearly shows.

The discussion of the risks of the different regimes begins in the following paragraphs: first, with the risks posed by regimes based on local currencies exclusively; then those subject to spontaneous dollarization; and finally those posed by formal dollarization.

The main risk posed by regimes based on a local currency exclusively is of the dilution of financial contracts through devaluation, inflation, or both. This risk is dismissed in most of the literature and even by the credit rating agencies, which normally give the debt in domestic currency a higher rating than they give to the external debt. This is because they estimate that governments are more able to repay the debts in the currency they can print than in the ones they cannot. This, of course, is true but only nominally, because the fact that they can print money actually reduces the probability that they will repay the local currency debts in real or in dollar terms. The very instrument that they would use to repay in nominal terms in case of necessity—printing money—leads to higher inflation and devaluations, so that if they use such instrument, it is virtually guaranteed that they will default at least partially in real and dollar terms.

While largely ignored in the literature, the association of the dilution risk with the ability to print money generates several other risks that have gravely negative consequences in the health of the financial system and the solvency of sovereign debts. Some of these risks are discussed below.

First, the shallow financial system characteristic of local currencies, which is a consequence of the risk of dilution, weakens the country's capacity to react to adverse external situations. All other things equal, a country's capacity to service its external and internal debts is proportional to its financial depth—that is, the ratio of deposits plus currency in circulation (M2) to gross domestic product (GDP). This is because the higher the level of financial intermediation relative to GDP, the higher the liquidity per unit of GDP that a financial system generates in any given period, broadening the sources of financing available and allowing debtors to refinance domestically external debts and vice versa. This is true for both the private and the public sectors. In other words, countries with deep financial systems have deeper pockets than those with lower ratios of M2 to GDP. Thus, their risk of default is lower. As discussed in part 1, countries that devalue less have deeper financial systems than those that devalue more.

Second, the potential to create money increases the risks of defaults caused by excessive interest rates. While the Brazilian real rates of interest are excessive even for developing countries' standards, these rates tend to be very high and variable in those countries and they can become extremely high very rapidly. This, in turn, increases the risk of default. An example of this problem was provided by the tequila crisis of 1994. The interest rates in domestic currency increased so much after the devaluation that many borrowers—actually, a majority of them—could not service their debts. The high rates lasted long enough to convert this into a permanent problem, as the debtors could not even service the interest payments and the balance of the debts escalated exponentially. It took many years to resolve this problem and, to this day, the credit granted by the Mexican banking system to the private sector is very scant. Housing was one of the sectors most negatively affected, as the present value of the balances on the mortgage debts grew above the value of the houses in the post-crisis era. Therefore, while many people could not service their debts, many others did not want to do it because they could get a new house with a lower debt. Through these mechanisms devaluations increase the losses accrued to the banking system in a financial crisis.

Third, the possibility of dilution also increases the risks of maturity and currency mismatches. As discussed in chapter 2, long-term credit is almost inexistent in the local currencies in developing countries. For this reason, the long-term credit that does exist in those countries is financed either with short-term deposits or with foreign currencies, so that banks run either a maturity or a foreign currency risk. Both risks increase the vulnerability of the system, particularly in times of crisis. In fact, countries with local currencies are bound to have currency mismatching problems, even if they do not allow foreign currency deposits. At the very minimum, those risks exist for the government through the external public debt. The effects of such mismatching can be grave, as they weaken the country's ability to service its debt precisely at the worst moment.

Fourth, as it has been shown uncountable times, the dilution risk leads to the endemic instability of the local currencies of developing countries, which in turn tends to result in unstoppable currency runs. Thus, it is amusing to hear that the main danger of dollarization is that by adopting a foreign currency they increase their risks of having crises. In fact, dollarization is equivalent to surrendering the ability to have currency runs.

Finally, through all these effects, local currencies also increase the risk of bank runs and of worsening them when they appear. All these risks tend to appear together, so that they combine with each other, producing an explosive mixture.

Spontaneous dollarization, the solution that most central banks have found to ameliorate the possibility of dilution, is a double-edged sword. By providing a local substitute for the weak domestic currency, partially dollarized countries capture resources that would otherwise leave the country. At the same time, however, they facilitate the currency arbitrage that renders useless their own monetary policies. The net result is that, even if the size of the financial system is larger than otherwise, the power of the three main instruments that central banks use to influence economic behavior—the rate of monetary creation, the rate of the devaluation, and the rate of interest—is drastically diminished or even nullified. In fact, as discussed before, in a partially dollarized economy, these policies mostly determine the direction and size of the changes in the currency composition of the operations of the banking system. Thus, at the very least, spontaneous dollarization drastically reduces the power of the central banks. In the worst cases, it eliminates it altogether.

Additionally, spontaneous dollarization introduces nonlinearity in the behavior of the banking system through the possibility of currency mismatching. The risk can take several shapes, depending on the specific nature of the currency mismatching.

- First, if the authorities force the banks to match assets and liabilities in different currencies, these can still incur in foreign exchange risk if they lend to borrowers whose incomes are subject to the risk of devaluation. This is what happens, for example, when a bank lends in dollars to, say, real estate developers. If the devaluation occurs, the borrowers will have severe difficulties in repaying their dollar loans.
- Second, the risk is even worse if the banks are not forced to match assets and liabilities because shifts in the exchange rate—either appreciation or depreciation—unleash nonlinear effects within the accounts of the banks.

In the first case, if deposits and loans are matched, banks may hope that a substantial portion of their debtors would be able to repay after a drastic devaluation if they refinance the loans at very long terms. Banks can negotiate an acceptable loss. In the second case, when deposits and loans are not matched, the loss is contractual, instantaneous, and final. There is nothing that banks can do. That is, banks run the worst of all exchange rate risks if they mix their funds in different currencies.

The case of the Mortgage Bank of Uruguay illustrates this point. The bank engaged in currency mismatching in an attempt to build up its housing portfolio in an environment in which the interest rates in pesos were too high to attract customers. To lower its costs, the bank took an increasing share of its deposits in dollars. However, it could not grant credit for housing and real estate in dollars because there were no takers—nobody wanted to run the risk of a serious devaluation. Thus, the bank took the exchange risk—borrowing in dollars and lending in pesos. When the big devaluations of 2002 came, the bank was caught with a peso loan portfolio financed with dollar deposits. The bank failed immediately; it survived only because the government recapitalized it at an enormous cost.

The magnitude of the risks imbedded in the accounts of the Mortgage Bank can be appreciated in table 6.1, which shows the accounts of a hypothetical bank whose only assets and liabilities were the actual credits and deposits of the Mortgage Bank in May 2001. It then goes through the actual devaluation of the local currency that took place between that date and August 2002. The exchange rate on the first date was 13.16 pesos per dollar and on the second, 28.8 pesos per dollar, making for a devaluation of 119 percent. As shown in the table, the capital of the bank would shift from 30 percent to minus 36 percent of the total assets of the bank as a result of the nonlinear effects of the devaluation.

One would expect that the heavy losses incurred by the bank would have benefited the debtors in pesos because the real value of their debts would have been reduced. Yet, as the annual interest rates on domestic currency increased from 50 percent to 159 percent from May 2001 to August 2002, while inflation between the two dates was only 20 percent, the burden of the service of the mortgage debts would have also increased substantially, to a point that would make such service unaffordable. This is shown in table 6.2 for a debtor owing one thousand pesos in a twenty-year mortgage. The table assumes that the wage of the debtor increased at the same rate as inflation. As seen in the table, total payments increased from 34 percent of the debtor's income—the internationally accepted ratio for mortgage payments—to 85 percent.

The two effects would be symmetrically damaging if the mismatching is the opposite—that is, if the deposits were mostly denominated in pesos and the loans in dollars. In this case, the bank would seem to gain by the devaluation, but it would lose heavily because of the immediate worsening of its debt portfolio.

Of course, the problems caused by devaluations are similar in countries with only a local currency. There, the banks are not exposed to cross-currency risks but are exposed to the interest rate effect. Still, bi-monetarism has all

Table 6.1: Devaluations and the Mismatch of Currencies: A Simulation
Based on the Mortgage Bank of Uruguay

| Devaluation factor May 2001–August 2002 | | 219% |
|---|---|---|
| Accounts of Mortgage Bank in Uruguayan Pesos | Assets | Liabilities |
| **Before Devaluation** | | |
| Credit $ | 979,161 $ Dep | 13,443,889 |
| Credit Pesos | 23,230,346 Peso Dep | 5,196,435 |
| Total Assets | 24,209,507 Total Liabilities | 18,640,324 |
| | Capital | 5,569,183 |
| Total Assets | 24,209,507 Total liabilities + capital | 24,209,507 |
| Capital % of assets in May 2001 | | 30 |
| **After Devaluation** | | |
| Credit $ | 2,142,845 $ Dep | 29,421,277 |
| Credit Pesos | 23,230,346 Peso Dep | 5,196,435 |
| Total Assets | 25,373,191 Total Liabilities | 34,617,712 |
| | Capital | (9,244,521) |
| Capital % of assets in August 2002 | 30 | −36 |

*Source:* Central Bank of Uruguay.

Table 6.2: Devaluations and the Impact on Debtors

| | May 2001 | August 2002 |
|---|---|---|
| Debt | 1,000 | |
| Annual Income | 1,600 | 1,924 |
| Interest payments | 499 | 1,592 |
| Annual Amortization | 50 | 50 |
| Total payment | 549 | 1,642 |
| Interest payments % of annual income | 31 | 83 |
| Annual Amortization % of annual income | 3 | 3 |
| Total payment % of annual income | 34 | 85 |

*Source:* Data on inflation and interest rates, Central Bank of Uruguay.

the risks of the single currency regime plus the dangers posed by the currency mismatching in the banking system.

On the other side of the ledger, spontaneous dollarization may reduce the risks of a transmission of panic from a currency crisis to a run on the banks. In all crises, dollar deposits fall at a much slower rate than those in local currency. This, however, gives banks only a temporary respite. If the government does not take advantage of this respite to stabilize the situation, the crisis keeps its course. After a while, the hemorrhage of peso deposits would signal to the population that the banks could fail. In some cases, like Argentina, this signal was accompanied by the open discussion of the need to convert the dollar deposits into pesos and then devalue the peso. This eventually led to a run on dollars as well.

This threat of a conversion of the foreign currency assets to the local currency is another risk of a partially dollarized economy. It brings back the risk of dilution to those assets. I discuss this risk later in this chapter, in connection with the fully dollarized economies.

All things considered, it seems that spontaneous dollarization is riskier than having only a local currency unless regulations force the banks to match the currencies of their assets and liabilities and ban lending in foreign currency to borrowers with incomes in domestic currency. This, of course, limits the volume of resources that banks can intermediate in the foreign currency to a small percentage determined by the central banks.

Dollarized countries do not present the risk of debt dilution. For this reason, they present much lower risks than those with local currencies in all the dimensions that have been discussed. There are, however, two risks that the dollarized economies have that those with only a local currency do not have. The first is the risk of conversion of the domestic foreign currency assets and liabilities into newly created pesos. The other is the risk associated with becoming a regional financial center.

Formally dollarized countries share with the partially dollarized ones the risk of pesification. Of course, if one government decides to dollarize, another government may decide to de-dollarize. While present, however, this risk is much lower in a formally dollarized economy than in a partially dollarized one. The risk is actually very low because there are no cross-currency risks in the banking system, which is the main reason why partially dollarized economies have converted the dollar accounts into pesos. Without this problem, there is little that a government could gain in the midst of a crisis by converting financial obligations into a new domestic currency for the following reasons:

• In terms of speeding the resolution of a run, de-dollarizing the economy would backfire because doing that would generate all the additional complications of a currency crisis. It would be crystal clear to the population that the only reason for the change would be to devalue the newly introduced currency. This would accelerate the run.

- The government would put itself in the reversed liquidity trap even if no run was taking place at the moment of de-dollarizing. While the government may decree that all the banking accounts are denominated in the new pesos, people would refuse to give in their dollar bills for the obviously weaker local currency. As the government increased the supply of the new currency to buy the dollars, the higher their price would be, and the higher the incentive for people to hold on to them. Creating a currency to get immediately into a currency run is not a good idea.
- De-dollarization would also backfire in terms of the service of the external debt, which would increase as a percent of the government revenues as a result of the devaluation.
- It would also backfire in terms of easing the conditions after the crisis, because of the surge in both the inflation and the real interest rates that would accompany the introduction of the new currency and its subsequent devaluation.
- The surge in real interest rates would magnify the loan portfolio problems of the banking system.

That is, without the problem of having a currency mismatch inside the banking system, there is no incentive for the government to pesify the economy. Additionally, the political problems associated with the substitution of a strong currency with an obviously weaker one are much higher if the currency is fully dollarized.

Some critics of dollarization hold that pesification could become inevitable, citing the example of the creation of the patacones (negotiable IOUs) by the Argentine provinces during the cash squeeze of 2001. These obligations were currency substitutes that circulated at a heavy discount in the markets.

The critics clearly assumed that, once created, the patacones would become the new currency. Yet, there was nothing to prevent the government from redeeming those IOUs with dollars at the end of the crisis, rather than adopting them as the new currency of the country. The critics forgot that the government of Panama issued similar IOUs during the fiscal crisis that preceded the invasion of the marines that ended with the capture of General Omar Torrijos. After the crisis ended, the government redeemed the IOUs and the situation returned to normal because, for the reasons sketched above, there was no gain in adopting these as the currency of the country.

Thus, the risk of a pesification of a formally dollarized economy can be considered negligible. This creates a sharp contrast with the partially dollarized economies, where cross-currency risks exist in the banking system, and governments can feel the temptation of converting the currency of the dollar deposits and loans to eliminate them. Some economists are of the opinion that countries should pesify while things are going well. This, however, assumes that people are fools. In fact, pesifying a stable country is the safest recipe to create a crisis out of nothing.

The second risk specific to dollarized economies is that of sudden withdrawals from nonresident depositors when they have become regional financial centers. This problem has never affected Panama; however, it affected Uruguay, a country that is not formally dollarized but has more than 90 percent of the deposits denominated in dollars. The case of Uruguay is unique, even among international financial centers, for four reasons:

- First, the high concentration of the bank's international deposits from the nationals of one single country, Argentina;
- Second, the smallness of the Uruguayan economy relative to that of Argentina;
- Third, the protracted instability of Argentina, which pushed the Argentines to deposit a considerable portion of their savings in Uruguay. In December 2001, Argentines had deposited in Uruguay an amount equivalent to almost 9 percent of the total deposits in the Argentine banking system; and
- Fourth, these risks combined with the currency mismatch present in the Uruguayan banking system to create a uniquely explosive situation.

Uruguay got into this situation because it had long exploited the high monetary instability of its neighbor, Argentina, by offering dollar deposits. After having increased rapidly during the 1980s, the deposits of the nonresidents remained flat at $2 billion from 1990 to 1995. Yet, they began to grow after the tequila crisis of 1995, when it seemed that the currency board would collapse. From then on, their deposits increased steadily, tripling to $6 billion in the following six years. By 2001, they represented approximately 45 percent of the total deposits in the Uruguayan financial system.

Then, in 2002, as the Argentine government prevented the access of its citizens to their bank accounts, the Argentines began to withdraw funds from the Uruguayan banks. Their heavy withdrawals combined with the cross-currency risks to create a crisis in the Uruguayan banking system that led local depositors into a parallel panic. As shown in table 6.3, the residents withdrew proportionally less than the Argentines. Still, they withdrew 37 percent of their deposits before the government was forced to decree a bank holiday in early August 2002.

An inspection of the data shows that the Argentine deposits increased quickly as the Argentine crisis deepened and that they began to fall immediately after the "corralito" was established in their country at the end of 2001. At that moment, the Argentines needed the cash they had deposited in Uruguay. The deposits of the Uruguayan nationals began to fall one month later, when what was happening to the nonresident deposits became clear to the locals.

Thus, this was a run that started not because of an initial lack of trust in the Uruguayan banking system but because the nonresident depositors needed their cash. As the resident depositors saw the hemorrhage of cash caused by the nonresidents, however, they also started to withdraw their deposits, leading to the run that ended with the August bank holiday.

In this way, the risks presented by the Uruguayan banking system combined to create the worst crisis of recent times. As a comparison, while the Argentine banking system lost 24 percent of their deposits from March to December 2001, the Uruguayan banks lost 50 percent of theirs from December 2001 to August 2002.

However, this combination of risks and the losses coming from them are unlikely to be present in other partially or fully dollarized economies, mainly because the Argentina factor that started the panic is not present in other cases. The case of Panama, where this kind of problem has not existed, shows that the concentration of risks was the crucial problem in the case of Uruguay.

Table 6.4 compares all the risks discussed in this chapter for the two regimes plus the mixed one:

The table shows that the risks of fully dollarized economies are less numerous and are lower than those of the other two categories with one single exception: international withdrawals, which only applies when the country is a regional financial center with highly correlated risks.

Much has been said about the impact of the loss of seigniorage entailed by a formal dollarization. Certainly, dollarized economies lose the revenues from

Table 6.3: Withdrawals of Residents and Nonresidents in Uruguay

|  | Deposits in December 2001 ($) | Fall in deposits through August 2002 ($) | Fall in deposits through August 2002 (%) | % of total withdrawals |
|---|---|---|---|---|
| Residents | 7,395 | 2,725 | 36.8 | 40.6 |
| Nonresidents | 6,193 | 3,981 | 64.3 | 59.4 |

*Source:* Central Bank of Uruguay.

Table 6.4: Comparison of the Risks of Different Monetary Regimes

| Risk | Local currency only | Partially dollarized | Fully dollarized |
|---|---|---|---|
| Dilution of domestic currency debt | Yes | Yes | No |
| Interest rate risks | High | High | Low |
| Risks caused by low intermediation levels | High | Lower | Low |
| Reversed liquidity trap | Yes | Yes | No |
| Needs dollars to act as a lender of last resort | Yes | Yes | Yes |
| Risk of bank runs resulting from currency risks | Yes | Yes | No |
| Magnitude of crisis increased by devaluation | Yes | Yes | No |
| Difficulty to stop bank runs | High | High | Lower |
| Likely cost of crises | High | Higher | Lower |
| Peso-ization | No | High | Negligible |
| International withdrawals | No | Yes | Yes |
| Mismatching with external debt | Yes | Yes | No |
| International banks' withdrawal of short-term credits | High | High | Low |
| External mismatching | Yes | Yes | No |

seigniorage; yet, this loss is much smaller than normally assumed, and it can be taken as the premium paid for an insurance against the higher risks presented by local currencies.

In this respect, we may note that very few developing countries actually collect seigniorage. To see this point, we have to trace a sharp distinction between seigniorage (the revenue accruing to the currency issuer by its meeting the demand for money) and the inflation tax (the revenue that the issuer collects by forcing money into the hands of the people). Seigniorage is produced by the normal growth of the economy and its increased monetization, which raises the demand for money. It is therefore the price of a service. The inflation tax is very inefficient tax. It works in the same way as Dema Gogo used it. The government prints money and uses it to buy goods and services at the current prices. The increased demand raises prices. People pay the tax through the price increases. Most developing countries extract government revenues from the inflation tax rather than from seigniorage. In fact, seigniorage in those countries may be negative in real terms, as people tend to rid themselves of the local currency when the inflation rate is high. Taking away the government's power to impose the inflation tax is not a problem of dollarization. It is actually one of its advantages.

In contrast, the loss of seigniorage is a disadvantage of dollarization; this loss, however, tends to be small.

The collection of seigniorage is not costless or uniformly efficient. It is collected on the monetary liabilities of the central bank: currency in circulation and the deposits of the commercial banks in the central bank. The crucial point is what portion of the currency issued by the central bank is really seigniorage and what portion is actually a monetary obligation. To see this point, we can examine the case of a central bank functioning as a currency board: printing money only when selling it against foreign currencies. The behavior of the demand for local money can be more easily measured in this regime. People manifest their demand by purchasing the local currency. Under this rule, of course, the central bank would constitute foreign currency reserves against each unit of local currency issued. There is no float in this environment. All the reserves are deposited abroad and earn an interest.

In this case, a prudent fiscal management would take as income only the differential between the interests paid on the local currency issued and the interests obtained from the international reserves acquired from them. Currency does not carry interests, so that the entire amount of interests generated by the corresponding reserves can be taken as seigniorage income. The deposits of the banks in the central bank, however, can carry interests, and the higher they are, the lower the seigniorage income. Many developing countries choose not to pay interests. However, as we saw in the case of Brazil, this increases the spread of the banking system, so that in this case, seigniorage becomes an inefficient tax on financial intermediation. It is inefficient because people can avoid it by shunning the formal financial markets, perversely distorting financial operations. It also increases the lending interest rates, negatively affecting investment and the economic activity in general. These negative effects are of a higher level of importance than the government revenue acquired through them, which can be obtained through other, more efficient tax mechanisms.

Thus, if improving the efficiency of financial intermediation is an objective of policy (as it should be in developing countries, given the poor state of such intermediation), the best policy in this respect is to transfer to the banks the interests obtained from the reserves built with their deposits, with only a nominal charge to cover the costs of the management of the deposits abroad. This reduces to zero the seigniorage that can be obtained from the banks' deposits in the central bank. Therefore, in a country aiming at having an efficient financial system, seigniorage can be collected only from the currency with the public.

The amount of currency with the public, however, diminishes as the financial system becomes more efficient and people use checks, credit and debit cards, and other electronic means to effect their payments. Thus, the income that can be obtained from seigniorage tends to be very small. In El Salvador, for example, while the deposits in the banks were on the order of 40 percent of GDP, currency with the public was about 2 percent to 3 percent of GDP. When multiplied by the rate of interest in triple A instruments in the international markets, the result was on the order of 0.05 percent of GDP. Seigniorage may be higher in other countries with higher ratios of currency to GDP, but not by much. What can be much higher is the inflation tax, which, as previously discussed, is a very inefficient way of raising revenue.

If we compare the seigniorage revenue with the risks associated with the use of local currencies, losing it seems to be a low insurance premium against such risks, particularly if we take into account the risks of currency runs leading to financial crises.

In summary, the financial advantages of the formally dollarized economy stem from two fundamental properties of international currencies: First, they minimize the risk of dilution. Such minimization is crucial. All the other risks of the local currencies are related to this risk. Because of the dilution risk, people transfer their standard of value to a foreign currency, and all the other risks of local currencies are higher than those of fully dollarized economies.

Second, the dollarized regime is the only one that can conceivably operate with just one currency—inside and outside its borders—thus eliminating the currency risk altogether. When forced to operate in other international currencies, dollarized countries have access to the deep currency hedging markets that exist in the international currency areas.

Chapter 7 analyzes how this risk—the currency risk—has been the fundamental cause of all the financial crises in developing countries.

# Chapter 7 The Currency Origins
of Financial Crises

The expression *financial crisis* evokes two different phenomena. First, it can be used to refer to cataclysmic runs on banks, such as those that took place during the Great Depression of the 1930s. Second, it can be used to refer to widespread insolvency in the banking system, even if there is no run on the banks. In this chapter, I deal with the two phenomena; for clarity, however, I reserve the expression *financial crisis* for the cataclysmic events associated with severe lack of liquidity.

Banking runs are always associated with illiquidity, and illiquidity is frequently associated with insolvency. However, solvent banks can become illiquid if caught in a confidence crisis. Conversely, banks can be insolvent for decades without becoming illiquid if people trust them, if their deposits keep on growing, and if they do not experience a shock that triggers their illiquidity. Everybody knows, for instance, that the Japanese financial system has been insolvent since the early 1990s. However, there has been no run on the Japanese banks. On the contrary, their deposits and other domestic market sources of funds increased by 2.2 percent per year from 1989 to 2002. This has been enough to keep them liquid (credit from the central bank to the banks increased by only 1.2 percent of the total market resources during the decade).[1]

Insolvent but liquid banks are also common in many developing countries. The environment is more propitious there for these walking-dead institutions, not because people trust their banks more than in developed countries, but because inflation helps weak banks to survive. Figure 7.1 shows how a hypothetical bank can manage to survive for twenty years even if it is insolvent from day one. The simulation assumes that the bank pays 10 percent interests on its deposits, charges 17 percent on its loans, and incurs in administrative costs equal to 5 percent of its loans. The bank keeps a ratio of bad loans to the total loan portfolio of 18 percent throughout the period. At that ratio, the bank makes increasing losses every year. However, since its deposits are growing at a rate (8 percent) that keeps its net cash flow positive, the bank survives quite easily for the entire period, even if by the twentieth year it has lost five times its initial capital. Since liquidity is a nominal variable, inflation helps insolvent banks to survive because with inflation deposits increase in nominal terms even if they fall in real terms.[2]

Of course, this bank is in danger of collapsing suddenly if any of the variables that determine its cash flow shifts negatively. A reduction in the inflation rate, a reduction in the growth of deposits for other reasons, the introduction of competition that would reduce the intermediation margin, or a small increase in the ratio of bad loans would turn the bank illiquid and a run would follow. Also, a large devaluation or a currency crisis could trigger the process through which the bank would rapidly become illiquid.

In all the crises of developing countries, the trigger has been a currency run associated with a cycle of currency appreciation and depreciation. During these cycles, the prices of nontradables have increased quickly relative to those of the tradables, leading to a boom in nontradable asset prices. Then, the prices of these assets have fallen, leading to a bust. The change in the direction of the shifts in relative prices has triggered a currency run, which has forced the devaluation of the currency. This, in turn, has worsened the speed of the collapse of the prices of assets. Thus, local currencies have been at the center of the crises.

These cycles generate the two dimensions of a financial crisis: illiquidity and insolvency. While currency runs create *liquidity* crises in the banks, the violent shifts in relative prices have a negative impact on the *solvency* of the banks.

Banks are quite vulnerable to shifts in relative prices because of the asym-

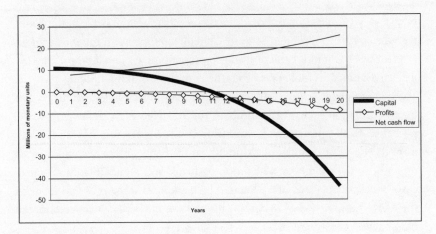

Figure 7.1: A long-living insolvent bank.

metric way in which they take their risks. We can see the difference by imagining that there are only two assets in a country, A and B, and that their relative prices fluctuate in such a way that if one gains value, the other loses it in equal amounts. Initially, the value of each of the assets is fifty. We may assume that the value of A falls to zero while that of B duplicates to one hundred. If you are operating in the stock market and had invested half of your portfolio in each of the assets, this shift in relative prices would not affect your wealth. You would have lost fifty in A but gained the same amount in B. Banks cannot hedge in this perfect way. A bank having 50 percent of its loans in A and 50 percent in B would lose 50 percent of its portfolio as a result of the collapse of A. The duplication of the value of B, however, would not compensate for this loss because the bank cannot collect from B more than the value of the loan plus the interest rate, which is an amount much smaller than the capital loss in A. Thus, banks are particularly vulnerable to drastic shifts in relative prices, which is what exchange rate movements elicit in the economy of developing countries. In fact, such movements aim at shifting relative prices. It is the reason why they exist as a policy variable.

While banks that have been weak for a long time are the first to go when a crisis hits, even banks that are healthy when the cycle of boom and bust begins may also fail. This happens because the shifting relative prices in the upswing lead them to lend to the activities that collapse in the downswing. Table 7.1 illustrates how rapidly the shift in credit allocation can be during the upswing with the case of Indonesia during the years that preceded its 1997 crisis.

Table 7.1: Bank Property Loans in Indonesia

|                           | 1993 | 1994 | 1995 | 1996 |
|---------------------------|------|------|------|------|
| Bank loans/GDP            | 45.6 | 49.6 | 51.9 | 55.4 |
| Property loans/GDP        | 6.6  | 8.8  | 9.5  | 11.1 |
| Property loans/total loans| 14.5 | 17.6 | 18.3 | 20.1 |
| Mortgage loans/GDP        | 1.9  | 2.7  | 3.0  | 3.1  |

*Source:* Mary Pangestu and Manggi Habir, *The Boom, Bust and Restructuring of Indonesian Banks*, IMF Working Paper WP/02/66, IMF, Washington D.C., 2002, p. 11.

In other words, even banks that are sound before the monetary-induced cycles can fall victim to misguided monetary and exchange rate policies. It is important to notice that, in all crises, monetary policies have been procyclical in both phases of the process, creating or accentuating the initial appreciation and then worsening the downswing shift in relative prices through the inevitable devaluation.

Of course, fully dollarized economies can experience drastic shifts in relative prices, caused, for example, by catastrophic shifts in their terms of trade. However, their risk of falling into a cataclysmic crisis is low for two reasons: First, they do not have a monetary policy to magnify the two phases of the cycle of boom and bust. Second, they do not have a currency to devalue. Thus, they do not experience currency runs. These two advantages are crucial. The effects of local currencies in crises have been devastating. The rest of this chapter illustrates these points with a review of several of the most notorious financial crises of the last few decades.

The Chilean crisis of the early 1980s was one of the worst crises ever to hit a developing country. In the previous years, there was a tremendous boom in all the asset markets, which was followed by a collapse of the asset prices. The cycle was engineered by the government through its monetary and exchange rate policies.

Monetary and exchange rate policies were not the only reasons for the inflation of asset prices during the upswing. The Allende government had nationalized practically all the big enterprises in the country and in the mid- and late 1970s, the new Pinochet administration decided to privatize all of them. At the time, the economy was depressed and there were few takers for the shares, so that the few adventurous entrepreneurs that bought the first of them experienced huge capital gains, particularly as the economy recovered under the first wave of the Pinochet reforms. This primed the public's appetite for buying shares of the firms that were still under privatization and of the already privatized firms that were experiencing the high capital gains.

The initial buyers formed giant conglomerates with their companies, organized around the privatized banks that they had also purchased, and financed their subsequent purchases of companies with credits provided by these banks. Thus, credit to borrowers linked by ownership to the lender— a deadly practice—became pervasive in the country. Naturally, banks did not analyze these credits because the main interest of the group was to finance its new acquisitions, not to prudently manage the bank.

At the same time, there were monetary factors at play. Credit was growing very quickly and the country had fallen into a classical vicious circle of inflation and devaluation. The two variables were growing at around 35 to 40 percent per year. The high inflation rate magnified the environment of rising asset prices.

The country was in this vicious circle because credit was expanding too fast; this propelled devaluations and inflation. The solution was to slow down credit creation. Yet, the government thought that stopping devaluation would stop inflation as well. In early 1979, it started to slow down the rate of devaluation and then, in June, it fixed the exchange rate at thirty-nine pesos to the dollar, announcing that it would never devalue again. It did so when the inflation rate was about 35 percent. Since the growth of credit did not abate, the rate of inflation remained high during the next two years. In December 1980 it was still 31 percent, and in June 1981, 21 percent.

While the country was already unstable, fixing the exchange rate in these conditions was the measure that created the bubble. The inflation of assets overtook overall inflation, propelled first by the rush to acquire privatized companies and then by a self-fed rush to get the capital gains produced by the combination of a fixed exchange rate with high rates of inflation. This rush was financed by the rapidly growing domestic credit.

The combination of fixed exchange rates and high inflation also created incentives to borrow abroad. Peso deposit interest rates were 47 percent, while the lending rate in the United States was 11.7 percent when the government fixed the exchange rate. Thus, it was possible to borrow dollars in the United States at that rate, convert the proceeds into pesos, deposit these in the banking system, withdraw them after one year, paying the dollar loan and making a 30 percent profit in dollar terms. In the subsequent months, the spread of the deposit rate over the lending rate in the United States diminished. Still, it was more than 10 percent throughout the period leading to the 1982 crisis.

The gains were much higher from the perspective of investors who could use the dollar loans to invest directly in Chilean assets. When the rate was fixed, the lending rate in pesos was 65 percent, or 47 percent higher than in the United States. Thus, there was a strong incentive for investors to borrow heavily abroad to buy assets in the burgeoning stock and real estate markets. While the government had strict controls on foreign borrowing, the big business groups were able to borrow large amounts abroad through their companies that produced tradable goods.

Figure 7.2 shows how the cycle progressed. It compares the real capital gains realized in the stock market and the real lending interest rates prevailing in the country from August 1978 (before the fixation of the exchange rate) to December 1982 (after the devaluation). Interest rates remained high in nominal and dollar terms but began to fall in real terms, pushed down by the capital inflows. This trend was reaffirmed when the government fixed the exchange rate. From then on the rate of interest kept on falling faster than inflation, so that it was shrinking in real terms, even if it remained high in nominal and therefore in dollar terms. In August 1980, the real interest rate reached almost zero. With falling real interest rates and asset prices increasing quickly, speculators got enormous capital gains, which reached (on a twelve-month basis) about 175 percent by mid-1980. These gains were even higher for those who borrowed in dollars; for them, dollar rates were negative in real terms.

Then, suddenly, the prices of both stocks and real estate stopped growing in June 1980, one year after the fixation of the exchange rate. Worse still, while interest rates had gone down during the upswing as a result of the capital inflows, they started to increase in real terms precisely at that moment because the rate of inflation was finally declining. While speculators still continued to make profits when measured annually, those profits began to dwindle fast. By mid-1981, the real interest rate overtook the annual rate of capital gains, propelled by an ever-growing demand for credit. This time, however, debtors demanded credit not to acquire assets or expand operations, but to refinance defaulting loans. Since interest rates were high and increasing, the amounts required to refinance debts were much larger than the original loans. The appetite for credit was insatiable. Buildings, which had been bought and sold several times under construction in the speculative rage, were finished and

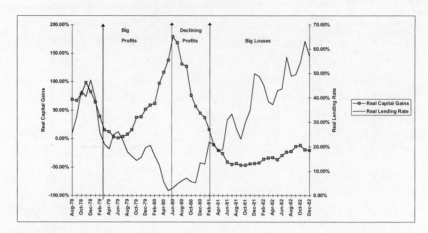

Figure 7.2: Real capital gains and real interest rates in Chile before, during, and after the crisis. *Source:* International Financial Statistics of the International Monetary Fund

had to be sold to people who would use them. Buyers did not appear at the highly inflated prices that the owners had paid for them. Also, although slowly, the overall inflation rate kept on declining, generating liquidity problems in companies that had expected prices to keep on growing at the same pace as before. The loan portfolios of the banks started to deteriorate quickly. Speculators were trapped in a classical scissor: Asset prices were falling while real interest rates were increasing. The combined effect crushed the investors and their bankers.

As the liquidity of the banks dwindled, the government facilitated their survival by abolishing the controls it had on private borrowing abroad. Taking advantage of this possibility, from mid-1980 on, the banks borrowed abroad in increasing amounts just to maintain their liquidity. The international banking community had not yet realized that the Chilean banks and the entire country were bankrupted and continued extending credit to them. This credit, however, served no useful purpose. It was used to refinance loss-making borrowers, so that the banks and their borrowers became more insolvent by the day. About $7 billion entered the country during 1980–1982, mostly to conceal the hemorrhage of losses.

As shown in figure 7.3, since the international banks ignored the true situation of the country, the inflow of foreign funds kept on increasing and reached record levels one year after the collapse of the asset prices. It was only in 1982 that capital inflows declined and it was only in 1983, after the devaluation, that they became negative.

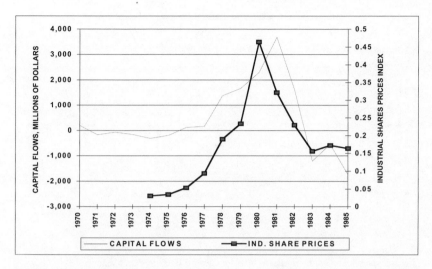

Figure 7.3: Chile: Capital flows and real share prices. *Source:* International Financial Statistics of the International Monetary Fund.

Figure 7.4 shows that it was clear by early 1982 that a currency run was on, months before the banking crisis exploded (the central bank started to lend large amounts to the banks in mid-1982, marked with a vertical line in the figure). Even if capital inflows reached a peak in that year, the net foreign assets of the central bank started to fall at an accelerating pace. While the international banks were still pumping in, the Chileans were already pumping out.

As the liquidity of the banks dried up in spite of the enormous amounts of capital inflows, the central bank resorted to quickly increasing its domestic credit. By May 1982, the central bank's credit was growing at 28 percent per year, while the exchange rate was still fixed. This further financed the hemorrhage of dollars. The final blow came in mid-1982 with the devaluation of the peso, which went from thirty-nine for the dollar in May to forty-six in June and then to seventy-five in January 1983. All prices went up, except those of assets. People who were caught owing dollars were finished. People owing in pesos were also finished because of the extremely high real rates of interest in pesos, which by December 1982 had reached a staggering 60 percent. It was only at the end of 1983 that confidence in the banking system returned, the central bank started to reduce the credit growth rate, and the trend in the international reserves reversed itself.

As it would happen in Venezuela a decade later, the losses in the banking system were enormous. The country's gross domestic product (GDP) declined

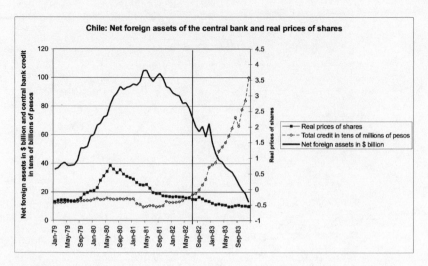

Figure 7.4: Chile: Net foreign assets of the Central Bank and real share prices. *Source:* International Financial Statistics of the International Monetary Fund.

by about 25 percent in the next two years. It took the government several years to untangle the problems created by the cycle of boom and bust.

It is important to notice that the entire cycle was caused by the combination of monetary and exchange rate policies. The large upswing that led to the ultimate catastrophe started precisely when the government fixed the exchange rate while the inflation rate was very high. The problem was not the fixation of the exchange rate. There are many countries that have fixed their exchange rates for decades without having a crisis. The mistake was to fix it while inflation was running high as a result of the also high credit growth rates. In these circumstances, the subsequent devaluation was inevitable. The Chilean crisis was self-inflicted through a particularly nasty combination of monetary and exchange rate policies.

The story in Venezuela, ten years later, is similar to the Chilean one. During the late 1980s and early 1990s, there had been privatizations of important companies; groups had been formed to buy them and control banks. Credit to related borrowers was as pervasive as in Chile. Also as in Chile, the country went though a boom-and-bust cycle during which it had a currency and a financial crisis, with the first starting well before the second exploded. In both cases, the swing can be traced to gross mismatches between monetary and exchange rate policies. Yet, while in the case of Chile the crisis was the result of a misguided but definite policy, in Venezuela it was the result of chaotic decisions of the central bank accumulated one on the other.

While the economy had been quite unstable during the 1980s, the main symptoms of the incoming crisis began to take shape early in 1990. From January 1990 to December 1993, the central bank increased its net domestic credit (net of the government deposits in the central bank) at an average rate of 64 percent per year. Most of this credit went to the government and to the nonbank public financial institutions, which are in charge of financing politically preferred activities. After some sterilization, this resulted in inflation rates that averaged 50 percent per year, while the devaluation rate was 35 percent. Thus, the currency was rapidly appreciating in real terms in the midst of very high rates of inflation. With the central bank pumping money into the economy, a cycle of boom and bust very similar to that of Chile rapidly developed.

Starting in January 1990, the real price of the industrial shares (deflated by the consumer price index, CPI) and the real rates of interest trapped investors in the same scissors that had trapped their Chilean colleagues. First, the currency appreciation with high rates of inflation led to negative real interest rates while the boom of asset prices was going on. Then, as in Chile, the movement of the two variables changed direction almost simultaneously, and the story turned sour.

The share prices kept on falling, until they somehow stabilized in November 1992, at a level that was just 40 percent of their value eleven months before. The same reversal of relative prices was taking place in the real estate markets, where the fledgling financial groups had also invested heavily. The financial groups were losing money at an amazing pace.

Naturally, the already insolvent banks concentrated their liquidity in refinancing the companies owned by their financial–real estate groups, and then in refinancing all other loss-making companies whose failure could bring about the bankruptcy of the bank. As in Chile, the banking system turned into a machine to transfer resources to insolvent borrowers.

People started a run on the currency. Figure 7.5 shows how the international reserves of the central bank started to fall right after the collapse in the assets' prices, and then fell at the same rhythm as the price of assets. As the central bank sold foreign exchange, receiving payment in local bolívares, the supply of bolívares declined, and the bolívares' liquidity in the banking system

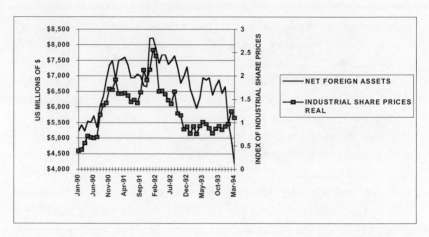

Figure 7.5: Real prices of industrial shares and net foreign assets of the Central Bank of Venezuela. *Source:* International Financial Statistics of the International Monetary Fund.

shrank. People were selling assets and buying dollars. Deposit interest rates reached 70 to 90 percent, while the rate of inflation was 35 to 45 percent. Lending rates were much higher.

In mid-January 1994, the Banco Latino, the second largest bank in the country, suddenly stopped operations. A run on the other banks started, complementing the run on the currency that was already raging. By the early summer, it was clear that the solvency crisis was general. Starting after the collapse of the Banco Latino, the government issued prison warrants against scores of people involved in the management and supervision of banks. Most of them, however, could not be located. The exchange rate jumped from 1.18 to 1.70 bolívares per dollar from April to July 1994. Eventually, the government was able to control the crisis, but not before losing enormous amounts of international reserves. The losses incurred by the banks were estimated at 25 percent of the country's GDP.

Thus, as in Chile, the crisis was domestically engineered through monetary and exchange rate policies. Also as in Chile, the currency run preceded the bank runs. Of course, as shown at the extreme right of figure 7.5 above, the reserves fell even faster when the run on the banks started. People took their money away from the banks and converted them into dollars, accelerating the loss of reserves of the central bank.

The history of the tequila crisis is very similar to the Chilean and Venezuelan ones: There was a boom in asset prices, followed by their collapse.

This took place while domestic credit was expanding at unsustainable rates, pushed by the central bank.

By 1994, Mexico had experienced substantial instability and a protracted recession for more than a decade. In 1982, all the banks had become insolvent and the government had suffered an external debt crisis. In 1989, the country suffered another scare. By the early 1990s, however, the government had resolved the external debt problems and had carried out substantial structural reforms, including the liberalization of trade and financial markets, the privatization of banks and public enterprises, and the signature of the North American Free Trade Agreement (NAFTA). The rate of inflation had been coming down, from almost 20 percent in January 1992 to a one-digit figure in early 1994. Mexico had become a very attractive country for foreign investment, and investment was coming in large amounts.

As shown in figure 7.6, the price of industrial shares in Mexico went up steeply from 1990 on, following the same path as the net international reserves of the Bank of Mexico. The two variables moved almost synchronically throughout the years. By the end of 1993, the real price of shares was six times its value in 1989. Then, as suddenly as it had happened in Chile and Venezuela, in January 1994, the prices of assets began to fall and one month later, the Bank of Mexico started to lose reserves at a very fast rate. The currency crisis had started, while the financial crisis was still almost a year into the future.

In Mexico, the events that seem to have triggered the simultaneous fall in asset prices and the international reserves of the central bank were the emergence of a rebel movement in Chiapas and the assassination of the most popular candidate in the presidential elections, which were due at the end of the year. Fear invaded Mexico in spite of the announcement of the signature of the NAFTA treaty. It is understandable, then, that a crisis of confidence would take place. The important point, however, is that such crisis started against the currency, not the banks. As shown in figure 7.6, the government was able to forestall the fall in the net foreign assets from April to October. It did so, however, by issuing short-term debt denominated *in dollars*. Up to that moment, the government's ability to repay was not in question. It was only the currency. That is why the government was able to sell the notorious tesobonos (bonds denominated in dollars), in Mexico and abroad.

Because it was an electoral year, the central bank printed pesos to create an environment of buoyancy while it kept on borrowing dollars with the tesobonos to avoid the fall in the international reserves. In the months that preceded the November 1994 crisis, the Central Bank of Mexico expanded its

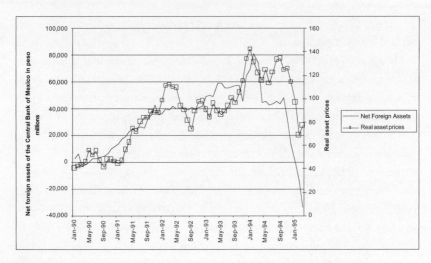

Figure 7.6: Real prices of shares and the net foreign assets of the Central Bank of Mexico. *Source:* International Financial Statistics of the International Monetary Fund.

credit at annual rates that surpassed 250 percent while keeping the rate of devaluation much lower to prevent an increase in the inflation rate. Rather than preventing the incoming crisis, however, the increased peso liquidity brought it faster and made it worse. As shown in figure 7.6 above, the prices of shares collapsed again in September, and in October, a second run against the currency began. The ample credit provided by the Central Bank of Mexico funded the capital flight.

The banking crisis exploded only when it became known that the government had difficulties in paying the tesobonos. Then all the problems were complicated by the large devaluation of November 1994, which was the beginning of a fast slide of the peso. By March 1995, the exchange rate against the U.S. dollar was twice as much as it had been one year before. The nonlinear effects of the devaluation in the balance sheets of banks, enterprises, and common citizens devastated the financial system. The Mexicans took it patiently. It was the fourth crisis in an election year in a row, all of them created by monetary mismanagement.

The story was similar in yet another crisis, that of the Dominican Republic, which took place in the early 2000s. In this case, the general assumption is that causality ran in the other direction: that a banking crisis created the currency run.

For about a decade, the Dominican Republic had attained very high rates of real economic growth based on a spectacular growth of exports. Then, suddenly, the country fell into a deep financial crisis, caused by the failure of its largest bank in March 2003. In the months that followed, both the peso- and the dollar-denominated deposits fell. Thus, it would seem that this was a purely financial crisis that affected the deposits in the two currencies.

There is no doubt that the banks were very weak in the Dominican Republic. As in other crises, they had engaged in credit to related borrowers and had lost enormous amounts in speculative activities. Yet, the evidence shows that a currency crisis had been in the making for some time before the financial crisis exploded. As in the other cases, it was the currency run that brought the problems of the banks to the surface.

The central bank started to lose international reserves around April 2002, one year before the banking crisis, while the deposits in the banking system were still increasing in both peso and dollar terms. The fall in the net foreign assets was so pronounced that they became negative by September, meaning that the central bank had to borrow abroad to keep its international liquidity. Thus, even if at the time it was not granting credit to the banks, and even if the dollar deposits were increasing, the central bank was losing dollars at a very fast rate. Then, as in Argentina, some depositors shifted their peso deposits into dollars, while others just took the dollars out of the country, further depleting the net foreign assets of the central bank.

The shift of currencies in the banking system was apparent between October 2002 and February 2003, still before the banking crisis exploded. Between those dates, dollar deposits went up from $1.6 billion to $2 billion, while the peso deposits went down in dollar terms from $4.4 billion to $3.2 billion. It is obvious that depositors perceived the currency risk as higher than the banking risk. Otherwise, they would have not increased their deposits in dollars. Then, in March 2003, the largest bank in the country stopped payments and the run on the banks started. Dollar deposits fell for the first time. Yet, by May, they stabilized at about the level they had three months before. At this time, the peso deposits were falling precipitously. By June 2004, deposits in dollars had increased *in dollar terms*, reaching a level that was 27 percent higher than their level in January 2002. In contrast, the peso deposits were 36 percent below their level at that date.

Of course, one can only speculate on what would have happened if the Dominican Republic did not have a local currency. Still, everything suggests that the initial run on the currency weakened both the banks and the central bank and this fed back into the people's confidence in the banking system. The fact that the dollar deposits never went below their level in January 2002 shows that, if the local currency had not complicated the events, the problem would have been much less grave.

The banking run did not start in a vacuum; it began within the pressures created by the currency run. The currency crisis did not start in a vacuum either; it was caused by an inconsistency between the central bank's monetary and exchange rate policies, the nemesis of local currencies in developing countries. The central bank had steadily increased the growth rate of reserve money, which had reached 40 percent at the end of 2001, while keeping the rate of devaluation at almost zero. It was the old story. The central bank had created a monetary problem, which then made it necessary to devalue the currency.

The risk factors that we have identified in these three Latin American crises were also present in the East Asian crises. In those countries, related credit was pervasive. The interrelationship among banks, government, and enterprises was so close that a new term, "crony capitalism," was invented to describe the system they created. These countries also went through a boom of asset prices propelled by a wrong combination of monetary and exchange rate policies. However, there are two puzzles in the East Asian crises. The first is that these factors do not seem to justify the magnitude of the collective crisis. The macroeconomic imbalances of the countries, while significant, were far from being as bad as in the Latin American crises. Indonesia, one of the hardest hit by the regional crisis, had experienced fiscal surpluses for several years in a row when the crisis began. Inflation was low throughout the region and, while all the countries had substantial current account deficits, they were not of the magnitude that would predict what happened after July 1997 in one country after another. The second puzzle is precisely the synchronization of the crises. Even if all developed in different ways, they all started in July 1997, when the baht, the Thai currency, collapsed.

There are three keys to resolve these puzzles. First is the order in which the two dimensions of the crises started: As in Latin America, the currency runs preceded the financial crises by an ample margin. In fact, the currency runs started simultaneously as soon as the Thai baht collapsed, while the financial crises appeared after a lag that varied across the countries. This, the close synchronicity of the currency runs in the different countries, is the second key. A study conducted by International Monetary Fund (IMF) staff shows that a 1 percentage average depreciation of the currencies of the four other countries was associated with a 0.38 percent depreciation of any of the countries' own exchange rates (the sample contained Indonesia, Korea, Malaysia, the Philippines, and Thailand). Equally, a fall of 1 percent in the average stock market prices of the other four countries was associated with a fall of 0.64 percent in the countries' own stock prices a day later.[3]

The third key is that the financial crises appeared in all countries only after the currency was devalued, sending to illiquidity and insolvency not only the companies that had borrowed in dollars and the banks that had financed their local currency loans with short-term dollar obligations but also those that had borrowed in the local currency and faced higher interest rates and a collapse in demand. That is, contagion went from one country to the others through the weakness of their local currencies. This was the triggering event.

In Thailand, the classic boom went from 1993 to 1996, largely caused by an excessively expansionary monetary policy combined with a fixed exchange rate. This attracted enormous amounts of capital flows to the country. Most of the domestic credit, however, was in baht. It was the banks that took the bulk of the foreign exchange risk, arbitraging interest rates on the idea that the exchange rate would not move, as had happened in Chile. The central bank also took substantial foreign exchange risks, as it committed a good portion of its own reserves to forward operations. In these operations, when banks or companies imported capital and sold the dollars to the central bank in exchange for bahts, the central bank promised to sell them the dollars back at the same price. While many companies and banks did not use this facility, the volume of the operations made a big difference between the apparent international reserves of the central bank and the amount of dollars it could use to resolve a crisis.

The end of the boom in 1996 triggered the familiar run on the currency, which resulted in a catastrophic fall in the reserves of the central bank during the first six months of 1997. Figure 7.7 shows how closely the fall in the net foreign assets of the central bank was associated with the fall in the real price of assets during the six months leading to the July financial crisis. This, together with the fact that the banks were not still in crisis, suggests that people were liquidating their positions in the stock exchange and were converting the proceeds into dollars to take them out of the country. This is what happened in Latin America. As discussed below, this was also happening in the other countries in the region.

The situation was much worse in June than portrayed in figure 7.7. As

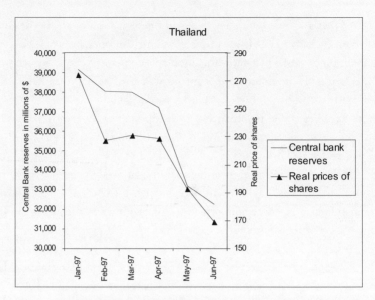

Figure 7.7: Real prices of shares and net international reserves of the Central Bank of Thailand during the six months preceding the financial crisis. *Source:* International Financial Statistics of the International Monetary Fund.

shown in figure 7.8, the apparently high reserve position of the central bank was counterbalanced by a highly negative position in dollars of the commercial banks, which were borrowing abroad at a very fast rate to invest in the domestic boom. By 1994, three years before the crisis, the reserves of the consolidated financial system (including the central bank) had already become negative. The difference had been invested in the booming domestic assets and then had leaked out through the widening current account deficit. The apparently strong reserve position of the central bank was in fact quite compromised, particularly because, as I mentioned earlier, the central bank had also taken forward positions to sell dollars for bahts with its reserves at the exchange rate prevailing before the crisis. Thus, the numbers shown in the figure grossly overstate the true amount of effective reserves it had. While the figure shows that by June 1997 the central bank had more than $30 billion in liquid reserves, by that month the usable reserves were actually very close to zero. For this reason, it had to let the baht go.

Figure 7.8 also shows a very important fact for our discussion: The banks were still able to borrow abroad in net terms in early 1997, when the run on the currency had already started and the central bank's reserves were already falling. I drew two vertical lines to show that period, which spanned from

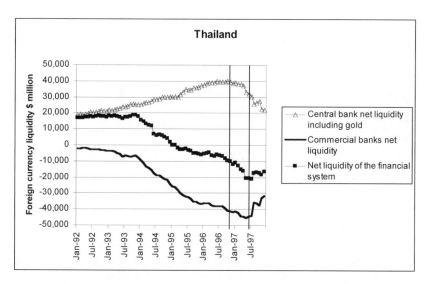

Figure 7.8: The international liquidity position of the financial system in Thailand. *Source:* International Financial Statistics of the International Monetary Fund.

January to July 1997. That is, for six months, the crisis only involved the currency run and this was purely domestic. The domestic banks were not demanding credit from the central bank, and the foreign banks were not recalling their loans. They were even increasing them. It was only in July, when the central bank let the currency go, that external creditors got scared and the banks had to start repaying the large capital inflows they had borrowed in the previous three years.

Figure 7.9 shows how the crisis unraveled. In July, when the central bank's reserves adjusted for forward commitments had fallen to zero, the government floated the currency and the banking crisis began. It was at this time that the central bank began to extend credit to the banks. As shown in the figure, it had to borrow large amounts of dollars to do it. The magnitude of the domestic run can be appreciated by the fact that the central bank's reserves continued to fall despite the large currency devaluations.

Thus, it is clear that the problem started with the currency. The currency troubles were rooted in the classic wrong combination of monetary and exchange rate policies. In the years leading to the crisis, the central bank had expanded the supply of reserve money at very high and erratic rates (reaching 22 percent in 1995) while keeping the exchange rate fixed. The rate of inflation remained low, but the current account in the balance of payments widened,

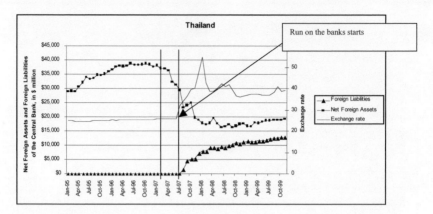

Figure 7.9: Net foreign assets and foreign liabilities of the Central Bank of Thailand. *Note:* The foreign liabilities of the Central Bank were deducted from the foreign assets to estimate the net foreign assets. The foreign liabilities are shown to illustrate the point that the country had to borrow heavily abroad, starting in July 1997, which is when Thailand devalued the currency. *Source:* International Financial Statistics of the International Monetary Fund.

financed with large capital inflows, which, as in Latin America, were reacting to the ongoing assets boom.

Why would people convert their bahts into dollars and export these? When the stock exchange collapsed in the United States in the early 2000s, people obviously took their money out of the markets. They, however, did not convert the proceeds into euros. The Europeans did not convert their euros into dollars or yen when their own stock exchanges collapsed. The difference is that in Thailand, as in all other crises in developing countries, people mistrusted the currency. Such mistrust led to the fall in the central bank's reserves, and this to the sudden devaluation, to the apparition of Thai authorities in Washington to borrow dollars, and to the recall of the foreign lines of credit. Lurking beneath all these events was the weakness of the baht, which, even if stronger than most currencies in the developing world, proved not to be strong enough in the critical circumstances of 1997. Like Chile, Venezuela, Mexico, and all the other countries that fell victims to crises, Thailand was caught in the reversed liquidity trap. Thus, as it had happened in all other crises, the Thai crisis was domestically engineered through a monetary policy that was too expansionary for the exchange rate. The weakness of the local currency exacerbated the crisis and gravely complicated its solution.

The case of Korea was so similar to the ones already discussed that the analysis of the subject can become boring. As in all the other countries, there was a boom in real assets, propelled by a bad mixture of monetary and exchange rate policies and a pronounced cycle of international capital flows associated with the boom. These flows were intermediated by banks owned by large conglomerates, called chaebols in Korea. These banks borrowed short-term in the international markets and passed on the proceeds to their related companies in the form of long-term loans denominated in wons. In this way, they took enormous maturity and foreign exchange risks that the bank supervisors should not have allowed. When the Thai currency crisis extended to the region, Korea experienced large losses in reserves and was forced to devalue. The currency crisis brought to the surface the weakness of the banking system, and the financial crisis began.

As shown in figure 7.10, the currency run began well before the banking run. The fall in the net foreign assets of the financial system started in June 1997. It was only in November, when the central bank let the won float, that banks began to falter and the central bank started to provide massive amounts of credit to them. The net foreign assets became negative after February 1998, as the central bank was able to support the banks only at the cost of heavy borrowing abroad.

The opportunity for the speculation that led to the crisis was once again the result of a serious mismatch between the rate of monetary creation and the rate of devaluation.

As in the other cases, Indonesia had been pursuing contradictory monetary and exchange rate policies for a long time. The central bank allowed the supply of reserve money to grow at an accelerated pace in the six years before the crisis exploded. It reached a growth rate of around 40 percent per year in the twelve months preceding the crisis. While this was happening, the exchange rate was depreciating at just 5 percent on average.

As shown in figure 7.11, in Indonesia the problems also started with the currency. In July 1997, just days after the first devaluation of Thailand, the net foreign assets of the central bank began to fall at a very fast rate along with the real price of shares. At the same time, the rupiah began to devalue rapidly. It was only four months later, in November, that the financial crisis started and the central bank began lending to the banks.

The case of Indonesia was notable because of the incredibly high rate of

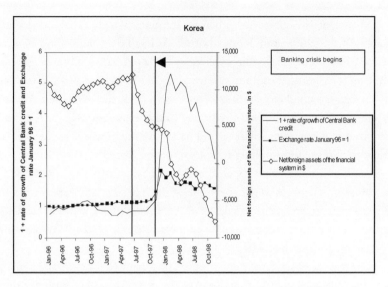

Figure 7.10: Rate of growth of central bank credit and foreign exchange reserves of the Korean financial system. *Source:* International Financial Statistics of the International Monetary Fund.

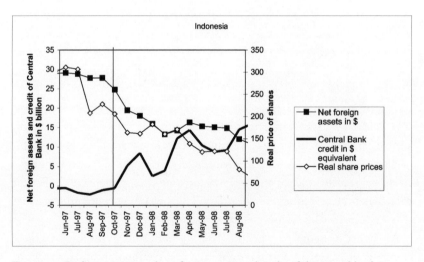

Figure 7.11: Real asset prices and net foreign assets and credit of the central bank in Indonesia. *Source:* International Financial Statistics of the International Monetary Fund.

depreciation of the rupiah. It went from 2,500 to 14,900 rupiahs to the dollar from July 1997 to June 1998 before appreciating again to 6,726 in June 1999. While large devaluations always cause serious disruptions in developing countries, the disruption that they caused in Indonesia were so grave that even devaluation-happy economists said that the currency should not have been allowed to depreciate so much. For example, in a country with thousands of islands, the cost of oil became prohibitive and transportation between many of the islands was interrupted.

The most common idea regarding the Argentina crisis is that its exports fell catastrophically in the aftermath of Brazil's large devaluation in January 1999. The idea is that the country's inability to devalue at that moment sealed its fate, setting into a course that required devaluation for trade reasons.

There are four problems with this idea, some of which I already noted in chapter 3. First, Brazil devalued its currency because its current account deficit was too large. It was importing too much, including from Argentina, and had to reduce those imports drastically. Thus, if Argentina had devalued, Brazil would have been forced to devalue again, entering into a game that in the 1930s was called "competitive devaluations." Second, as shown in figure 7.12, while exports declined in 1999 along with a sharp decrease in export prices that had started back in 1995, they recovered by 2000 as these prices increased modestly. Certainly, after the 2000 recovery, the country's exports did not grow relative to their 1998 level, but this was true of most of Latin America in those years. Third, the trade balance improved quite rapidly after 1998, so that the country attained substantial trade *surpluses* in 2000 and 2001, before the devaluation. Brazil, the counterexample, attained a trade surplus only in 2001, two years after its large devaluation. Thus, contrary to common belief, the fixed exchange rate did not cripple Argentina's international trade. Fourth, as it is obvious in the figure, the real problem was the reversal in the capital flows. The magnitudes involved in this reversal dwarfed that of the movements in the level of exports.

As capital inflows fell at an accelerated pace, the economy experienced a grave recession. GDP per capita fell by 8.5 percent from 1998 to 2001 after having grown fast on average in the previous five years. This drastic fall also has been attributed to the currency board regime that Argentina established in 1993. Certainly, the currency board was a risky regime. It left the local currency in place while introducing rigidity in its management. Additionally,

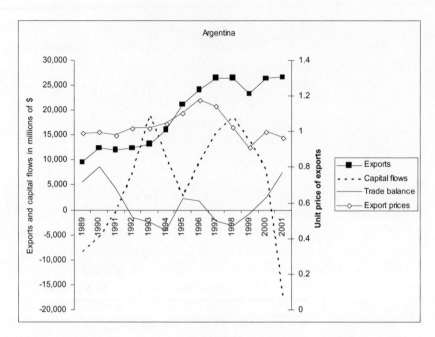

Figure 7.12: Exports, export prices, and capital flows in Argentina. *Source:* International Financial Statistics of the International Monetary Fund.

the government allowed the existence of cross-currency risks in the banking system.

Argentina's problems, however, seem to need a wider explanation than the exchange rate regime. As shown in figure 7.13, the country has been suffering from drastic falls in its income per capita at constant dollars purchasing power parity (PPP) for almost three decades now, under different exchange rate regimes. These ranged from plain fixed exchange rates to preannounced devaluations to floating exchange rates to the currency board and then again to floating.

Thus, as also shown in table 7.2, the crisis was not unprecedented. Up to 2001, when the currency board collapsed, income per capita had fallen by 10.4 percent when measured in international dollars PPP at constant 1995 prices. This was lower than the fall of 1987–1990, which totaled 15.3 percent. Once we take into account the year that followed the collapse of the currency board, 2002, the total fall of the crisis amounts to 18.0 percent, which is in the same order of magnitude as the 1987–1990 one. Overall, Argentina experienced declines in its GDP per capita in thirteen of the last twenty-eight

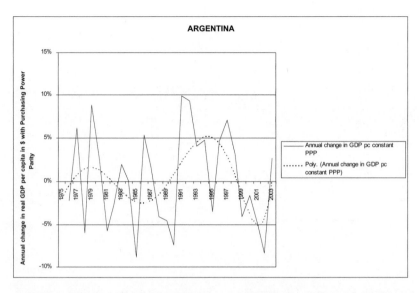

Figure 7.13: Argentina: Changes in GDP per capita measured in dollars with purchasing power parity (PPP) at constant 1995 prices. *Source:* World Development Indicators, World Bank.

Table 7.2: Crises and GDP PPP Per Capita Reductions

|  | Fall during crisis (%) | Worst annual fall (%) | Year of worst annual fall |
|---|---|---|---|
| 1976 | −2.27 | −2.27 | 1976 |
| 1978 | −6.04 | −6.04 | 1978 |
| 1980–1982 | −8.32 | −5.74 | 1981 |
| 1985 | −8.76 | −8.76 | 1985 |
| 1987–1990 | −15.31 | −7.45 | 1990 |
| 1995 | −3.57 | −3.57 | 1995 |
| 1998–2001 | −10.44 | −4.95 | 2001 |
| 1998–2002 | −17.95 | −8.38 | 2002 |

*Source:* World Development Indicators, The World Bank.

years, from 1976 to 2003. In eleven of those years, the fall was of 4 percent or worse.

Internationally, the country defaulted in 1828, 1890, 1982, 1989, and 2001. Thus, the country is quite unstable even by developing countries' standards. As shown in figure 7.14, the income fluctuations have been associated with

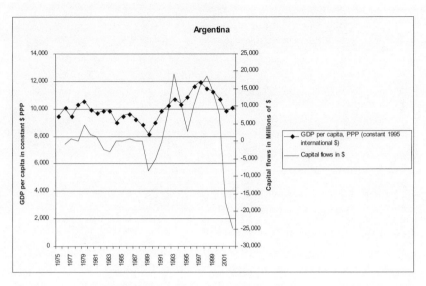

Figure 7.14: Argentina: GDP per capita in dollars PPP and capital flows in millions of dollars. *Source:* World Development Indicators, World Bank, for the income per capita and the International Financial Statistics of the International Monetary Fund for the capital flows.

the capital that has flowed in and out of the country. As visible in the figure, capital flows have been extremely volatile and this is reflected in the volatility of income. As in Brazil, the economy grows when it gets capital inflows and collapses when it does not.

As can be observed in the figure above, capital inflows fell sharply in 1995, mainly as a result of the tequila crisis. The problems caused by the tequilazo in Argentina were so deep and sharp that for a while it seemed that they would force the abandonment of the currency board. The people's confidence in the fixed exchange rate seemed broken. They started to hedge against it in the following years. We can see this by examining the behavior of the deposits of the nonresidents in Uruguay, who, as we know, are Argentines. There was a break in the tendency of the deposits of the Argentines in that country precisely in 1995. Before that year, they remained flat around $2 billion. Then, after the tequila crisis, they started to grow quickly, so that by 2001 they had tripled to $6 billion. The Argentines had started to hedge.

The nervousness of the Argentines is quite understandable. The currency has always been a problem in their country and this has generated cynicism in the population. If you had bought a dollar's worth of Argentine local currency in 1975 and held it, the current value of your asset would be

0.00000000021 dollars, practically air. Said in another way, your pesos would have been worth 4.8 billion times more in 1975 than they would in 2003. In the midst of this nominal devaluation, the country experienced a real appreciation of about 33 percent—that is, the rate of devaluation was slower than the differential between the Argentine and the U.S. rates of inflation. Thus, you can imagine what the inflation rate was. Following the example I posed in the introduction, this is as if you boarded a very long and fast train in Baltimore that went in the direction of New York and ran against the direction of its movement until you got to Buenos Aires.

The nominal devaluations, combined with the also chaotic real appreciations and devaluations, have caused enormous redistributions of resources between people who hedged with foreign currencies and those who did not; and among the people who held peso-denominated financial assets and those who held liabilities in the same currency. One Buenos Aires taxi driver told me once that he had bought an apartment in the 1970s and shortly after that he repented because the installments were too high for his income. Nevertheless, urged by his wife, he kept it. Five years later, he repaid the entire loan because the cost of driving to the bank to make the monthly payments was higher than the entire balance of the loan. He only regretted not having bought a mansion. Of course, the depositors who had financed him had seen the value of their financial assets collapse from the equivalent of an apartment to less than half a gallon of gasoline. These violent shifts must affect productivity. In this environment, you cannot blame the Argentines, and the people dealing financially with them, if they are quite nervous about the value of their currency.

They were nervous in the years that preceded the 1998–2002 crisis, much more so than about the health of the banks. Actually, the fact that the government was able to convince the people that the currency board was safe and that the peso was equal to the dollar is amazing given the credibility track of governments in this subject. This is particularly amazing after 1998, when the national and international calls for devaluation and pesification of the dollar accounts were becoming more frequent and visible. Although many people hedged, many others believed that their dollar deposits would be respected. They actually thought that dollars would protect them against an eventual abandonment of the currency board, which the data shows they thought increasingly probable. As can be observed in figure 7.15, while peso deposits stagnated after mid-1997, dollar deposits continued growing until December 2000, at the end of the second year of declining GDP per capita

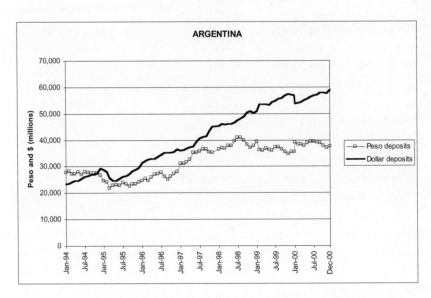

Figure 7.15: Deposits in pesos and dollars in Argentina, January 1994–December 2000. *Source:* Ministry of the Economy, Argentina.

and capital flows. Under the influence of the dollar deposits, the total deposits of the banking system continued growing until that date. This shows that there was no lack of confidence in the banks or in the dollars. The mistrust was related to the pesos.

The withdrawal of dollar deposits started only in February 2001. This can be taken as an early manifestation of mistrust in the banks. It may be, although the evidence shows that the problem worrying the Argentines was still mostly the currency. The difference in the way people saw the two currencies is visible in the fact that they withdrew more pesos than dollars. Figure 7.16 shows the data by month from January 2000 to November 2001, two weeks before the currency board collapsed. Even by October, the dollar deposits had fallen only 7 percent from their level in January, while peso deposits had fallen by 31 percent during the same period. A fall of 7 percent of deposits in ten months is a problem that banks can handle easily with their liquidity reserves and by not renovating short-term loans. A fall of 31 percent is a run. Moreover, dollar savings deposits, held by small savers, *increased* in dollar terms during the months leading to the collapse, while peso savings deposits were falling dramatically in the same terms.[4] The resilience of the dollar deposits is evidenced by the fact that their withdrawals remained moderate even in the midst of

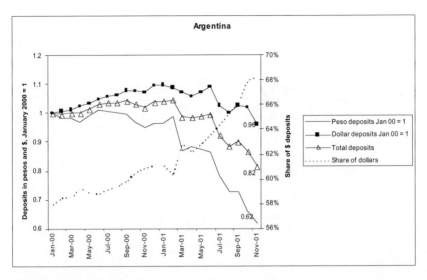

Figure 7.16: Deposits in dollars and pesos in Argentina in 2000–2001. *Source:* Ministry of the Economy of Argentina.

increasing proposals to pesify the dollar deposits to subsequently devalue the peso.

These figures suggest that without the dollar deposits, the impact of the run on the currency on the liquidity of the banks would have taken place at a much earlier stage and by much larger magnitudes.

International creditors, belying their bad reputation as footloose among some analysts of financial crises, also showed a remarkable trust in the banks up to a very late moment. International flows of credit to Argentine banks remained positive until the end of 2000. It was only in 2001 that they turned negative as the foreign banks recalled their loans. The outflow of capital caused by the repayment of the banks' obligations, however, was less than half the problem—it was $7.9 billion; the total capital outflow in that year was $17.4 billion. This was equivalent to 6.5 percent of GDP.[5] This was not a run of the international banks; it was a generalized one.

How could people extract so much liquidity out of the country? It amounted to 88 percent of the total domestic liquidity that existed at the end of 2000 (as represented by all the currency bills plus all the demand deposits). Figure 7.17 shows that starting in January 2001 the central bank of Argentina violated the rules of its own currency board and extended credit to the gov-

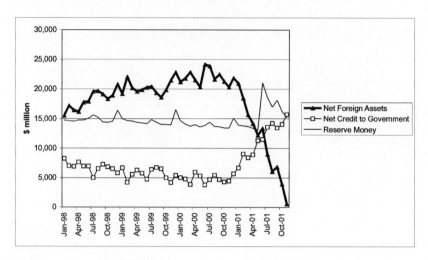

Figure 7.17: Credit to the government and net foreign assets of the Central Bank of Argentina. *Source:* International Financial Statistics of the International Monetary Fund.

ernment by an amount that by November 2001 reached about $10 billion over the previous balances. It is clear that most of the money created by the central bank in those months was not to support the drain of dollar deposits in the banking system. In fact, the central bank's credit to banks increased by just $2.4 billion. Most of the new money went to the government, which spent it to cover the provincial governments' deficits. People used that purchasing power plus a good portion of the $11 billion they withdrew from the banks in pesos to buy dollars. In the process, the central bank lost $20 billion in reserves against the $13 billion it had created through credit to the government.[6] Figure 7.17 also shows why the government had to let the currency board go in December. It had no more of the money that people demanded: dollars. Being in excess demand, the dollar then jumped to 3.7 pesos in the months that followed.

Thus, the Central Bank of Argentina funded the exportation of all the liquidity in the country. Many people would argue that extending credit to the government was the least that the central bank could have done in a situation in which the provincial governments could not pay their salaries and other indispensable expenditures. After all, the economic contraction induced by the loss of domestic liquidity caused by the capital outflows was terrible. Argentina was clearly in a liquidity trap. The economy needed liquidity to function. According to this argument, the central bank had to act.

*$ cleane by the C.B*
*✓ did ho some the profits*

Yet, the evidence shows that the money created by the central bank did *✓ $ /et,* not help to resolve the problem. It did not remain in the country. The more it created, the more it lost reserves, and this was happening as the country's current account deficit was narrowing from $8.9 billion in 2000 to $4 billion in 2001. That is, the problem was not in the current account; it was in the capital flows. The liquidity trap of Argentina was not of the normal variety; it was a reversed liquidity trap. The liquidity that people wanted was in dollars.

In addition, they wanted them abroad. Unfortunately, government after government has taught the Argentines that the best place to locate their savings is abroad. The six governments that managed the situation beginning in early December 2001 confirmed this teaching. To the applause of the international community, the dollar accounts were converted into pesos at an exchange rate that implied severe losses to the depositors. Many of the people who applauded would not have done so if their savings had been denominated in the money that was forcibly converted and then devalued.

Everybody assumed that the devaluation would stop the capital outflows. This was not so. As visible in figure 7.14 above, capital outflows were larger after the devaluation than in 2001. They amounted to $24 billion, 42 percent more than in the previous year. GDP per capita fell by an additional 8 percent. The burden of the external debt ballooned as a percent of GDP. This might not have mattered in the short term because the government defaulted on its debts and offered its debtors the repayment of only a very small fraction of their obligations. In 2003, the economy experienced growth again. At a rate of 2.4 percent as measured in international dollars with purchasing power parity at constant 1995 prices, the recovery was very modest, particularly taking into account that the government was not servicing its debts. In 2004, the country grew at record rates—but, of course, without servicing its external debts. By 2005 growth was weakening again as the short-term gains of default were exhausting themselves.

Thus, our review of the most representative of the crises that have afflicted the developing countries in the last few decades shows that all of them were *crises caused by* caused by monetary and exchange rate manipulations that started years before the crises erupted; and that in all cases, the crises were triggered by a currency run, which was a manifestation of the reversed liquidity trap. None of these things can happen in a dollarized economy: They cannot engineer artificial booms from the central bank and they cannot experience a run of people exchanging the local currency for dollars. For these reasons, financial crises are less likely to happen in dollarized countries and, if they happen, they would be much more easily resolved than in developing countries with their own currencies. It is much simpler to resolve a banking crisis than a combination of a banking and a currency crisis.

The case of Argentina shows that currency boards are not able to avoid the reversed liquidity trap. People distinguish between an image in the mirror and the real thing, and they are right. The problem that Argentina faces today is that the government has shown again that the real thing exists only out of its frontiers.

There is, however, the idea that, for all their deficiencies, local currencies allow for the existence of a lender of last resort, which is a guarantee of a prompt solution when a country falls into a financial crisis. This argument is somewhat strange. To accept it, we would have to believe that central banks can resolve the crises they have created through excessive monetary creation by creating even more money. In the logic of the reversed liquidity trap that dominates the crises, central banks could stop the conversion of local currency into dollars by not creating money and, if possible, by sterilizing the existing currency. However, this would not resolve the crises because they arise from the panic of the population trying to get dollars. As discussed before, in such circumstances, the government would have to increase the interest rates to levels that would signal to the population that a large devaluation is coming. This would worsen the currency run. Thus, central banks are powerless in those circumstances.

The only solution for them is increasing the supply of what people want: the foreign currency. That is, they have to go to Washington and New York to borrow dollars. Argentina found the needed dollars by not repaying the dollars it owed. The panic ends only when people are satisfied that the government has enough dollars to support the local currency, at an exchange rate that, by that time, is grossly depreciated. I examine this subject in the next chapter.

# Chapter 8 The Myth of the Lender of Last Resort

One of the most popular arguments in favor of local currencies is that they allow countries to have a lender of last resort to support their banks in times of crisis. I would respond that if this were true, ministers of finance and central bank governors would not rush to Washington and New York to get dollars when they have a financial crisis. They would stay comfortably at home, printing money, saving themselves the bad moments they go through when questioned by bankers and listening to the conditions imposed by the International Monetary Fund (IMF) to provide the money which, according to the conventional idea, they should not need.

Surprisingly, however, many people argue that these gentlemen visit New York and Washington only because their banks have dollar deposits and people are withdrawing them. Then they reassert that central banks do not need dollars to print domestic currencies. In their view, if such deposits did not exist, ministers and governors could rest at home while the printing presses worked.

In fact, they engage in those peregrinations because they desperately need dollars for three reasons: First, they need them to print domestic currency because financial crises in developing countries are always associated with currency runs, so that people take their pesos and convert them into dollars. Second, they need dollars to cover the dollar foreign obligations of the domestic banks that are coming due and are not being rolled over. These two reasons exist in all developing countries, even in those where dollar deposits are not allowed. The third reason is the dollar deposits. There is no doubt that if people decide to withdraw them, they also increase the need for dollars. However, in most cases, the foreign currency deposits have actually protected the banks during the initial stages of a crisis. As already discussed, practically all the financial crises in developing countries have started with a currency run. At that stage, many people have exported their savings, but many others have shifted their local currency deposits into dollars and left them in the local banks. For this reason, foreign currency deposits have fallen less than the local currency deposits and in some cases they have increased. People have begun to withdraw their dollar deposits only when the currency run has raged for some time, obviously weakening the banks. In some cases, as in Argentina, people did not withdraw their dollar deposits in significant amounts until the very edge of the crisis, while they had been withdrawing their pesos in dangerous amounts for months.

The fact that central banks do need dollars to print their domestic currency is most alien to Americans because even the expression *international reserves* does not carry much meaning for them. After all, because the dollar is a reserve currency, the Federal Reserve can create international reserves at will. Thus, even when keenly conscious that the current account deficit in the balance of payments will deteriorate if the fiscal deficit escalates in the United States, many Americans tend to forget that to pay for this deficit, they need a substance that comes so naturally to them: dollars. This need for dollars always exists, although it increases exponentially during crises, as the reversed liquidity trap acts on the monetary markets.

There are very simple reasons why dollars are needed to print domestic currencies. No country is self-sufficient, and finished goods and production inputs need to be imported from abroad. Thus, even in equilibrium, a portion of the aggregate demand will leak through imports, paid for either by exports or by capital inflows from abroad. The connection between printing money and the deterioration of the balance of payments, of course, is not automatic. With the economy growing, people would demand increasing amounts of money to carry out their transactions. If the central bank printed money only to meet those increased needs, inflation and the current account balance would not change because the new money would be used for the increased domestic transactions. Central banks create money in this way when they print local currency by purchasing foreign currencies.

If, however, the central bank decided to expand the supply of money beyond what people demand for transactions (which is what central banks do when they want to spur economic growth or finance an excessive fiscal deficit), people would find that they are carrying cash balances in excess of what they need and would spend the excess, increasing domestic demand. Naturally, this would increase imports at the rate given by the marginal propensity to import of the economy. Since the increased domestic demand was created by printing money, not by increased exports or autonomous capital inflows, the additional dollars needed to pay for the new imports would have to come from some other source—the international reserves of the central bank. If the central bank did not take compensatory measures, its reserves would continue to fall until *all* of the excess monetary creation is exhausted through imports.

The central bank has two mechanisms to restrict the losses of reserves measured in foreign currency. The first—devaluation—does not reduce the amount of domestically created money that leaks out of the system, but reduces the dollar equivalent of such leakages. The other action is sterilization of part or the total of the newly created money. As discussed in previous chapters, central banks can sterilize money through forcing commercial banks to deposit with them a portion of their deposits from the public (establishing or increasing legal deposit requirements) or selling obligations to the banks. These actions actually destroy part or the total of the newly created money, so that less is left to leak through imports and to increase domestic prices.

Table 8.1 illustrates this process in two panels. For simplicity of exposition, the example assumes fixed exchange rates. The top panel shows the case where the only leakage in the multiplication is imports. In this case, given a marginal propensity to import of 0.4, nominal domestic demand (money spent by the public) would increase by two and a half times the amount of excess money created. Demand would stop expanding until all the excess money had leaked through imports. The lower panel simulates a double leakage. In addition to imports, money leaks into legal reserve requirements of 25 percent, going back to the central bank. In this case, the increase in imports would be lower than the excess money created.

Thus, monetary printing in excess of the natural increase in the demand for transactions always results in a reduction in the international reserves of the central bank, the magnitude of the decline being determined by several

## Table 8.1: The Multiplier of the Banking System and Imports

Multiplication if imports are the only leakage, propensity to import = 0.4

| Round | Excess money | Spent | Imports | Intermediated by banks |
|---|---|---|---|---|
| 0 | **100** | 100 | 40 | 60 |
| 1 | | 60 | 24 | 36 |
| 2 | | 36 | 14.4 | 21.6 |
| 3 | | 21.6 | 8.64 | 12.96 |
| 4 | | 12.96 | 5.184 | 7.776 |
| 5 | | 7.776 | 3.1104 | 4.6656 |
| 6 | | 4.6656 | 1.86624 | 2.79936 |
| 7 | | 2.79936 | 1.119744 | 1.679616 |
| 8 | | 1.679616 | 0.671846 | 1.00777 |
| 9 | | 1.00777 | 0.403108 | 0.604662 |
| 10 | | 0.604662 | 0.241865 | 0.362797 |
| Total | | 249.09 | **99.64** | 149.46 |

Multiplication with legal reserve requirements of 25 percent

| Round | Excess money | Spent | Imports | Deposited in banks | Available for lending |
|---|---|---|---|---|---|
| 0 | **100** | 100 | 40 | 60 | 45 |
| 1 | | 45 | 18 | 27 | 20.25 |
| 2 | | 20.25 | 8.1 | 12.15 | 9.1125 |
| 3 | | 9.1125 | 3.645 | 5.4675 | 4.100625 |
| 4 | | 4.100625 | 1.64025 | 2.460375 | 1.845281 |
| 5 | | 1.845281 | 0.738113 | 1.107169 | 0.830377 |
| 6 | | 0.830377 | 0.332151 | 0.498226 | 0.373669 |
| 7 | | 0.373669 | 0.149468 | 0.224202 | 0.168151 |
| 8 | | 0.168151 | 0.067261 | 0.100891 | 0.075668 |
| 9 | | 0.075668 | 0.030267 | 0.045401 | 0.034051 |
| 10 | | 0.034051 | 0.01362 | 0.02043 | 0.015323 |
| Total | | 181.79 | **72.72** | 109.07 | 81.80 |

factors, including the amount of the sterilization carried out by the central bank. While devaluations do not affect this process, they do reduce the foreign exchange equivalent of the resources leaked abroad. On average, however, central banks in developing countries tend to lose reserves when printing money in excess of the natural growth of demand for money even if they devalue their currency.

The need for dollars becomes more pressing when the possibility of capital outflows and dollar deposits withdrawals is taken into account. In this case, demand for dollars may reach 100 percent of the money created in the first round.

The relationship between the international reserves of the central bank on the rate of discretionary monetary creation exists in all countries except when they have remarkably large inflows or outflows of foreign currencies. Inflows of foreign currencies make room for discretionary monetary expansions without losing reserves, as the demand for the domestic currency is increasing relative to the country's gross domestic product (GDP). This, for example, was the case of China during the 1990s and the early 2000s. The inflows of foreign exchange coming from large surpluses in the balance of payments allowed the Central Bank of China to expand its discretionary monetary creation at moderate rates (lower than the rate of growth of the country) while still gaining reserves. For this reason, there is no correlation between discretionary monetary creation and changes in the net foreign assets of the country. Symmetrically, outflows of foreign currencies reduce the room for such expansions, to the point that central banks lose reserves even if they do not create more local money or reduce its creation to rates lower than those of the decrease in its demand. This is the case in the currency crises that lead to full-fledged financial crises.

The idea that central banks in developing countries can be the lenders of last resort by printing local currency is based on the assumption that people stage runs on banks in those countries only because they are afraid that the banks will fail. However, if people only want to take their money out of the banks during those crises, the creation of money to stop bank runs should not result in inflation, current account deficits, capital outflows, declines in reserves, or devaluations. People would not spend the new money but would hold it. This is what they did in the bank runs of the 1930s in the developed countries, to the extent that, as Keynes noted with his liquidity trap theory, they depressed the economy for lack of demand for goods and services. Rather than inflation, purebred bank runs created deflation. This would be the case if bank runs in the developing countries had the same causes as those old scares in the 1930s.

Yet, everybody knows that this not what happens in developing countries in crisis. On the contrary, the rate of inflation goes up, the dollar reserves go down, and all the symptoms of excessive nominal domestic demand acutely appear. These symptoms show that people do not withdraw their money from the banks to hold and caress it. On the contrary, they want to be rid of it, spending it on whatever they can get, driving inflation up, and purchasing dollars, driving the reserves down. In fact, the domestic currency is the commodity they want to be rid of because its price is falling or is about to fall. Issuing domestic currencies in these circumstances only provides the funds for people to move to other assets, preferably the dollar or any other internationally tradable currency.

As a manifestation of this, all crises stopped when the government demonstrated undeniably that it had enough foreign exchange to back the currency at the exchange rate of the moment—which in most cases was already highly devalued—not when the government recapitalized the banks (something that takes years to do). After exchange rate credibility had been achieved, governments have recapitalized the banks by buying the bad debts with government bonds—that is, with a promise to provide the banks a steady cash flow through the years to compensate for the cash losses caused by their bad portfolios. People showed that they were not afraid the government would be unable to support the capital of the banks by accepting the gradual recapitalization and by returning their deposits to the banks. What they doubted was the government's ability to keep the exchange rate in place.

Some governments in crises (as in Indonesia) issued deposit guarantees in two periods: once when the currency run was raging, and then when that had abated even if the banks were still insolvent. Yet, it has been only in the second occasion that the dual runs have stopped. Why would people at first not believe and then believe the same promise? The difference has been that in the first occasion, the higher risk—that of further devaluations of the currency—was present, while it was not in the second. This shows that the main fear of the population is the loss through devaluation, rather than the loss of bank failures. In fact, this is why governments and international institutions give first priority to stabilizing the currency when these crises are raging, knowing that in all cases, currency uncertainty has led to bank runs, not the other way around. For this reason, developing countries in crisis have always needed dollars to support their banks.

The failure of the central bank to act as a lender of last resort without dollars can be exemplified with the crisis in Dominican Republic. Figure 8.1 shows the close correlation between the monthly changes in the credit granted by the central bank to the commercial banks and the monthly *fall* in its net foreign assets (i.e., the higher the curve, the higher the loss of reserves).

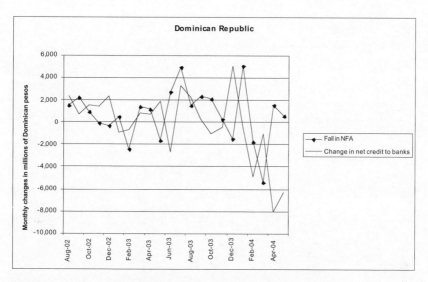

Figure 8.1: Dominican Republic: Net credit to banks and fall in net foreign assets, monthly changes. *Note:* The net credit is equal to the central bank's credit to banks minus deposits of banks in the central bank minus securities sold by the latter to the banks. *Source:* International Financial Statistics of the International Monetary Fund.

This was not an exclusively Dominican phenomenon. Domestic monetary creation has led to losses in international reserves in all financial crises in developing countries. Figure 8.2 shows how central banks needed dollars to print local currency during the crises in Indonesia and Thailand, figure 8.3 in the Chilean and Mexican crises, and figure 8.4 in the crises in Ecuador and Venezuela. In all these cases, the government faced the same situation that was exemplified with the case of the Dominican Republic: It had to borrow dollars heavily in the international markets to save their banks.

These cases show that, regardless of the cause (people exchanging pesos for dollars, foreign banks not rolling over their loans, or a run on dollar-denominated deposits), central banks do need dollars to control a financial crisis in our times. If central banks cannot create local currency without dollars, they have lost their ability to play their role of lender of last resort in an autonomous way. As Guillermo Calvo once told me, central banks are no longer lenders of last resort; they are in fact *borrowers* of last resort. In this capacity, they are in a similar situation as the ministries of finance in formally dollarized economies. That is, globalization has eliminated the purported advantage of nondollarized over dollarized economies in this respect. None of

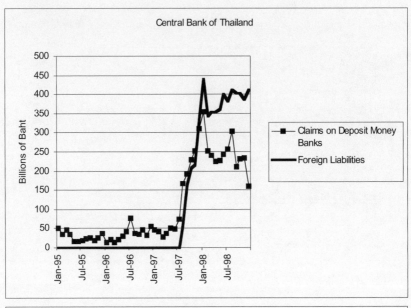

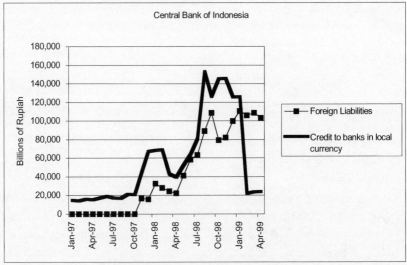

Figure 8.2: Credit in local currency equals dollar borrowing: Thailand and Indonesia.
*Source:* International Financial Statistics of the International Monetary Fund.

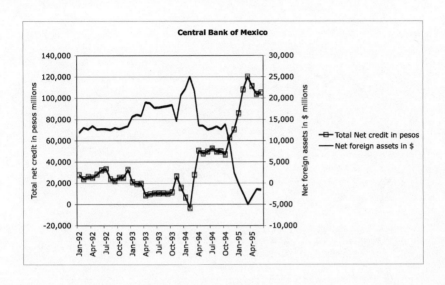

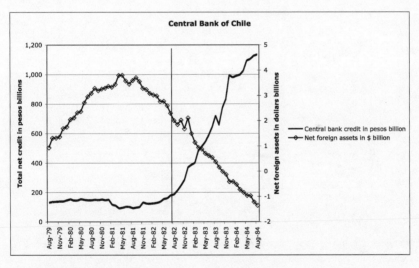

Figure 8.3: Credit in local currency equals dollar borrowing: Mexico and Chile. *Source:* International Financial Statistics of the International Monetary Fund.

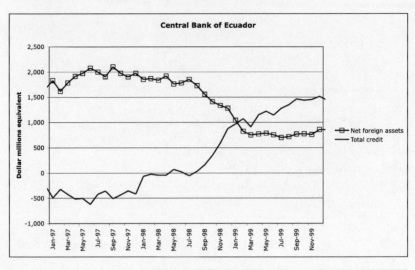

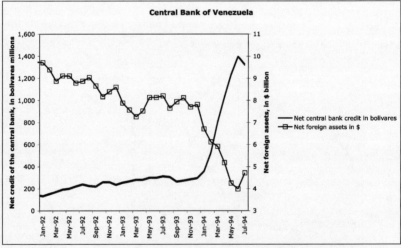

Figure 8.4: Credit in local currency equals dollar borrowing: Ecuador and Venezuela. *Source:* International Financial Statistics of the International Monetary Fund.

them have a lender of last resort that can save banks without getting dollars to back its credits.

It could be argued that, even if it is true that central banks lose reserves when they create money in a crisis, they do not lose them in a one-to-one proportion. In other words, there is a portion of the monetary creation that is absorbed by the population. This, however, does not detract from the argument. Even in the midst of a crisis, people need transaction balances, and these increase in nominal terms with the rate of inflation, which increases with the higher monetary creation. Thus, when they get the currency created by the central bank, they need to keep some of it as transaction balances to keep on living. In the process, however, they buy as many dollars as they can, eventually leading to the depletion of the international reserves of the central bank. The converted amounts can be amazingly large in terms of the domestic economy. In practically all crises, people have converted into foreign exchange more than the monetary base that existed before the crisis, which was the total liquidity of the system. The argument that being able to replace the entire liquidity of the system is an advantage of countries with local currencies is void because the conversion to a foreign currency takes place only because there is a local currency. There are no runs against international currencies.

We may notice in this respect that the very ability to create money that supposedly gives central banks the power to act as lenders of last resort is what has prompted the need for such a lender in all the crises in developing countries. The lenders of last resort, however, have not been the central banks but the IMF, the other public international financial institutions, and, in some cases, the Treasury of the United States. They had what people wanted: dollars.

Thus, we may conclude that the difference supposedly existing between nondollarized and dollarized economies, in terms of the existence of an autonomous lender of last resort that can save the banks without needing dollars in the former and not in the latter, does not exist in reality. It is a myth.

The weakness of central banks in both crisis and normal times is that people can escape from the monopoly game board. This was not so in the old times, when the Bretton Woods system was created. In those years, countries had in place drastic restrictions on international capital movements and it was illegal to hold other countries' currencies. Additionally, central banks controlled the interest rates. Central banks in developing countries could save banks by printing the domestic currency because people had no other choice but to accept it. Not able to buy dollars, they bought any real assets they could, driving their prices up. Central banks were not necessarily unhappy about this; they could set the interest rate at a level much lower than inflation, so that all debts were diluted in real terms. The banks were thus saved, although their depositors lost their money in episodes similar to that old story of the doctor who reported on an operation: "intervention successful, patient died." Some would call this a Pyrrhic victory, but a victory it was.

The weakening of the central banks started with the elimination of the controls on international capital flows, which were removed because governments were no longer able to make them work because of the development of electronic transfers of money. This put an end to the monopoly powers of central banks. Yet, the idea that central banks can act as they used to do has lingered, and this is the origin of the idea that central banks can act as lenders of last resort without having to borrow dollars.

A final argument to prove the point is that the IMF owes its power to being the key for developing countries to get dollars, particularly during crises. If dollars were not needed to resolve crises, the IMF would be powerless to impose conditionality on countries in crisis. Conversely, if the IMF did not have dollars nobody would turn to it in times of crisis.

**Chapter 9** The Solution of Crises

and the Aftermath

Do local currencies help in the solution of crises? In the previous chapter, we found that the powers of the so-called lender of last resort are mythical in the case of developing countries. Now, the question is, do they help in other ways?

The evidence suggests that they do not help, and actually complicate the solutions for exactly the same reasons that turn them into the trigger that unravels the crises. We can see that the solution of crises in countries with local currencies requires calming down two markets in panic—the currency and the financial ones—while in a dollarized country without a local currency, you would deal with only one market. We can also notice that the currency market holds the key to resolving the overall crisis.

This point is easily illustrated with the case of Ecuador. Figure 9.1 shows how the January 2000 decision to dollarize the economy not only stopped the run on deposits that had been taking place in the previous years but also generated an immediate increase in them, which by mid-2002 had resulted in almost a full recovery of the total deposits in the banking system.

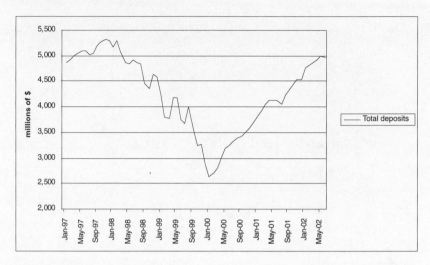

Figure 9.1: The recovery of deposits in Ecuador. *Source:* International Financial Statistics of the International Monetary Fund.

Why would the people in Ecuador suddenly recover their confidence in their banks? In January 2000, everybody knew that the banks were not only illiquid but also bankrupt, and that this was the result of both the terrible devaluations of the previous years and bad practices that had prevailed in the system for many years before. Scandals about the banks were erupting by the day. Nevertheless, people returned their funds to the banks because they trusted that once the main problem had been resolved, securing their savings against devaluations, the government's promises to recapitalize the banks would become a reality.

Local currencies complicate the solution of crises and increase their costs through another mechanism: the disruption caused by the devaluations them-selves. These magnify and reinforce the environment of crises in unpredictable nonlinear ways and worsen the situation of the banks. A manifestation of these problems is the high interest rates, prompted first by the fear of deval-uation and then by its reality. As discussed before, this negatively affects the ability of the banks to collect their loans.

The negative effect of the large devaluations that have accompanied the crises in developing countries on the solvency of the banks and their customers has not been limited to the interest rates, though. As previously discussed, devaluations also shift relative prices all over the economy. Such shifts are unpredictable because the speed of transmission of the new prices varies in different sectors. Even those shifts in relative prices that were intended can be distorted in perverse ways. In all the crises, the disruption has caused a decline in production of both tradables and nontradables for prolonged periods.

This happened, for example, after the Thai crisis exploded with the July 1997 large devaluation of the baht. David Dollar and Mary Hallward-Driemeier conducted a survey of 1,200 manufacturing firms in the last quarter of 1997 and the first quarter of 1998. In answer to their questions, the managers of these firms ranked the causes of their output declines in the following order: the negative effect of the devaluation on input costs; the lack of domestic or foreign demand; and the high cost of capital and the lack of credit.[1] It is important to note that both exporters and producers for the domestic markets mentioned the high costs of imported inputs brought about by devaluations as the worst problem they faced. While Dollar and Hallward-Driemeier did not pursue the question, it would seem that the problem was the result of the drastic increase in transaction costs that devaluation had brought about, both domestically and abroad. This finding contradicts the common assumption that the producers of tradables benefit from real devaluations because while these increase the price of imported inputs, they also increase the selling prices. If the latter are too high for the domestic market, the producers of tradables can immediately compensate for the declining domestic demand by increasing their exports. In fact, this reasoning is widely used to argue that devaluations result in increased exports.

Yet, Dollar and Hallward-Driemeier also noted that while the tradable industries that they surveyed should have benefited from the devaluation, their capacity utilization and employment had fallen between the first half and the second half of 1997 because their productive facilities had been tailored for the domestic market. Since the devaluations increased the relative price of tradables in the domestic market (one of the intended effects of devaluations, aimed at forcing them to export), domestic demand for their products collapsed while they could not increase their exports because their products were not fit for exporting.[2]

The theoretical model that advocates devaluations as a means to increase exports cannot explain these responses because it is too simple. The only relative price that it includes is that between the tradables and nontradables in general, without dissecting the tradable and nontradable contents that all products have in a modern economy and without noticing that what looks like a tradable may actually be a nontradable. This is very common in developing countries, where, mostly because of protection, locals are forced to buy products that people living outside their borders would never buy, at any price. How much would you pay for leaky diapers, for example? Or for towels that do not absorb moisture?

There were other surprises in the survey results. For instance, we could have expected that the companies that had borrowed in dollars would have fared worse after the devaluation. According to Dollar and Hallward-Driemeier, however, those that had borrowed in baht were in the worst financial situation. It was only the very large and efficient companies with ties to foreign companies that tended to have their loans in dollars, and most of them were better off because they had long maturities.[3] These facts show that the interrelationships existing in a modern developing economy between costs and foreign exchange rates are so intricate, even if this economy does not have foreign currency deposits, that a large devaluation is a leap into the unpredictable.

Were countries better off because of the devaluations, even if they worsened the solvency and liquidity positions of both banks and their customers? The main argument to answer positively would be that devaluations improve the countries' capacity to export and, through this, they also improve their overall rate of growth and their international solvency. Our previous analysis of the relationship between devaluations and export growth casts a shade of doubt on this. However, even if we assume that this positive effect took place, we would still have to balance the effects of the devaluations on this dimension with the negative effects on the burden of the debts denominated in foreign currency.

The trade-off between the capital loss inflicted by devaluation through the increase in the ratio of the external debt to gross domestic product (GDP) and the subsequent growth of the economy can be simulated in very simple terms. Assume that there are two countries, A and B. The external debt of both is the same, $1 billion, and they owe it at ten-year maturities at an interest rate of 8 percent per year. For both, the ratio of the debt is 40 percent of GDP and that of the service of the debt 2.7 percent. Then A devalues by 50 percent in real terms. The ratio of its debt goes up to 60 percent of GDP and the burden of the annual payments increases from 2.7 percent to 4.1 percent of GDP.

In cash flow terms, this means that 1.4 percent of GDP, which previously had been used to fund expenditures that improved the welfare of people, now will have to be used to make ends meet in the service of the debt. We should note that the sacrifice of the citizens in A does not represent a benefit for the foreign creditors, who keep on collecting the same amount in dollars every year. Thus, the citizens of A do not have even the excuse of saying that their burden has increased because some greedy banker is squeezing them. The citizens of country A would be covering a cost that country B does not have. It is not a cost that provides any benefit to them; it is just kindly delivered by their local currency.

We can say that 1.4 percent of GDP is a figure that can be easily compensated through higher growth. The smallness of the increase in the debt service is as deceptive as the schemes to sell very expensive items with a low quota and a long maturity, however. Sooner or later you pay the price. In stock terms, the net wealth of the citizens of A would have been reduced in peso terms by 20 percent of GDP. We must believe that this loss would be more than compensated by the higher growth produced by devaluations to think that these are beneficial.

What would be the additional growth rate of real GDP that A should attain over that of B to get back in parity with B in terms of the net wealth of the population, adjusted for present value? For this calculation, we assume that both countries continuously roll over their debts. We also assume that the rate of discount of both countries is 2 percent and that the ratio of total capital to GDP is 2.5. This ratio allows us to estimate the value of the total assets of the country and the net wealth of its citizens by deducting the debt from such value.

Under these assumptions, A would have to grow at substantially higher rates than B in order to catch up with it. For example, for the adjustment to take place in three years (a reasonable period for the new exchange rate to produce its benefits), the A economy would have to grow 5 percent more per year during the next three years, so that if B grew at a moderate 2 percent, A would have to grow at 7 percent per year compounded during this period, or 22.5 percent total in the three years. This is a tall order. If the country does not grow in the first year, it has to grow at 10.7 compounded in the next two years to meet that requirement.

Experience shows that countries do not recoup their capital loss through higher rates of growth. We can see this with the case of Thailand, which devalued its currency relative to the dollar in 1997–1998. As shown in figure 9.2, the external debt at the end of 1996 was $113 billion, equivalent to 64 percent of the gross national income (GNI). Since the devaluation, Thailand started to repay its debt, so that by the end of 1998 it had reduced it to $105

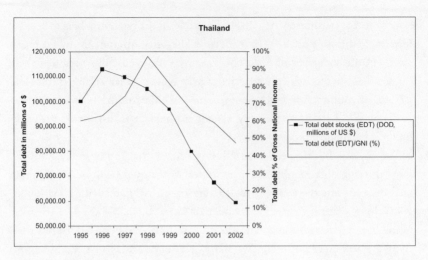

Figure 9.2: Thailand: External debt in millions of dollars and as a percentage of GNI. *Source:* Global Financial Indicators, World Bank.

billion, or 7 percent lower than in 1996. Yet, the ratio of the debt to GNI had increased to 97 percent, or 53 percent higher. If Thailand had not devalued but repaid at the same rate it did, the ratio would have fallen to 59 percent of GNI. If the country had devalued and had not repaid, the ratio would have increased to 104 percent of GNI, assuming in both cases that the country's GNI would have remained equal to that of 1996 in dollar terms.

The total capital loss of the Thai population was equivalent to 40 percent of GNI, estimated as the difference between the ratio of the debt to GNI in 1998 without repayments (104 percent) minus the same ratio in 1996 (64 percent). Valued at the 1996 GNI, this magnitude was equivalent to $45 billion, or 65 percent of the total debt of the country at the end of 1996. Compensating for this loss is the benchmark that the devaluation would have to match with its benefits to start being profitable.

We can see that the country's 2002 GNI measured in dollars (the currency in which the debt was measured) fell quite short of the mark. In fact, it was $53 billion *lower* than in 1996. This was five years after the crisis. Faced with these stark numbers, you wonder whether there was a solution different from devaluation to the Thai crisis. The answer, unfortunately, is most probably not because the run against the currency was unstoppable. If this run had not occurred, it is almost certain that the problems of the bad debts could have been resolved in a more economic way. A renegotiation of debts when the debts are 64 percent of GNI is less costly than one carried out when such ratio is 104 or 97 percent. The fact that Thailand has been able to service even the post-devaluation higher ratios shows that the country had the potential to service the lower pre-devaluation burden.

Of course, the counterargument is that Thailand would not have been able to service anything if it had not devalued. However, if we look at the real side of the economy in 1995–1996, it is difficult to find symptoms that would predict that the Thai economy was on the verge of a collapse as catastrophic as the one that took place. Certainly, as we saw in chapter 7, there were serious monetary misalignments. Also without a doubt, the economic growth rate, measured in dollars with purchasing power parity (PPP), had slowed down. Yet, the drop was from 9.3 percent to 6.5 percent. This is hardly a rate that presages a terrible crisis. In fact, most developing countries would love to have the lower of these rates.

Nothing in those numbers suggests that the country had lost 40 percent of GNI in net wealth, which is the amount it lost as a result of the subsequent devaluation. Any bank would have been happy to quietly refinance the country had it not fallen into the currency crisis. The country would not have suffered from the terrible disruptions that the currency run and the subsequent devaluations brought about. The huge loss was caused by the possibility of devaluation against the dollar, which brought about the currency run and then the devaluation and the financial crisis.

It could be argued that the current account deficit in 1996, at 8.2 percent of GDP, was unsustainably high and had to be reduced by devaluation. Yet, the huge 1997 devaluations did not resolve this problem. The deficit increased to a record-breaking 10 percent in 1998 and then it went down to 8.2 percent in 2000, the same level it had in 1996. Then, until 2003, the deficit was a still considerable 5.3 percent.

Why don't these high current account deficits trigger a crisis today even if the Thai banks are still far from perfect? Because the Central Bank of Thailand has accumulated enormous free reserves in international currencies, which give security to the people that the government is able to defend the local currency. While it is true that the banks in Thailand were weak, the origin of the crisis was not in their weakness. The problem was monetary, not financial or economic. It was because of this monetary problem that the Thais paid such a high price for the crisis.

Yet another problem created by devaluations is the arbitrary redistribution of wealth and income that accompanies them and the attitude that this generates in the population in the long term. A World Bank study has documented it for the East Asian countries.[4]

Using data from this study, we can examine the changes in the level of employment by sector in the years before and after the crises. The evidence regarding employment is mixed. In two countries, total employment increased during the crises, while it declined in the other two. In the two countries where total employment went down—Korea and Malaysia—it remained lower one year later than in the year previous to the crises.

Yet, the results are clear regarding manufacturing employment. The conventional expectation is that devaluation would first reduce the real wage and then that this would increase employment in that sector. The East Asian devaluations met the first expectation. The real consumption wage in the sector fell substantially during the crisis. In Indonesia, the fall was 44.0 percent; in Korea, 9.8 percent; in Malaysia, 2.9 percent; and in Thailand, 6.3 percent. These wage reductions, however, did not result in an increase in employment. On the contrary, employment in manufacturing went down in all countries in the crisis year and, with the exception of Malaysia, it remained lower than before the devaluation in the year subsequent to the crisis. The worst fall in manufacturing employment was in Korea, where it fell by 13 percent. These figures are consistent with the findings of Dollar and Hallward-Driemeier, discussed earlier in this chapter.

Looking at the other sectors, it is clear that, in general, employment increased only in the sectors with lowest value added. Moreover, even if total employment went up in two countries, the unemployment rate went up in all of them as more people entered the labor market in the difficult circumstances of the crises. The overall unemployment rate increased from 4.7 percent to 5.4 percent in Indonesia; from 2.6 percent to 6.8 percent in Korea, and remained at 6.3 percent the year after the crisis; in Malaysia it went up from 2.6 percent to 3.2 percent; and in Thailand, from 0.9 percent to 3.7 percent and then on to 5.2 percent in the subsequent year.[5] All these figures show the pressure that the currency crisis and the devaluations exerted on the labor force.

While the impact of the crises on employment was different in each country, the impact on poverty was uniformly bad, showing the disruptive effects of the crisis and the effects of the devaluation in the population's income. Using data from the same study, we can see that the poverty head count worsened in all countries during the crises and their aftermaths. In Indonesia, poverty almost doubled; in Korea, it almost tripled. It is interesting to note that rural poverty in Indonesia increased from 12.4 percent to 23.0 percent, even if agriculture was the sector where employment increased the most during the crisis.

In Indonesia, as in all the other countries, the overall picture is that of a situation in which, as the real wage went down, more family members were forced to enter the labor force. For this reason, the unemployment rate went up even in the cases where employment increased. Altogether, even in the cases where employment increased, the overall income of families went down, particularly among the poor, who had to work more for less. The result was a drastic increase in poverty.

This result should not be surprising. As we have seen before, devaluations reduce the net wealth of the population in many ways, and they affect income distribution in many other ways. People able to convert their local currency savings into dollars before the large devaluations experience a capital gain in domestic currency terms, while the slow ones experience a capital loss. In many countries, debtors benefit at the expense of savers, as has happened in Argentina so many times. In other countries, it is the other way around. A study on the Mexican crisis shows that, even if depositors in pesos had a capital loss with the 1994–1995 devaluations, financial income increased thereafter at a much faster pace than wages as a result of the higher interest rates prompted by devaluation. The conclusion of the report is that financial income became a source of inequality in Mexico in the years after the crisis.[6]

The same kinds of effects take place in other dimensions, as relative prices adjust at different speeds and in varying magnitudes in the different sectors. As shown in the case of the Asian crises, manufacturing is one of the most negatively affected sectors, even if theoretically it should be one of the big gainers.

These chaotic redistributions do not improve the efficiency of the economy. In the longer term, they become a deterrent of investment, as potential investors take into consideration the possible costs of unpredictable redistributions in their decisions to invest. They also deter investment because, learning the lessons of crises, people hedge not only by depositing their savings in foreign currency accounts but also by depositing them abroad. The situation is even worse when, as in Argentina, countries default in their external debts. The default gives them room to grow in the very short term, as the resources that would have been used to service the debts can be used for consumption and investment. In the longer term, however, they reduce the availability of funds for investment and therefore increase its costs. It is not by coincidence that the countries that devalue the most need higher interest rates to attract the same percent of GDP than countries that devalue less.

Thus, in summary, bank runs are less likely to happen, more easily stopped, and less costly—in terms of recapitalization of the banks—in the formally dollarized economies than in the nondollarized and partially dollarized ones.

# Chapter 10 The Counterfactuals

What are the counterfactuals to this analysis of crises? The usual argument to defend devaluations is that they become inevitable when countries have severe macroeconomic and financial problems. This, however, happens only because they have a local currency vulnerable to devaluation.

There are two kinds of counterfactuals. The first is the behavior of foreign currency deposits during the crises of countries with local currencies. In all cases, they either kept on increasing while those in local currencies were falling fast, or, when the run on local currencies was already threatening the banking system, they fell at a much slower pace than the local currency deposits. In Ecuador, the run on the banks stopped and funds returned to the banks as soon as the government announced the dollarization of the country.

The other counterfactual is the behavior of countries using international currencies that they do not control when facing problems similar to those that have created grave crises in countries with their own currencies. We can look at two cases: Panama, the only country that has been dollarized for a long time; and Ireland, after the adoption of the euro.

Monetarily, Panama is boring. Its history has been one of remarkable stability within an unstable and macroeconomically exciting neighborhood. It is easier to analyze its monetary and financial performance by looking at what did not happen rather than at what happened.

What did not happen is significant. The Panamanian data shows that the country could have had crises as severe and maybe more so than those that afflicted its neighbors. For instance, the current account deficit amounted to approximately 10 percent of gross domestic product (GDP) in six of the last twenty-five years, including 1998 and 1999, when it reached 10.8 percent and 11 percent, respectively. These values would have prompted a crisis in countries with local currencies. Yet, you have never heard of a financial crisis in Panama.

Moreover, the large current account deficits of Panama resulted from very large fiscal deficits, on the order of 14 percent of GDP, which in other countries would also have caused grave crises. In fact, none of the countries we reviewed in the previous chapter even came near to this level of deficits during their crises, either fiscally or in the current account. Nevertheless, Panama sailed away from these problems without even an outburst of high inflation. Only in one year since 1950 (1975) did the local inflation exceed that of the United States by more than 4 percentage points.

Furthermore, in the late 1980s and early 1990s, Panama experienced one of the most dramatic shocks that a country can have. In those years, the country sank into a grave political crisis that culminated with the capture of the president by the U.S. Marines. Except for Nicaragua in the 1930s, no continental Latin American country experienced a similar crisis during the twentieth century. Yet, the spread of the Panamanian interest rates over the U.S. rates reached only about 5 percent during the period. We can compare this with the forty-odd spreads of the Brazilian lending interest rates against the lending rates in the United States, without marines, without invasion. We can also compare it with the spreads between the deposit interest rates in pesos and dollars in Argentina and the certificate of deposit (CD) rates in the United States during the Argentine crisis. While the spread of the dollar rates reached 11 percent by November 2001, three weeks before the devaluation, the spread on peso deposits reached 30 percent.

Also, Panama was impervious to the international crises that afflicted its neighbors in 1995 with the tequila episode and in 1998 with the Asian crisis. Even Chile, one of the strongest economies in Latin America, suffered from these crises while Panama, much humbler in many respects, did not even feel the effects of that problem.

This is not to say that dollarization is a carte blanche to enjoy large fiscal and current account deficits. Panama had to take painful adjustments in all the cases of excessive deficits. The point is that the pain was far less than that suffered by countries with local currency in similar circumstances. The difference is that in Panama there is no lack of confidence in the currency, and this allows for quiet solutions to the macroeconomic and financial problems.

It is very common to hear that the resilience of Panama is not attributable to dollarization per se but to the fact that the country is an international financial center. Since the banking system is owned by large international banks, the argument goes, these protect the country and bring capital whenever it is needed, in real time. This argument is weak for several reasons. First, Panama is not the only country where most of the banking system is or was owned by international banks when a crisis struck. For example, large international banks owned most of the banks in Argentina, and these did not "protect" the country in 2001. Second, the fact that Panama is an international financial center could actually make the country more vulnerable to macroeconomic problems because foreign depositors might get scared when these problems appear. Third, if it were true that the resilience of Panama is due to the solvency of the international banks, this would imply that these banks would not have any reason to care about the fate of Panama. Their customers would continue depositing their funds with them even if the country were sinking in macroeconomic turmoil. They would trust the banks, not the country. It would be like depositing in Miami. So, why bother about Panama? Fourth, even if we discard the idea that the banks are detached from the country, they clearly do not have any reason to care about the country's large current account deficits, which are the result of excessive consumption and investment of the Panamanians relative to their income. If the banks covered any current account deficit, just to be nice to their host, they would eliminate any budget constraint on the Panamanian people and government, something that would not be a good business proposition. There are other places where the banks could move if this were the case. After all, the argument goes, what is important is the foreign-owned banking system, not the dollar, not the country. Fifth, the banks located in Panama do not finance most of the public and publicly guaranteed debt of the country. The government finances its deficits primarily through bonds sold internationally, which represent 77 percent of the total public debt of the country.[1]

Another argument is that Panama has the canal. This has two variations: One is economic and the other political. Economically, it is argued that the canal provides a steady flow of dollars to the country, which permits any macroeconomic disorder. This ignores that any amount of dollars can be squandered, and also that all dollars are green, independent of the source. Other countries have exports, which of course Panama also has, and tourism, remittances, and the like, and these dollars have the same acquisitive power as those paid by the ships to go through the canal. Symmetrically, all current account deficits are similar. They represent a deficit of income relative to expenditures, independent of the source of income. That is, the argument ignores the fact that a country can be insolvent at any level of income.

The second, more sophisticated variety of the canal argument is political. According to this version, because of the canal the United States would never permit a grave crisis in Panama. This might be true, but this is no reason to make, say, Citibank feel obligated to pay the bills of the Panamanian government.

In the last fifty years, Panama has faced grave fiscal and financial problems without ever falling into the panics so common in countries that are similar in all respects except the currency. This is further evidence that such panics are motivated by the mistrust in the local currencies, not the fiscal or current account deficits or the weakness of the banks. When there is a financial problem in Panama, as it happens whenever their fiscal and current account deficits increase excessively, these problems can be resolved in their own terms, without the complications introduced by parallel runs on the currency. Moreover, without the possibility of creating money, the government does not have the power to complicate its fiscal deficits with expansive monetary policies, which, as we have seen in this part of the book, has been a crucial factor generating the crises of developing countries.

Ireland provides another example of what does not happen when a country uses an international currency that it does not control. Shortly after Ireland adopted the euro, it appreciated substantially relative to the dollar, the currency of one of the country's main trade partners, the United States. This problem is formally similar to that which afflicted Argentina a few years earlier.

It is important to note that Ireland does not control the international currency it uses. While theoretically Ireland participates in the management of the euro, in practice its influence in a central bank with more than twenty associates can be assessed as nil. The Central Bank of Europe targets inflation in the euro area as the objective of its policies, without any consideration to the specific problems of each of its associates. Curiously, the magnitude of the deviation of the local currency with the main trade partners is also similar in the cases of Argentina and Ireland. However, it seems as if Ireland is bent on showing that many of Argentina's problems were not inevitable.

Contrary to the idea that a depressive deflation is the unavoidable consequence of a situation like that of Argentina and Ireland, the rate of inflation in Ireland has remained positive. By June 2004, it was 2.3 percent on an annual basis. At about 2.2 percent of GDP in 2003, the current account deficit was low. There was no capital flight. Interest rates remained low. Long-term credit was available. There was not a shadow of doubt about the health of the banking system. No run against the euro has been observed in Ireland, Berlin, Paris, or any other part of the world as a result of the Irish problem. That is, there is no liquidity trap, and much less a reversed liquidity trap.

None of these things eliminates the problem of the appreciation of the exchange rate. Yet, they create the ideal conditions for the transformation that Ireland decided to carry out in its economy. Gross fixed investment remains unchanged at around 24 percent of GDP. The country's debt has not increased as a percent of GDP and the country has experienced no problem in servicing it on time. The country has continued growing in euro and real terms. Unemployment increased as the euro appreciated relative to the dollar, but by magnitudes that are not different from those suffered by the United States during the world recession of these years.

The comparison of Argentina and Ireland illustrates two opposing views of the role of a currency. While in Argentina the idea prevailed that a currency must help a country to remain as it is, in Ireland the prevailing idea was that it should help the country to become what it wants to be. Of course, this applies not just to the current but also to all transformations. It is obviously better to carry out such transformation in the environment of Ireland than in those of Argentina and Thailand.

The calmed environment in which Ireland is carrying out its transformation is something that only a solid international currency like the euro or the dollar could have provided. The currency makes a difference in the adjustment, but not in the direction that is frequently assumed. An international currency is much better than a local one to carry out the adjustment. Since in the new economy of the twentieth century it is certain that countries will have to transform themselves several times, this advantage of the strong international currencies is crucial.

Part Three  **The Optimal Currency Area
and the Choice of Currency**

# Chapter 11 The Conventional Optimal Currency Area Theory

What are the implications of the foregoing analysis for the fundamental question about the choice of a currency regime: Should a country have a currency of its own or adopt an international one?

This question is routinely dealt with using the criteria established by the conventional optimal currency area theory. According to these criteria, a country should have a currency of its own if it meets the conditions outlined in table 11.1.

Given all the facts that we have analyzed in previous chapters, we can ask ourselves how optimal the optimality of the conventional optimal currency area theory is. A cursory review shows that it has at least four grave faults. First, it focuses the optimality on the features of geographical regions, not on the services that a currency should provide in such regions to turn them into optimal ones. It does so because it assumes that the optimality is given by the possibility of manipulating the currency and not by the quality of the currency itself. Second, it assumes that local currencies will react to manipulations in ways we know are unrealistic in developing countries. Third, it focuses on trade, ignoring the financial dimensions of the

Table 11.1: Criteria to Prescribe the Use of a Local Currency under the Optimal Currency Area Theory

| Dimension | Criteria to prescribe local currency |
| --- | --- |
| Openness | The economy is relatively closed to the rest of the world |
| Size | The economy is big |
| Relationships with the international markets | Its geographic composition of trade, its business cycle, and the external shocks to which it is vulnerable do not coincide with those of countries that could share a currency with it |

choice of currency. For this reason, its application results in grave conflicts between the financial and trade aspects of the choice of currency. Fourth, the theory ignores the preferences of the populations and is therefore being overtaken by spontaneous dollarization.

Part 3 develops these points. In this chapter, I analyze the main faults of the theory, and in chapter 12, I propose a different set of criteria to define an optimal currency area, based not on the features of economic regions but on the services that the currency should provide to be considered optimal. Then the conclusions of our analysis are summarized in chapter 13. Finally, the epilogue addresses some of the questions that remained in the Devil's head after having trapped Dema Gogo, focusing on the international comparison of income.

By defining optimality on the features of geographical regions exclusively, assuming that any currency would be optimal when the conditions enumerated above hold, the theory leaves aside all the essential qualities that turn a currency into real money. As discussed in chapter 1, there are two dimensions to the role of money: one fundamental and the other accessory. The fundamental one is that it must establish a standard of value. The accessory one is that, once it has attained that objective, it can be used to manipulate economic behavior in desirable ways. Money cannot play the second role without having met the first one. Focusing only on the second leaves the theory not just incomplete but also misleading. Practically all countries in the world meet the conditions to be optimal currency areas according to the theory. They also manipulate their currencies, the ultimate objective of the theory. Yet, it is difficult to consider as optimal currency areas where inflation rates are as high as those that have been common in developing countries; where interest rates are high and financial intermediation low; where the danger of deadly currency crises is always present; where people cannot plan ahead because the value of the currency is always dropping; and from which people escape as soon as they see an opportunity to do it. It could be argued that the theory assumes that these problems would not exist. However, if the theory would not classify these cases as optimal, it does not say so explicitly. Moreover, it does not contain any recommendation regarding a second best when all the conditions set above were fulfilled but the currency itself would not meet the conditions established by people to consider it as real money. Finally, what is the use of a theory that assumes that countries will manage their currencies in a way that they don't do?

In part, these problems arise because of the second flaw of the theory: It assumes that currencies in developing countries would react to manipulation in an optimal way. The experience in the developing countries shows that such assumption is unwarranted. The ability to devalue the currency has failed to spur export growth in the long term and actually the countries that devalue the least are the ones that have experienced higher growth rates of both exports and general economic activity. Different from developed countries, the strategy of expanding monetary creation to spur economic growth backfires, as the devaluation results in increases in the interest rates. As central banks have pursued this strategy even if it backfires, the rates of interest in developing countries tend to be higher than in the international markets. Additionally, financial intermediation is weak. Furthermore, local currencies have been at the center of the grave financial crises that have afflicted many of these countries. Typically, the origin of these is the mismanagement of monetary policies before the crises, which then leads to currency runs, which in turn lead to financial crises. Then, the currency runs have gravely complicated the solution of the crises. The promise to afford a lender of last result has also proven hollow, as central banks cannot resolve currency runs without losing dollar reserves, which turn their effectiveness contingent on getting dollars from the International Monetary Fund (IMF), the other official international financial institutions, and the markets. Finally, local currencies have become an obstacle for the integration of their countries to the international financial markets and the benefits of financial globalization.

Of course, these problems affect developing countries in different degrees. Many of these countries apply prudent monetary and exchange rate policies. As we saw in the figures in part 1, these countries tend to have lower interest rates and to be more successful in terms of exports and overall economic growth. However, the previous paragraph describes the general situation of developing countries.

In fact, all these problems arise from the inability of the local currencies to establish themselves as standards of value—precisely the dimension of money that the theory ignores. It can be argued that this problem is particular to the circumstances of developing countries, including their tendency to fiscal irresponsibility. A theory that leaves out sets of circumstances that are common in the real world, however, is at best incomplete.

The theory compounds these problems by exclusively focusing on the trade aspects of the choice of currency. As we saw in part 1, local currencies have failed to deliver their promises in the trade area. At the same time, currency areas that are considered optimal in accordance with the conventional theory face serious foreign exchange risks on their financial operations. These risks have turned into grave currency and financial runs with devastating consequences for the optimally created currency areas. Ignoring the financial side of the currency areas has posed a serious challenge to the internal logic of the theory. These crises have generated the "fear of floating," which denies developing countries the supposed benefits of having created their own optimal currency area. Countries wanting to keep their own currency have two options to deal with such fear: The first is to surrender to it, adopting a fixed exchange regime and, through this, surrendering their power to manipulate their monetary variables. According to the theory, this would nullify the optimality of their currency area. More precisely, they would not be using the potential optimality of their already optimal area. The other choice is to sever as much as possible their financial links with the rest of the world—thus renouncing all the benefits of financial globalization. In other words, to remain optimal, a currency area must forgo those benefits. A theory that defines as optimal a currency area that confronts such a hard choice cannot be right.

In fact, it is doubtful that a theory that does not take into consideration the preferences of the people could define what is optimal. Spontaneous dollarization shows that these preferences may diverge markedly from what the theory dictates. Through their choosing of international currencies to denominate their domestic financial operations, people are creating currency areas that are, by the definition of the word in plain English, optimal for them. They choose the foreign currencies precisely because they allow them to escape from the local traps that the theory regards as optimal.

Spontaneous dollarization is a manifestation of the old Gresham's law. This law is frequently stated as asserting that bad money drives out good money from circulation. The rationale for this statement is that when a government forces debased money on people while a good currency is also available, people prefer to spend the bad money and save the good one. Gresham stated the law at a time when governments issued coins that mixed baser metals with gold, pricing them at the same value as the previously issued ones that contained only gold. Gresham observed that the good coins disappeared from circulation, as people wanted to rid themselves of the debased ones while saving the good ones. Shifting the perspective of the analysis, the law can be stated in a reversed way, saying that good money always drives out bad money as a standard of value and as the currency for saving and contracts. This is the process through which spontaneous dollarization has advanced throughout the developing world, and through which optimal currency areas expand, driven by the choices of the people.

Of course, the advantages of a currency increase with the number of users. By its own nature, money has enormous economies of scale in all the roles that it plays in society, so that the larger the number of people using it, the better the currency becomes for all the users. In this way, a desirable currency generates a virtuous circle, offering increasing benefits for its adoption.

Looking at the conventional theory from the point of view of Gresham's law, we can summarize its shortcomings. By failing to recognize that *currency* is the fundamental word in the expression *optimal currency area*, the conventional theory fails to see that it is the quality of the currency—not the features of a region—that creates an optimal currency area. This poses a crucial question: For whom should an optimal currency area be optimal?

There is no question that the possibility of manipulating local currencies affords tremendous power to both local and international monetary authorities. Ostensibly, these functionaries act on behalf of the people. Yet, the fact that people try to escape from their power suggests that monetary management has generated a classical instance of the principal-agent problem. By ignoring people's preferences and focusing on maximizing the ability to manipulate the currencies, the optimal currency area theory supports the case of the agents (those who manipulate currencies) against that of the principals (the people). The theory has other important shortcomings that plague it with ambiguities. I examine some of them below by looking at each of the criteria that the theory prescribes as defining an optimal currency area.

We can begin our analysis of the criteria provided by the conventional optimal currency area by making a fundamental distinction between the criteria to determine whether a country needs a local currency and the conditions that make the manipulation of such currency viable. The condition of being a closed economy belongs to the latter. There is no reason why a closed economy cannot use an international currency, except for the potential divergence between its business cycles and those of the issuer of the international currency—a condition that is covered by another criterion. There are, however, clear reasons why a local currency may not work in an economy that is too open. A local currency must meet one of two requisites through which the central bank can manipulate the economic behavior of the population: One is that it embeds the standard of value of the population; alternatively, the government must be able to force the people to use it. This is why the degree of openness of the economy is important. If the economy is not closed, people can escape the monopoly of the local central bank. People in open economies are too much in contact with international currencies and can introduce them in the country, legally or illegally, weakening the monetary control of the central bank. I know of no case in which optimal currency area theory has been used to recommend the abandonment of the local currency, even in countries that are widely open. Thus, in practice, this criterion has been at best irrelevant; at worst, it is just an argument in favor of the agents in the principal-agent problem.

Thus, we are left with criteria in two dimensions: size and relationships with the international markets. Regarding size, we have to recognize that bigness is relative. There are many economies and even regions within countries that are larger than any or most of all the developing countries taken together. China, the largest developing economy, has a GDP of $1.4 trillion and represents 3.9 percent of the world's GDP, about the size of California. Mexico, the second largest, represents 1.7 percent of the world's total, 14 percent of the Japanese economy, or 46 percent of that of California. The economy of the Netherlands, a country of sixteen million inhabitants, is about the size of that of Brazil, which is only 20 percent larger than that of New York City (and smaller than New York City and northern New Jersey together). At $10.9 trillion in 2003, the economy of the United States is 53 percent bigger than all the developing countries combined ($7.1 trillion). The European Union, at $8.3 trillion with the countries it had in 2003, was 15 percent bigger. Taken together, 52 percent of the world's economy works under two currencies. If we add Japan, which represents 12 percent of the global GDP, almost two-thirds of the world's economy works under three currencies. The other 38 percent works under more than one hundred currencies.[1] Many of these countries have a GDP that is equivalent to that of a few blocks in downtown London.

The three big economies are not only larger but also more diversified and complex than the economy of all the developing countries taken together. Like the developing countries, they produce commodities and basic industrial products; in addition, they produce sophisticated industrial goods and knowledge-based goods and services. They do it in different regions or, in the case of the European Union, in different countries. Each of these regions or countries is much larger than most developing countries (think of Germany, France, or Italy or the region of the Great Lakes). Yet, all these regions and countries share a common currency. Bigness in itself is not a criterion to determine whether an economy should have its own currency and, if it were, no developing country would reach the minimum size, which would be that of Japan or the United Kingdom.

Thus, we are left with only one dimension of criteria: the relationship with the international markets, which comprises criteria on the business cycles, the geographical distribution of trade, and the divergence of external shocks. The three criteria could be collapsed to only one, as all of them refer to the risk of external shocks, which may come from the differences in the business cycles and shifts in the geographical distribution of trade as well as from other kinds of events, such as natural disasters. Collectively, using these criteria to create a local currency would make sense only if we assume that monetary management in developing countries can produce countercyclical effects. Unfortunately, this is not the case in most developing countries, where the classical responses to external shocks of any kind, devaluation, tend to be quite depressive.

In addition to these problems, when each of the trade-related criteria is examined more closely, we find that the theory is also vague. It is difficult, for example, to pinpoint what kind of divergence between the business cycles of two places is acceptable within an optimal currency area. The vagueness extends to all other criteria, including the implicit real exchange rates of different regions or cities within a country.

For example, during the second quarter of 2004, the rate of inflation in Houston was 4.31 percent, while in San Francisco it was 0.9 percent. The other twelve largest cities in the country had rates between these two. This means that the dollar was appreciating in real terms in Houston relative to San Francisco. The fact that the cost of living is substantially different in different cities and regions in the United States shows that this is not a passing phenomenon. Prices must have grown at consistently higher rates in New York than in Tulsa, Oklahoma, to explain the wide differences in the prices of nontradable services in the two places. In the theoretical jargon, the American dollar of New York would be overvalued in terms of the American dollar of Tulsa, Oklahoma. Consequently, New York should be growing at a slower pace than Tulsa. Yet, New York has been more expensive and has grown at a faster pace than Tulsa for generations. Certainly, many activities that were characteristic of New York disappeared in the process as they became too cheap for the city's costs. One example of this was the leather products industry that used to thrive in Manhattan. That industry disappeared, but the city kept on growing by shifting to activities with increasing value added.

In this respect, it is interesting to note an optimal currency area criterion that was included in the original statements of the theory but was dropped later: the possibility of migration within the currency area as an essential condition that should be present for two countries to share a currency. The idea was that, since the rate of unemployment would be a function of monetary policy, and this is a reaction to the particular stages of the business cycle in the currency area, adopting the currency of some other country would create unemployment in the adopting country when the business cycles diverged. The only solution to this problem was to have free mobility of labor between the two countries. Even if not said explicitly, we can deduct that this job arbitrage would result in an equalization of the unemployment rates across the two countries.

Nevertheless, in the second quarter of 2004, the unemployment rate in New York City was 7.07 percent, while in neighboring Boston, Newark, Philadelphia, Baltimore, and Washington, D.C., it was 4.37, 4.97, 5.20, 4.43, and 3.07 percent, respectively.[2] That is, the unemployment rate of New York City was more than twice as high as that of Washington, D.C., and substantially higher than those of its neighbors, including Newark, which is just across the Hudson River. This should prompt a massive migration from the first to all the other mentioned cities. If there is an area in the world where migration is easy, it is this region; in fact, many urban economists reckon the region as one single megalopolis. Yet, the substantial differences in unemployment rates do not result in massive migrations within the megalopolis.

Dropping this condition was understandable given these facts. Yet, dropping it seriously damaged the internal logic of the theory. It was the only criterion that referred to the capacity of reaction of the economy to an external shock. The other criteria referred to the shocks themselves, so that by dropping it, the optimal currency area is defined exclusively in terms of the problems it can face.

To grasp how badly the theory was damaged by dropping this condition, we can look at the currency area built by the dollar in the United States. Given the previous discussion, we can alternatively conclude that the theory does not make sense or that all the cities of the Eastern megalopolis should have different currencies, so that, for instance, New York could devalue its dollar to reduce its unemployment or appreciate it to reduce its rate of inflation. Since other criteria tell us that the dollar area is as close to optimal as any area can be, we have to discard the idea of fragmenting it into as many currencies as divergences in growth, inflation, and unemployment there are among its regions, cities, and neighborhoods. Having access to a hugely diversified economy working under the same currency is what really turns the United States into an optimal currency area. This is what maximizes the possibilities of substitution when the exchange rate moves. This is what allows the financial system to be as large as it is. This is what reduces transaction costs, uncertainties, and unexpected monetary shocks between trade partners. Therefore, whatever the differences in growth, inflation, or unemployment, it is optimal for these regions and cities to belong to this area. Consequently, we can say that, if this is true for the economies of the regions and cities in the United States, which are larger than most developing countries, it should be true for countries adopting the dollar as well. The answer to this assertion used to be that people in the United States could migrate within the currency area to compensate for the asymmetric effects of the common monetary policy. Now that this answer has been dropped, there is no other answer to this assertion. The possibility of internal migrations was the hidden foundation of the conventional optimal currency area.

The discussion in the previous paragraphs dealt with the first two conditions established by the conventional currency area and found them wanting. Regarding the criterion of commonality of business cycles, we can measure the divergences of the business cycles of different regions in the world to see whether the conventional optimal currency area theory gives us a clear idea of which of them should have a currency of their own. We can use two important countries that share a currency—Germany and France—as the yardstick to see what is acceptable in terms of divergences in the business cycles. These countries are neighbors, industrial, and share the euro.

It is commonly assumed that the divergence of the developing countries' cycles relative to those of the developed countries is much larger than that between countries that share a currency. Figure 11.1 shows that the order of magnitude of the divergence between the business cycles of the two leading countries of the European Monetary Union is about the same as the divergence between the developing and the developed countries taken as a whole. Moreover, the two curves seem to coincide, with varying lags, in the direction of their movements.

An analysis by region shows some differences within the aggregates used in the previous figure. The next three figures show the divergences between the business cycles of the different regions of the developing world and those of the United States, compared with the divergences between France and Germany. As shown in figure 11.2, the business cycles of South Asia and Latin America diverged quite markedly from those of the United States during the highly inflationary 1970s and 1980s. Yet, they have been comparable with the divergence between France and Germany since the early 1990s. This shift seems to raise the suspicion that the business cycles of developing countries are heavily affected by their own monetary manipulations. The period of high divergence coincides with one of high instability in the developing countries. These countries suffered from high rates of inflation and large current account deficits during the 1970s and early 1980s. Then, during the 1990s they reduced the rates of inflation and the current account deficits. As they did that, their business cycles came much closer to those of the United States, to the point that their divergences are within the range of those between France and Germany. Based on their performance of the last fifteen years, each of these regions could have used the dollar as much as the two European countries use the same currency (remember that the possibility of internal migrations is no longer among the criteria of the optimal currency area).

The top panel of Figure 11.3 shows that the divergence of the Middle East and North Africa followed a path similar to that of the two regions shown below. The case of Sub-Saharan Africa, shown in the lower panel, is somewhat different from those of the other regions. While the divergences of the other regions with the United States have been larger at the beginning of the period and smaller at the end of it, the divergence of Africa has been on the same order of magnitude as that of France relative to Germany throughout the period.

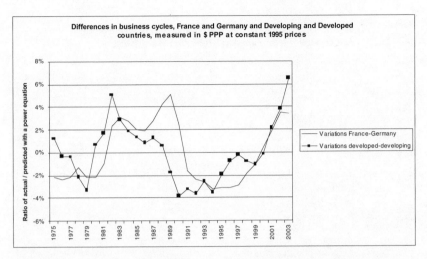

Figure 11.1: Divergences in the business cycles of developing and developed countries compared with those of France and Germany. *Note:* The variations between A and B were estimated running a log-log regression of A as the dependent variable and B as the independent one. The variations shown in the figure were the exponentials of the residuals, which is the same as the ratio of the actual over the predicted values. A was France in the first regression and the developing countries in the second. Thus, the cycles of Germany are very similar when seen from the perspectives of France and the developing countries. *Source:* World Development Indicators, World Bank.

The only region that showed consistently large deviations in its business cycles relative to the United States was East Asia and the Pacific, which includes the Asian Tigers. This is shown in figure 11.4. There, the differences fluctuated from +10 percent to −10 percent in two and a half cycles. The cycles are not just pronounced but they are also frequent. Curiously, however, several of the larger countries in the region, prominently China, peg their exchange rates to the dollar. Thus, with the exception of East Asia and the Pacific, the divergences of the regional business cycles of developing countries relative to the United States are within the same magnitude of the two economies (Germany and France) that most people think are the most closely tied economies in the world.

Of course, we can find divergences within the European Monetary Union larger than those between France and Germany. One example, with variations up to 10 percent in each direction, is provided by Belgium and Greece, shown in the top panel of figure 11.5. These are of the same order of magnitude as the divergences between any of the developing regions (including East Asia

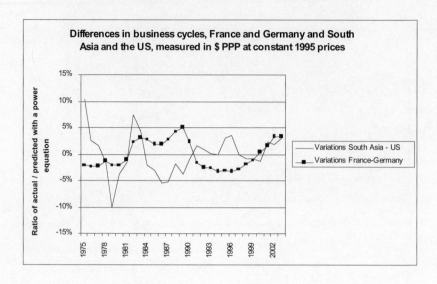

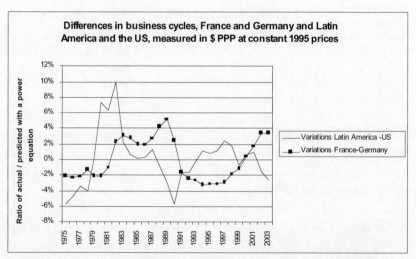

Figure 11.2: Divergences in the business cycles of South Asia and the United States and Latin America and the United States compared with those of France and Germany. *Source:* World Development Indicators, World Bank.

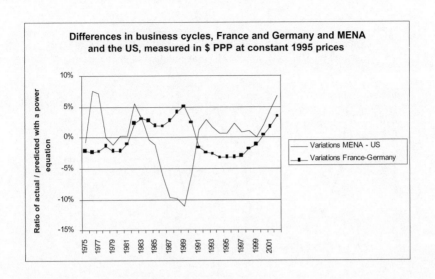

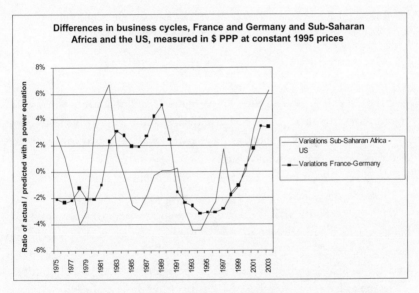

Figure II.3: Divergences in the business cycles of the Middle East and North Africa and the United States and Sub-Saharan Africa and the United States compared with those of France and Germany. *Source:* World Development Indicators, World Bank.

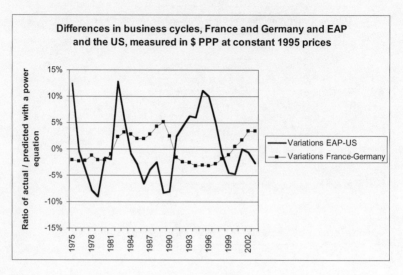

Figure 11.4: Divergences in the business cycles of East Asia and Pacific and the United States compared with those of France and Germany. *Source:* World Development Indicators, World Bank.

and the Pacific) relative to the United States. The lower panel of the same figure shows the divergences between Ireland and France, which are of an even larger magnitude—about twice the ones we found between East Asia and the Pacific and the United States.

Moreover, the business cycles of developing countries may be much closer to those of a developed country than to a neighboring developing one. Figure 11.6 illustrates this point in the case of two countries that many people assume should share a currency because their business cycles are very close. The top panel portrays the deviations of Argentina's GDP relative to those of Brazil and the United States. It is clear from the figure that Argentina's business cycles are as far away from those of Brazil as from those of the United States. The deviations against the two countries are quite substantial, having fluctuated in ranges up to −15 percent to +15 percent from 1975 to 2003. In fact, as shown in the lower panel, the business cycle of Brazil is closer to that of the United States than to that of Argentina. While in the 1980s the deviations of the Brazilian cycles relative to those of the United States were significant (although less so than those relative to Argentina), the range of variation since 1990 has been around 6 percent (2 up and 4 down).

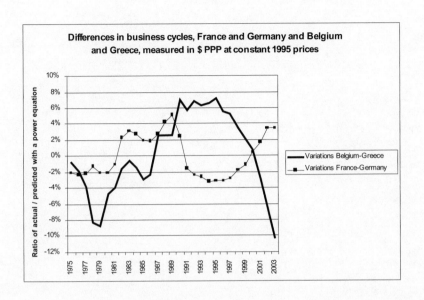

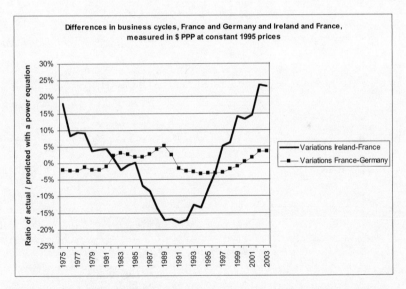

Figure 11.5: Divergences in the business cycles of Belgium and Greece and Ireland and France compared with those of France and Germany. *Source:* World Development Indicators, World Bank.

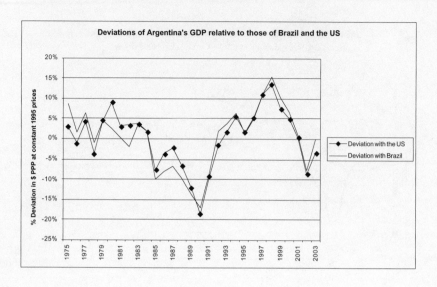

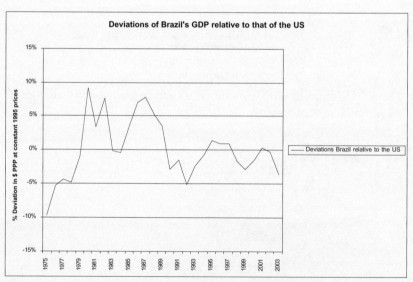

Figure 11.6: Deviations of Argentina's GDP relative to Brazil and the United States and of Brazil's GDP relative to that of the United States. *Source:* World Development Indicators, World Bank.

Both panels tend to confirm the idea that a good portion of the business cycles in developing countries is domestically induced by monetary instability. As the Brazilian economy stabilized in terms of inflation and devaluation, the divergences between Brazil and the United States tended to shrink through the years. Also, they show that the deviations between the cycles of Brazil and the United States were in the same order of magnitude as those between Belgium and Greece, even during the initial period of Brazilian high instability—which would not have taken place if Brazil had had a stable currency. Since the stabilization of the mid-1990s, the Brazilian cycles have been extremely close to those of the United States. If we applied the logic of the business cycles to Brazil, it seems that the dollar would be a better currency for this country than a Mercosur (a trading zone among Brazil, Argentina, Uruguay, Paraguay, and Venezuela) hybrid, which would lead to protracted conflicts due to the large divergence with the cycles of Argentina.

The Netherlands provides an example of a successful mix of commodity and sophisticated industrial and agricultural production within a single monetary area, even if those products tend to have different business cycles. This is a good example because the monetary problems generated by the conflicts between the prices of the commodity this country produces (oil) and the rest of the economy were vilified with the name of "the Dutch disease." This disease was pronounced incurable, and it is so when seen through the looking glasses of narrow trade models. Yet, not only did the patient live, but it also attained an impressive transformation into a highly sophisticated economy based on knowledge. It even succeeded in competing with the developing countries in the production and marketing of another commodity, flowers, a field in which the latter seemed to have all the comparative advantages. This feat was attained with the strong Dutch local currency, now substituted by the euro, with a soil that freezes for a long period every year, in a country where the sun disappears behind clouds for months, and where land is more scarce and expensive than in any developing country, and where salaries are many times higher than in those countries. It would be difficult to argue that the Netherlands should have had a currency with its value based on the price of a commodity, in this case oil, as many propose developing countries should do. The interaction among the different sectors of the highly diversified Dutch economy provided the solutions for both oil and the traditional activities that this threatened. Thus, if the case of Europe establishes the limits to which divergences in the business cycles are acceptable within a currency area, it seems that most developing countries are well within such limits in relation to the dollar and the euro.

There is another dimension of the problem of the divergences among the growth rates of different countries that, while not included in the formal criteria to have a local currency, is taken as a reason to devalue a currency in the long term: the divergence not in the business cycle but in the long-term growth trends. The idea is linked to the relative growth of productivity between two countries. It prescribes devaluation when a country's total factor productivity is growing at a slower pace than those of their trade partners or competitors. The prescription is based on the notion that if the relative productivity of one country is declining, it would be left with nothing to do, as all their activities would be taken over by its competitors. The population would just starve in front of an amazed world. According to this logic, the only solution is to devalue the currency to reduce the real wage of the population, turning the country competitive again and thus preventing unemployment. In other words, following this logic, countries must have a currency to adjust for changes in their total factor productivity relative to that of other countries.

This idea, however, ignores that monetary instability may negatively affect total factor productivity. As discussed in part 1, continuously devaluing the currency to keep the existing activities profitable blunts the market incentives to advance to a higher stage of value added. Japan tried that strategy in the first few years after World War II and then abandoned it, aiming at a strong yen. The shift in strategy was successful. In fact, no country has developed based on a weak currency.

Moreover, devaluing the currency would lead to higher rates of interest, higher inflation rates, lack of long-term credit, higher external debt burdens, and higher economic volatility, all of which tend to reduce the total factor productivity. Following this prescription, which theoretically seems unbeatable under its own assumptions, would condemn countries lagging in productivity growth to a low-level equilibrium.

It is also important to note here that, because of comparative advantages, countries can always find activities where, with their resource endowment, they can be more productive than others. The incentives to make the shift, however, must be there.

Regarding external shocks, most economists assume that the existence of a local currency gives countries more flexibility to adjust to them. Yet, this assumption does not follow mathematically from theory. It is open to empirical evidence, particularly in developing countries, where devaluation means increased interest rates and pressures to increase wages, among other reasons why devaluations may be depressive in those countries.

For example, the evidence shows that these assertions are untrue in Central America and the Caribbean. A recent study of the subject analyzed the long-term vulnerability to external shocks of the countries in the region. The analysis was conducted when El Salvador had not yet dollarized. Yet, it did have a de facto fixed exchange rate for several years, so that four different regimes were present in the region: dollarized (Panama), fixed rate (El Salvador), crawling-pegs, and floating.[3] The study defined Panama and El Salvador as "credible pegs" to differentiate their regimes from those of the other countries. It reached the following conclusions:

- "As expected, changes in terms of trade are positively correlated with changes in GDP. The coefficient of the interactive term [a dummy variable that is one when the country has a truly and credible fixed exchange rate and zero otherwise], however, is negative (although not statistically significant). This suggests that in our sample of Central American countries, more flexible regimes are no better than fixed ones in terms of the ability to protect the economy from external shocks."[4]

- Regarding the cyclical behavior of interest rates, the authors of the study say, "we find a significant anti-cyclical interest rate in Panama and El Salvador (Panama is dollarized and El Salvador has a formally flexible but de facto fixed exchange rate), a pro-cyclical interest rate in Costa Rica (which has a crawling peg) and a neutral interest rate in Guatemala (which has a flexible exchange rate)."[5]

- In general terms, the study concludes: "Our analysis suggests that beyond the reduction in inflation, dollarization may reduce financial fragility by reducing the volatility of key relative prices in the economy, as well as to contribute to the development of the financial system. Although higher inflation and more volatile relative prices are clearly undesirable outcome under flexible exchange rate regimes . . . they might just be the result of a rational choice, in which the government decides to trade some credibility for more monetary independence and output stabilization. The analysis [of this paper], however, seems to indicate that this is not the case. The Central American countries with flexible exchange rate regimes appear to be worse off than their counterparts with credibly fixed regimes [Panama and El Salvador] in terms of the volatility of their nominal variables, without any noticeable gain in terms of the volatility of the real variables. We therefore conclude that although Central American countries with flexible regimes paid a large cost in terms of credibility, they did not appear to gain very much in terms of the benefits of monetary independence."[6]

Among the results of this study, it is interesting to focus on the conclusions about the relationship between the interest rates and the economic cycles. Contrary to what everybody expects from the assertions of conventional theory, the rates of interest in the countries that did not devalue during the period of the study were anticyclical (i.e., they were low when the economy was in a downswing and higher when it was in the upswing) while those of the crawling peg were pro-cyclical. They increased when the economic growth rate was declining. This is quite logical in the real world. It was during the downswings that the countries with the crawling peg devalued the most. With the standard of value set in the foreign currency, the rates of interest tended to increase with the devaluations, making for the anticyclical response of interest rates.

Regarding the adjustment in trade, the study concludes that the flexible rates were no better than the fixed ones to protect the country against shocks in this dimension. In fact, El Salvador not only outperformed all of its neighbors (all of which devalued repeatedly during the period) in terms of overall growth of exports but also all of Latin America from 1992 to 2004. In fact, the adjustment to external shocks through devaluation suffers from all the problems associated with devaluations that have been discussed throughout this book, including prominently the transference of the standard of value, the reversed liquidity trap, and all its consequences.

The case of Central America shows that it should not be assumed that flexible exchange rates actually deliver higher protection against external shocks. In fact, the depressive responses of developing countries to devaluations suggest that this is not true generally. The burden of the proof that they help in dealing with external shocks must be placed on the local currencies.

The geographical distribution of trade is included among the criteria because of reasons that are closely related to those of the business cycles and the external shocks. The idea is that countries must have currencies that move as closely as possible with the currencies of their trade partners to avoid situations in which their nontradable costs put them out of competition. There are two possible policy conclusions from this reasoning: One is that countries must share a currency with their main trade partners; failing to meet this condition, they must have a local currency that they can devalue if the trade partners devalue. If the currencies of their trade partners move in different ways, then the best policy is to take a weighted average of these movements and change the value of the currency in accordance to such average. Appreciation when the partners appreciate is rarely advised, although it may happen if the country uses an automatic formula to adjust its currency. In reality, however, the case is also rare.

The case for devaluation when dealing with shifts in the geographical distribution of trade seems compelling. Yet, as in the rest of the criteria of the optimal currency area, such case depends crucially on the ability of developing countries to counterbalance the business cycle, trade problems, and external shocks. This ability is quite weak and efforts to apply it prove counterproductive in many cases. As discussed before, a developed country with an international currency has this ability because its currency gives access to a thoroughly diversified economy, so that when it is devalued, the substitution effect of the devaluation (the substitution of local production for imports) predominates over the income effect (the increase in domestic prices). This is not so in developing countries, where devaluations tend to be depressive, inflationary, or both. It does not make much sense to increase interest rates and the burden of the external debt to counterbalance a depressive shock.

Thus, it is much better to share a currency with trade partners or, alternatively, belong to a currency area with a well-diversified economy, which would allow for substitution effects to overcome the income effects of shifts in the exchange rates. Such a currency area would be truly optimal, much better than one where income effects are the main response to these shifts.

In summary, the features of the actual currency areas in the developing countries are far from optimal, even if all of them are optimal in accordance with the conventional optimal currency area theory. They are so far away from optimality that people spontaneously substitute their currencies with foreign ones in their domestic operations, even if this introduces substantial foreign exchange risks. People, however, find it better to face those risks than to save and operate financially in the official currencies of the supposedly optimal currency areas. That is, people assess the risks posed by the local currencies as higher than the exchange rate risks, which we know are substantial.

These problems should be sufficient to revise this theory. Definitely, no country aiming at reducing the risks posed by the globalized world should use it to choose its currency regime. The issues involved in such a choice are much more complex than those contemplated in the limited scope of the theory. As a manifestation of the incompleteness of the theory, the decision to adopt a local currency, which is as far as the theory goes, is not sufficient to resolve the problem. Such decision triggers the need for many other decisions, some of them having to do with the monetary regime, others dealing with specific challenges. In this way, countries taking this option would have to make a decision on the way they would manage their currency. A first dimension of the choice is whether they would stick to a certain foreign exchange regime or change it from time to time—changing, for example, from fixed to floating or a sliding peg, depending on the circumstances. Then the decision of what shape the regime would take (permanently or initially) would be needed. All of these decisions, of course, would be linked to decisions regarding the stance the government would take regarding the objectives of monetary policy. The monetary policy could target, among other objectives, a certain inflation rate, the level of interest rates, or an exchange rate to a foreign currency. Not all of these options are open for all the foreign exchange regimes.

Once these decisions were made, the governments would still need to put numbers to their policies. Then, each time there was a relevant event in the international or domestic markets, they would have to make decisions on how to manipulate their instruments to best face the challenge. These decisions would become more complex as the countries integrated with the international markets because the increased number of currencies involved would affect the relative prices of inputs and final products. Each shift in the exchange rate relative to all the other currencies would create both income and substitution effects. The possibility of converting the former into the latter diminishes with the number of currencies the country would have to deal with. Moreover, the complexity of these effects easily overcomes the capacity of macroeconomic models to predict and even measure their impact on the welfare of the countries. Finally, the theory would say nothing about the relationship between financial and trade variables that should exist in the monetary regime, except for stating that borrowing abroad is a source of exchange rate rigidity.

At the end, one discovers that the optimal currency area can be optimal only if the currency is managed optimally—case by case, event by event, day by day—and, still, optimality would be in the eye of the beholder because the theory does not say a word about the subject. It is well known that macroeconomists who passionately believe that currencies must be managed may hold extremely different opinions on how this management should be conducted in any given set of circumstances. Of course, all of them believe that the currency should be flexible, but their opinions will always diverge on the particular way in which the currency would be flexible and on what monetary policy should be applied within such flexibility. These issues, and many others, will always be present.

Moreover, the designers of a currency regime cannot assume that future governments will manage the exchange rate in order to adjust smoothly to external developments all along. In reality, the management of the exchange rate opens many other possibilities, some of them very perverse, which appeal to politicians. As history proves, governments may decide to appreciate a currency to reduce inflation and generate a domestic boom. This is irrational in the long term but may be rational politically in the short term—for example, generating the boom to win elections or leaving the task of dealing with the subsequent crisis to the next government. We know that these cases are not rare in the developing countries. The only consolation would be that, according to the theory, the currency area would be optimal regardless of what the central bankers or politicians were to do with the currency. In this sense, the theory is reassuring. In chapter 12, we look at the features that make for a truly optimal currency area.

# Chapter 12 Toward a Redefinition
# of an Optimal Currency Area

The objective of a monetary regime must be to maximize the probabilities of a smooth adjustment to the unpredictable developments of a globalized economy. The conventional optimal currency area theory seeks such flexibility through the freedom of the currency to change its value relative to that of the others. As we have seen previously, this approach has failed in most, if not all, the developing countries. In fact, the theory provides little guidance beyond rating as optimal regions that share some common external problems.

As discussed in chapter 11, we need a definition of what an optimal currency area is, based not on the features of geographical regions but on the quality of the monetary environment. That is, a currency area must be optimal not because its members share the same problems but because they obtain optimal services from the currency that covers it.

To identify these features, we can look at the experience of the successful currency areas: those covering the United States, Europe, Japan, and the United Kingdom. Drawing from this experience, we can say that a currency area would be optimal if it maximizes the possibilities that substitution effects would dominate the income effects coming from external shocks of any nature (divergences in the business cycles, devaluations of other currencies, or changes in the patterns of trade partners). The maximization of such a possibility is what turns a currency area optimal both from the trade and the financial points of view.

From the trade perspective, if exports to some countries suddenly declined because of exchange rate movements, optimality would mean that exporters would be able to find other markets within their own currency area. This also applies to imports; if some of these became too expensive, the currency area should be able to substitute for them at the equivalent prices and quality, so that neither consumers nor producers would suffer from significant price increases.

Size and diversity also help to absorb changes through other mechanisms. The larger and more diversified an economy, the less it will be affected by drastic changes in one sector. If a technological advance turns some products obsolete (like slide rules or dedicated word processors, for example), a large and diversified economy would be able to absorb their disappearance with lesser macroeconomic effects than would be suffered by a smaller economy. The fact that different products have different business cycles helps to ensure that none of them would bring down aggregate demand. This makes the system more stable for everybody.

Contrary to what could be surmised, this criterion does not prevent countries from trading with other currency areas. The volume of trade among the three major currency blocks is enormous. Diversification, however, helps them to absorb any shock that can come from the other two blocks. The U.S. economy provides an enormous natural hedge to American exporters to Japan. Smaller and less diversified economies cannot provide such a hedge.

On the financial side, the criterion of diversity would mean maximizing the access to large and deep financial markets, capable of providing credit at all maturities and at different levels of risk, as well as derivative instruments to manage the risks. In addition to facilitating development through the access to deep financial markets, having an identity between the currency used in domestic and international operations would resolve one of the main problems now faced by most developing countries. Obviously, such identity eliminates the risk of a sudden shock caused by exchange rate movements on the burden of the external debt. This would increase the efficiency of exports in promoting economic growth, as a part of them would not have to be used to pay for the additional burden of debt caused by devaluations relative to the currency of international borrowing. Moreover, the access to a large and diversified financial system allows people within the currency area to explicitly hedge their foreign exchange risks in their operations with other currency areas. They can hedge many other risks as well, which they cannot do in a small monetary environment.

The interaction among the trade, monetary, and financial dimensions would also be optimal and mutually reinforcing in this conception of the optimal currency area. With substitution effects dominating the income effects, the inflationary pressures would be much weaker, facilitating the task of keeping inflation rates low and real wages stable. This, in turn, would allow the domestic currency to become a standard of value, helping to keep the interest rates low even when the currency is devalued.

Thus, the degrees of freedom of adjustment to external shocks can be maximized through a completely different and much simpler approach than the continuous adjustments advocated by the conventional optimal currency area. Rather than adjusting individually to each change, trade resilience can be attained by maximizing access to unrestricted diversification within the same monetary area. This, in turn, would maximize the probability of turning income effects into substitution effects whenever there is a trade shock. This maximization would be the only criterion in the choice of both a currency regime and the currency that would give reality to it. Maximizing such access would be necessary and sufficient to choose a currency. That is, under this other approach to the optimal currency area, the criterion to choose a currency would be that the area covered by the chosen currency must be as large and diversified as possible.

Notice that this condition diverges in two dimensions from the criterion of size in the conventional optimal currency area. First, it includes both size and diversification. Second, size is not taken as a criterion mandating the creation of a local currency once a critical size has been reached; instead, it is a magnitude that the chosen currency must maximize. In the sense I am giving to the criterion, a currency covering two large countries is better than one covering only one of them. For example, because of economies of scale and diversity, the euro provides more services for each of its users than the sum of the services of the currencies that it substituted. It gives all the services of each of these currencies plus the overarching ability to reduce transaction costs as well as to open more possibilities of substitution among inputs and outputs within the same currency area.

Looking at the optimal currency area from the perspective of diversity also creates a sharp contrast with the conventional views on the desirability of sharing currencies across countries with different degrees of development. Asymmetries in the economic features of the countries that join the currency area are not undesirable when the issue is looked at from this perspective. Under the conventional approach, it is frequently assumed that competing countries tend to share business cycles and external shocks, so that if they decide to share a currency with someone, it should be with similar countries, à la the euro. As we saw in the case of Europe, the assumption that countries with similar economies tend to have the same business cycles is not based on reality. More fundamentally, however, while sharing a currency area would be profitable for competing countries, it would be even more so for countries that are in different stages of development, are complementary in trade, and have diverging business cycles. The uniform monetary space would help them to create international chains of production with the certainty that the relative prices of inputs (among them and relative to the price of the output) would not be disturbed by arbitrary decisions made in central banks. Thus, mixing countries producing commodities with industrial countries would be ideal from the point of view of trade.

The identity of the currency used in trade and financial operations would render additional benefits in terms of trade. There would be no conflicts for traders between the two aspects of monetary matters, and a deep financial market would allow traders to hedge those risks that they would be forced to take. Also, exporters, operating in a deep financial market, would be able to provide financing to their customers, something that is a problem in all developing countries. David C. Parsley and Shang-Jin Wei provide another advantage. In a recent paper, they show that currency unions result in a closer and faster price convergence among the participants.[1] Since prices are a major source of information for exporters and traders in general, trade is facilitated when the prices prevalent in the domestic market are similar to those in the export markets. By adjusting their production functions to be profitable in the domestic markets, producers can be profitable in the foreign ones as well.

Of course, short-term capital flows, which worry the supporters of the optimal currency area to the point of prompting them to ban their flows, would not be a problem. A big and diversified currency area eliminates the contradictions now present between what the conventional theory says is optimal and financial flows.

Within this environment, the stability of any transformation would be guaranteed. Macroeconomic problems would not trigger lethal currency runs.

This would reduce the probabilities of having financial crises and would decrease their costs if they become inevitable. The absence of the nonlinear effects from both the expectation and the reality of devaluations would restrict the impact of crises and simplify their solution. Moreover, spontaneous dollarization, now a big threat to the monetary stability of countries, would disappear.

Having defined what an optimal currency area would be, we can begin to look at the features of the currency itself that would make it eligible to create an optimal currency area. The first such feature should be that, regardless of its exchange rate volatility, the currency must provide domestic price stability (considering as domestic all the goods and services available in the currency area), as well as low interest rates. Obviously, the size and diversity of the area helps in meeting this criterion for the reasons discussed in the previous paragraphs, particularly the elimination of the income effects from exchange rate movements. Yet, it also requires that the monetary policy applied by the issuer should result in low levels of inflation.

The second feature would be liquidity—that is, the largest possible number of people must accept the currency. The optimal in this respect would be a currency that is accepted all over the world.

Given these conditions, the rate of devaluation or appreciation of the currency relative to other international currencies is not relevant within a wide range. Of course, there is always a magnitude of depreciation that will impair the substitution effect, so that inflation will increase, triggering a host of undesirable effects. This range, however, has proven to be very wide in the last several decades. Table 12.1 summarizes the conditions that make for an optimal currency area from the point of view of the diversification of risks.

It could be objected that the criterion of access to a large and diversified economy assumes that all the countries belonging to an optimal currency area would be totally open to trade with those sharing the same currency. It does not. The criterion says that maximizing such access should be the primary consideration in the choice of currency. The access provided by all the potential currencies, including the local one, should be compared with each other and then the decision should go in the direction of the currency that maximizes it. In most cases, we can be sure that the local currency would not be the chosen one, nor would a currency issued by a group of developing countries.

Table 12.1: The Revealed Preferences for the Qualities that Define a Standard of Value

|  | Criteria | Practical Manifestations |
|---|---|---|
| Features of the currency area | Open and diversified economy | On the trade side: Provides substitutes for demand or supply of goods and services when there are problems with other currencies<br>On the financial side: Provides the whole range of modern financial services |
| Features of the currency | Stability<br>Liquidity | Low inflation<br>Accepted worldwide |

Moreover, in a series of papers on the subject, Andrew K. Rose has shown that common currencies promote trade between the monetary partners in magnitudes that he himself finds extraordinary. He has proven this point with gravity models as well as with meta models that include the results of studies carried out by many other scholars on the subject. The analysis of the point is marred by the scarcity of data regarding currency unions, which have been rare. Nevertheless, the results are so strong statistically that the probabilities that he might be wrong are negligible.[2]

Thus, countries can choose between two different approaches to attain a smooth adjustment to the unpredictable developments of the modern globalized economy. The first, based on the conventional optimal currency area, seeks resilience through creating independent, flexible currencies that could fluctuate against the others. The second, based on a different interpretation of what is an optimal currency area, seeks resilience through the maximization of the substitution effects and the minimization of the income effects of external shocks. The best course to attain these objectives is to adopt an established international currency.

In the conventional theory, optimal currency areas are determined by the characteristics of regions; in the other approach, they are determined by the features of a currency and have no geographical limits. In fact, while the first approach aims at maximizing the fragmentation of currencies subject to an unspecified lower limit to the size of the economies that can have one, the second approach aims at maximizing size and diversity within the same monetary areas, so that these improve as they become larger. The focus of the first is on the possibility of manipulating economic behavior through variations in the supply of money and shifts in the exchange rate; the focus of the second is to assure that money provides the services it is supposed to provide. The first creates tensions between the trade and the financial sides of currency choices; such a contradiction does not exist in the second. The first one affords a seigniorage; the second does not. The first reassures countries that by having a local currency they are within an optimal currency area; the second provides access to a truly optimal currency area.

Developing countries tired of being an optimal currency area in the midst of obvious suboptimal monetary conditions have two choices regarding their integration into a truly optimal currency area: one is to create it; the other is to enter into an existing one, which means adopting one of the major international currencies. Creating an optimal currency is obviously more difficult than adopting an existing one. Actually, it may be impossible for most developing countries to generate it because they lack the necessary size and diversity. To be fully diverse, a developing country aiming at creating an optimal currency area would have to entice some *developed* countries to adopt its currency. The probabilities of this happening are zero. Thus, becoming part of an optimal currency area entails adopting an international currency. In practical terms, this means adopting the dollar, the euro, or the yen. Some countries may also consider the pound sterling.

Once the decision to become part of an optimal currency area has been made, the country should choose a currency that is naturally related to its economy in trade and financial terms. If there is a contradiction between the two, the choice should favor the one that is the standard of value of the population. This would give finality to the decision.

This sounds extreme, but only because we grew up in a world in which having a currency is considered essential. For this reason, the burden of the proof is placed on the arguments in favor of joining an already developed international currency area, as if the natural thing were for each country to have its own currency. In fact, monetary fragmentation is the source of so many problems that the burden of the proof should be on the other side. The question should be why a small and poorly diversified economy (as all developing economies are) should create a currency when it has access to a well-established international one.

Of course, a country adopting an international currency would not have the ability to conduct monetary policies. Given the problems that monetary policies have created in the developing countries, this could be taken as one of the advantages of joining an optimal currency area.

It may be objected that the problem is not just that the country would not manage its own currency; it would be that the issuer of the currency would manage it in ways that could be contradictory with the country's circumstances. In other words, the issuer might apply restrictive monetary policies when the user country needed an expansionary one. This argument forgets four things. First, monetary management in developing countries has failed to produce countercyclical behavior. It does not make sense to miss the ability to conduct policies that result in higher interest rates when lower ones are needed. Second, the range of variation of interest rates in international currencies is just a fraction of the range of variation of the rates in the local currencies. Third, interest rates in developing countries tend to be higher than the international ones, regardless of the phase of the cycle. Finally, developing countries cannot defend themselves against a rise in the international interest rates. While interest rates may increase in developing countries as the international rates go down, those countries can reduce their rates when the international ones are going up only at the cost of accelerating the substitution of international currencies for the local one, domestically or through capital flight. In a world of reversed standards of value, the movements of domestic interest rates relative to those prevailing in the international markets do little more than shift the currency composition of the supply of financial savings.

Thus, the range of the outcomes of losing the ability to conduct monetary policy spans from irrelevant to positive in most developing countries.

The official adoption of another country's currency, however, may be politically difficult because it elicits strong emotional reactions in developing countries. Curiously, there is a contradiction between the public posture and the individual choices in these countries. Publicly, most people in those countries reject the idea of dollarization; privately, however, they deposit large portions of their savings in foreign currency accounts, engage in contracts denominated in foreign currencies, and judge the adequacy of their sources of income denominated in the local currency (profits, rents, interest rates, and wages) based on the standard of foreign currencies.

People reject in public what they do in private because there is the idea that having a currency is as essential to sovereignty as the flag and the national anthem. The association is strange because local currencies have been the vehicle through which many developing countries have lost their economic sovereignty to the International Monetary Fund (IMF). There are few developing countries that do not have to clear their economic policies with the IMF; most have to do so because of problems created by their local currencies. For those that do, the IMF representative and its mission leaders are more important than the governor of the central bank and minister of finance combined because if the former do not agree with something that the latter two propose, than the country loses access to the IMF credit and, with it, to the international markets. This is hardly conducive to sovereignty. Many civil society organizations blame this dependence on the IMF. It, however, stems from the problems created by the countries themselves and their penchant to manipulate their currencies in ways that make them dependent on the IMF. On average, local currencies have been source of dependence, not of sovereignty.

Moreover, the idea that the issuer could manipulate the currency in such a way as to harm the interests of one of its users is outlandish. Such manipulation would produce more damage in the issuing country than in the one using the currency.

There are also vested interests that oppose the adoption of a foreign currency. Local banks tend to be the most prominent among these. The rationale for this opposition is that weak local currencies act as protective barriers against foreign competition. Typically, international banks shy away from committing strong currencies in massive commercial operations in developing countries. Where they operate, they finance their operations with local currency exclusively, so that they become part of the local banking system, subject to the same constraints imposed by the weakness of the country. The common mechanism to do this is to commit the minimum capital and then extract it back through services provided by the international headquarters. They commit foreign exchange resources only to a small number of elite exporters and to companies with which they have ties abroad. Their behavior is rational. Channeling large amounts of foreign exchange to the domestic market would expose them to the foreign exchange risks of currencies against which there is no possible hedging. This, of course, keeps the margins of intermediation comfortably high in the local markets. Local banks can be profitable even if they are highly inefficient. With the adoption of an international currency, the exchange risk is eliminated and transferring money from abroad becomes attractive for international banks. Margins of intermediation go down and the market is spoiled by competition. There is no need to emphasize the strength of the opposition coming from the people in charge of monetary management, their advisors, and the people who aspire to be among them.

Politicians are also enticed by the possibilities provided by the ability to create money. It allows them to collect the inflation tax, the only tax they can apply without having to obtain the approval of the national assemblies. Using the central bank as a source of unlimited credit for their pet projects and sectors is quite attractive. Once they discover the powers of sterilization, and particularly the ability it gives central banks to create credit for certain sectors and withdraw it from others, in a nontransparent way, they tend to love it too. Thus, even in countries where people reveal their preference for an international currency, dollarization may pose a political problem.

The possibility of creating regional currencies within the developed world has been proposed frequently. This proposal appeals to the myth of monetary sovereignty; yet, even in those terms, it is inadequate. There is a qualitative difference between managing a currency and half-managing it. As discussed in the case of Ireland, having a seat in the board of a central bank with several members cannot be called managing a currency. Trying to define policy opportunistically to meet each challenge (as the optimal currency area would have it), can only result in chaos and protracted internecine conflicts. Consider the differences between the business cycles of Argentina and Brazil and then picture the discussions in the board of directors of a hypothetical Mercosur Central Bank. Think of the weight of the opinions of Paraguay and Uruguay in such a bank. Think of the demands for credit of all countries to finance their fiscal deficits. Then imagine what would happen if one of the countries experiences a banking crisis and demands monetary creation to meet it—using dollar reserves of the entire community to save the banks of one of the members.

In fact, the only way to manage a regional central bank is to adopt impersonal rules, such as keeping the rate of inflation low throughout the currency area. Two of the additional rules would have to be that the communal central bank would not lend to the ministries of finance of the member countries and would do nothing in case of a crisis in one of these members. Otherwise, the set of incentives would be tilted in favor of imprudent fiscal and financial behavior. All the members would try to maximize their share of the credit of the collective central bank. Thus, the only viable solution is to impose the impersonal rules. Once these are established, each and every member of the board becomes irrelevant in terms of defining policy. Their only role would be applying the rules. That is, to be effective, the central bank would have to be the equivalent of a foreign one. This is the case of the European Central Bank, which does not lose sleep if one of its countries is having exchange rate problems. Rightly, it focuses on the quality of the currency, knowing that if it deteriorates, all the members would suffer and the euro would lose its legitimacy as currency.

More fundamentally, aiming at creating an optimal currency area by putting together a group of developing countries is as unrealistic as trying to create it within a single country. Even if all the developing countries joined together to create such a currency area, this would still be wanting in terms of size and diversity. The income effects would still dominate the substitution effects of devaluations. The currency would lack demand beyond the geographical borders of the currency area and the financial depth of a true international currency. Thus, it would still require financing in international currencies, so that the foreign exchange risk would remain embedded in the financial operation of the country. Devaluations would still increase the burden of the external debt. For these reasons, forming monetary unions of developing countries exclusively, although they initially could be instruments to raise the self-esteem of these countries, does not seem to be a promising idea.

In summary, a truly optimal currency area is defined not by the commonality of problems across geographic regions but by the quality of the currency serving it. Such quality depends on its ability to keep inflation rates low and its acceptance across a large and diversified economy, thus maximizing the possibilities of substitution in production and consumption within the area itself. Financially, the currency must provide access to deep and broad financial services and credit. Three or four such areas already exist—the dollar, the euro, the yen, and the pound sterling. Adopting one of them is the only practical possibility that developing countries have to access an optimal currency area.

As I finished revising the draft of this last chapter in January 2006, the fiscal and current account deficits of the United States had been escalating for several years, the dollar had weakened against the euro, oil prices had reached unprecedented nominal levels, the prices of all other commodities were going up, and the situation of the world's economy was becoming increasingly similar in some respects to that of the early 1970s. In those years, the pressure on the weakening dollar became unmanageable under the Bretton Woods system then in place. Countries were accumulating dollar reserves and some of them, particularly France, demanded the conversion of those dollars into their equivalent in gold. The United States responded by demonetizing the gold, which meant that the dollar would float from that moment on. In the ensuing years, the rate of inflation increased dramatically, from 4 percent in 1972 to 11 percent in 1974 and then, after a temporary decline, to 13.5 percent in 1980. During that period, commodities boomed and inflation went up to two digits in most countries. It was only in the 1980s that inflation in the United States returned to its traditionally low levels. Slowly, inflation abated in the developed countries. In 2006, commodity prices were increasing again in dollar terms. The countries that were accumulating dollar obligations were in Asia. They could not ask for redemption in gold or in any other quantity. However, they could stop buying them. People worried what would happen to the dollar as an international currency and to the world's economic stability.

Do these troubles affect the conclusions of this book? Do they mean that it would be better for countries to keep to their peso rather than joining an international currency, at least when such currency is the dollar?

The answer to this question is no, for three reasons. First, the economy of the United States remains the largest and most diversified one in the world. Moreover, since it is the one with the highest productivity growth and the one that is marking the path of the connectivity revolution, it is fairly sure that it will remain the strongest and most diversified economy in the foreseeable future. That is, the United States will continue to meet the main criterion to be an optimal currency area for a long time. Second, in spite of the large depreciations, inflation and interest rates remain low in the dollar area, at least until early 2006. Third, the influence of the dollar in the global financial markets is such that if its inflation and interest rates increase, they will increase even more in the developing countries. This was the experience in the 1970s. It is also what can be expected today.

This, of course, is not to say that the deepening of the macroeconomic problems of the United States would not result in dire consequences for the country and the rest of the world. It only means that clinging to a weak currency, tradable in only one small country, gives no protection against such consequences.

# Chapter 13 Conclusions

We have reached the end of the book, and can answer the question I posed at its beginning—Why should a developing country surrender its power to create money by adopting an international currency as its own? The answer, in a nutshell, is that it is the only way in which it may access a truly optimal currency area.

This answer should not be surprising; it is in full agreement with the kind of economic reasoning that has become the mainstream of the discipline in the last two hundred years. In fact, the idea that countries should detach themselves from the worldwide money markets is very odd in the realm of economic thought. Who would seriously argue that the efficiency of markets increases with their size but just to a certain point, beyond which it starts to decline, thus creating an "optimal size of the markets"? Yet, this is the idea behind the optimal currency area. I cannot think of any other field of economics where adding participants to a market is seen as negative or one in which fragmented markets are considered more efficient than one that would integrate all of them. In all other fields, the optimal size of a market is the largest possible one.

The idea that detaching submarkets from bigger ones may be optimal also goes against the grain of globalization—a process that is increasing the productivity of all its participants by rearranging production in accordance with competitive advantages. In particular, as discussed in chapter 5, it goes against the grain of financial globalization. This is truly odd because monetary and financial economics are so intertwined that it is sometimes very difficult to ascertain when one ends and the other starts.

This is quite strange because, as in all other markets, everything seems to suggest that the benefits of a currency increase monotonically with the size of the group that uses it. If we imagine that a currency is used by $n$ people, it is clear that augmenting this number to $n + 1$ will benefit everyone. Of course, the highest benefits would be for the added one, who would get access to all the advantages of a currency area, where he or she would be able to trade, save, and think in terms of a common currency. It is like a child learning a language, who clearly benefits more than the rest of society taken as a whole from his or her new access to communication. Yet, the entire society (the $n$ in our $n + 1$) also benefits when the number of people using a currency, or speaking a language, expands. The $n + 1$ can do everything that the $n$ could do and more. That is, from the point of view of the services of money, there is no doubt that the optimal size of a monetary market is the largest possible one.

The idea that fragmented markets can be better than integrated ones is so alien to economic reasoning that even people who defend protectionism in trade tend to do so by portraying the protection they support as a temporary measure, aimed at giving infant or weak industries a respite to strengthen themselves before facing international competition. At the end of some period, the argument goes, protection would be eliminated and the detached market would be integrated again with the international ones. That is, not even these arguments deny that the largest market is the optimal one. People who argue that markets should be permanently fragmented do so when their aim is to protect a certain group inside society, not the benefit of society as a whole. Their arguments tend to be political rather than economic, precisely because it is impossible to demonstrate that restricting competition would increase the economic welfare of the entire population.

Monetary economics, in its optimal currency area dimension, is also the only field where competition is seen as negative and the creation and enforcement of monopolies is seen as positive. In all other economic fields, it is taken for granted that the welfare of the population increases with competition. Yet, central banks and the International Monetary Fund (IMF), the institutions in charge of maintaining the monetary order that the optimal currency area theory defines as optimal, staunchly defend the right of the central banks to have a monetary monopoly within their countries. This, in itself, denies the claims of optimality. If the currency area is optimal, why should it be protected against competition? Why are people trying to escape from these monopolies that are supposedly optimal for them? Defending such monopolies is really odd.

Of course, oddity is not a synonym of wrongness. Reality could be such that, unlike other markets, restricting the size of monetary markets would actually result in improved efficiency for the mutilated integrated market, for the portion taken away, or for both. Yet, it is obvious that the fragmentation of currencies now prevailing among the developing countries does not improve the efficiency of the international monetary and financial markets. As we have seen in this book, such fragmentation does not improve the efficiency of the monetary markets of the developing countries themselves nor the welfare of their populations. On the contrary, these countries get all the costs of operating within very small monetary markets, isolated from the mainstream of the international markets.

As in the case of language, people already using international currencies would gain from the integration of new people to their currency areas. Yet, the largest gain would be experienced by those gaining new access to them. That is, the developing countries would gain the most from enlarging the area of international currencies.

For this reason, we end the book by turning the initial question around and, rather than asking why a country should surrender its power to create its own money, we ask why a developing country should surrender all the benefits of using an optimal currency for the sake of having a currency it can call its own.

# Epilogue Werner von Bankrupt on the Art of Buying Countries with a Buck-Fifty

The Devil went to Dema Gogo's country with ten of his underlings six months after its catastrophic currency crisis. They had a great time. Everything was cheap for them, to the point that they could dine in good restaurants for two bucks—wine, desserts, and lavish tips included.

"These guys are in very good shape!" he told von Bankrupt when going back to headquarters. "Look how cheap everything is for them! I met a journalist with a prestigious magazine and he told me that this was because their dollar purchasing power parity, which he referred to as PPP, was very high. I don't get it. They went through a disaster and now the habitants live in a paradise of low prices. Please explain this to me for future operations."

Von Bankrupt smiled. "You are falling into a common fallacy, my dear Mephistopheles. You found that life is cheap in the country only because you arrived with dollars. The problem is that the people living inside the country don't have dollars. If you feel great that you can invite ten of your friends to dine in a good restaurant with only two bucks, think how the owner of the restaurant feels when he has to feed ten people to get only two dollars. His profit, of course, is smaller. Think of the waiters."

"You are telling me that life is expensive for them?"

"Of course! If a haircut is thirty cents, you have to cut the hair of three people to get close to one dollar. If you are a barber and want to buy a haircut for yourself, there is no problem. It's a one to one exchange. But if you want to buy something that is priced in dollars, or you want to pay debts denominated in dollars, you have a problem."

"This is confusing, doctor. Why did the journalist tell me that the dollar purchasing power *parity* in the country is very high when you are telling me that the dollar purchasing power of the country is very low? It's only one word of difference between the two statements, but what a heck of a difference!"

"For this, I have to explain how the international statistics are calculated," said von Bankrupt, "something I already did when you were convincing Dema Gogo."

"Do it again," said the Devil, choosing not to mind the insolence of the economist.

Von Bankrupt installed the projector and loaded a PowerPoint presentation. "As you may remember," von Bankrupt said after accepting a glass of cognac, "I made my argument when Dema Gogo had doubts about the convenience of devaluations. Someone had told him that the country's purchasing power in dollars would be reduced if he devalued in real terms. That, Gogo was told, meant that the international purchasing power of his country's gross domestic product (GDP) would fall as well. He was scared by that and, if I may say, my dear Mephistopheles, you too because you couldn't counter this argument. I then produced this counterargument, which, if you allow me to say, was brilliant."

"Yes, yes, but remind me of the counterargument," said the Devil, anxious to cut the avalanche of self-congratulations that von Bankrupt was about to launch.

"Well, we can start by saying that it's true that a country's international purchasing power is reduced when it devalues its currency. This is so obvious that I find it unnecessary to explain. If you could buy one thing in the international markets when your exchange rate was one to one, you would be able to buy only half of it when the exchange rate goes up to two for one. Then, since your GDP is produced in local currency terms, the amount of things that you would be able to buy in the international markets with it would be halved as well. The size of the loan in dollars that you would be able to service would be halved as well. Got it?"

The Devil refused to answer such an obvious question, thinking that he would have to find a way to discipline this bombastic man. Maybe one or two notches in the temperature of his furnace would do the job.

Von Bankrupt saw the stare in the Devil's eyes and decided to continue without an answer. "Then, the person who said this to Dema was right. Thus, I knew that I had to give a spin to the argument if I wanted to convince him that he should devalue.

"Fortunately, there are two widely used and respected indicators that provide such spin. They ignore and even reverse the effects of real devaluations in the international purchasing power of the population. These indicators are the GDP in constant dollars and GDP in dollars with purchasing power parity. People use these indicators to compare the GDP of different countries and their rates of growth. They are published in the World Development Tables of the World Bank.

"Let's start with the way GDP at constant dollar prices is calculated. You would expect that, when converting GDP from current to constant dollars, the GDP expressed in current dollars would be deflated by the rate of inflation of the dollar. It is surprising, then, that this is not the way the conversion is effected. The GDP measured in current dollars (which is the one that shows the impact of devaluations in the current purchasing power of the population in the international markets) is not even used in the calculation. The number is estimated by dividing the GDP in constant local currency units by the exchange rate with the dollar at some specified date—for example, by the exchange rate in 2000 if this is the basis for the constant prices. That is, all the figures in the time series of GDP in constant local currency are divided by the same number. The result is that, while the GDP figures are different in constant local currency and constant dollars, their rates of change are the same, regardless of the intervening devaluations against the dollar.

"Thus, we have the paradox of a measure of GDP in constant dollars that does not take into account the loss of value of the domestic currency relative to the dollar. This, of course, distorts the plain English meaning of the term *production at constant 2000 dollars*. It also inflates the rates of growth in constant dollars of countries that devalue in real terms because it ignores the declines in the prices of the local currency relative to the dollar.

"Now, this bias is even worse in the purchasing power parity estimations of production," continued von Bankrupt. "PPP numbers are estimated by dividing production in local currency by a special exchange rate. This exchange rate is the product of the multiplication of the nominal one by a conversion factor that is essentially a measure of the real exchange rate. It becomes lower the more a country devalues in real terms. When the denominator declines, the quotient, which in this case is the GDP PPP, increases."

Von Bankrupt paused to see if the Devil was following him. Then he continued, "The way this works in practice is amazing. Depending on the relationship between the numerator and the denominator, you can increase your GDP in current PPP dollars by just devaluing your currency in real terms, even when your output in constant local currency units is actually declining. And since dollars PPP are almost universally used to compare GDP across countries, you would seem to be growing faster than other countries that do not devalue as much as you do, or, worse still, do not devalue.

"Do not believe me. Look at the figures. Table E.1 shows the case of the Dominican Republic in 2002–2003. In that period, the country suffered a devastating financial crisis. According to the national accounts measured in constant local currency terms, real GDP declined by 0.4 percent. Given the impact of financial crises of comparable magnitudes in other countries, this in itself is amazing. It is not surprising, however, that, since the country drastically devalued the currency in real terms, the GDP measured in current dollars declined by 23 percent. You would expect that the GDP decline in constant dollars at 2000 prices would be 25.1 percent because the rate of inflation in the United States was 2.3 percent. Yet, as a manifestation of the way GDP in constant 2000 dollars is measured, the decline in dollars of this kind is just 0.4 percent, the same as in the local currency units. More surprising, however, is the next row, which shows the GDP in current international PPP *dollars*. My dear Mephistopheles, measured in this way, GDP actually increased by 3.8 percent!"

It was obvious that von Bankrupt was enjoying his own presentation. He continued, "Finally, when converting the current PPP dollars to constant 2000 dollars PPP, the income growth settles to a positive 2 percent. That is, according to this indicator, you can turn a declining GDP (as measured in real terms) into a growing one—not because the devaluation will actually increase production, but because the indicator will measure the decline as an increase. And this in an indicator that is called dollars! How could Dema Gogo resist this evidence? According to these figures, you can have a catastrophic currency

Table E.1: Converting a Declining Income into an Increasing One: The Case of Dominican Republic, 2002–2003

|  | GDP 2002 | GDP 2003 | Growth Rate (%) |
|---|---|---|---|
| GDP (constant Local Currency Units) | 114,793,600,000 | 114,334,500,000 | −0.4 |
| GDP (current US $) | 21,595,220,000 | 16,540,850,000 | −23.4 |
| GDP (constant 2000 US $) | 21,167,470,000 | 21,082,800,000 | −0.4 |
| GDP, PPP (current international $) | 57,432,090,000 | 59,622,410,000 | 3.8 |
| GDP, PPP (constant 2000 international $) | 55,245,830,000 | 56,324,740,000 | 2.0 |

*Source:* World Development Indicators, World Bank.

and financial crisis and still increase your purchasing power in the currency you devalued against!"

Von Bankrupt paused for effect.

"To see more clearly how this discriminates in favor of countries that devalue in real terms, we can compare how the indicator measured the evolution of the international purchasing power in three countries in crisis: Argentina, the Dominican Republic, and Ecuador. The crises in Argentina and Ecuador culminated with catastrophic devaluations against the dollar while Ecuador dollarized as its former currency was spiraling down uncontrollably.

"Let's look at Ecuador. When the exchange rate was falling, you could buy many an Ecuadorian thing for a buck-fifty. The salary of the population went down to a few dollars per month. Then, after the government decided to dollarize in 2000, it had to devalue further because the country's dollar reserves were not enough to buy the monetary base at the prevailing exchange rate. Then, after this date, relative prices readjusted to normal levels, wages increased so that people today can buy, say, TV sets, if they wish, while in the years of the depreciation it would have taken an entire life of income to buy one. Probably you think that the measure of their purchasing power should have increased. Amazingly, the opposite was true. The PPP measure of the country's GDP punished this increase in the purchasing power of the population because the increase in both wages and prices that took place after the crisis ended was equivalent to currency appreciation. Between 2000 and 2003, the conversion factor (the factor by which the current dollar income is divided to get the PPP dollars) was multiplied by 1.5. With the denominator increasing, the estimation of the purchasing power of the population through the PPP indicator fell immediately. This can be seen in figure E.1, which shows the inverse of the conversion factor. This gives the measure of the purchasing power of the population in PPP terms. As you can see in the figure, according to the PPP data, the international purchasing power of the Ecuadorians was at its best in 1999–2000, when they were mired in their crisis and could not afford even the barest essentials. Maybe you can use this line in future operations: 'Improve your PPP by getting into a spiral of uncontrollable devaluations!'

"On the other side of the spectrum, the income expressed in current dollars of the Argentines and Dominicans fell dramatically as a result of their devaluations in 2001 and 2002, respectively. Simultaneously, their purchasing power in international dollar PPP terms went up as a result of the same devaluations." Von Bankrupt paused for effect.

"In summary, the PPP figures penalized Ecuador's GDP as measured in current dollars by multiplying it by 0.66 of its crisis levels. At the same time, the indicator multiplied the devalued income of the other two countries, by 1.4 in the case of the Dominican Republic and by a whooping 2.1 in that of Argentina.[1] The Argentines then lost international purchasing power because their peso appreciated against the dollar in 2003.

"You can see what I mean if you estimate the ratio of the growth of GDP PPP at constant 2000 international dollars with that of GDP at constant 2000 dollars, and then compare that ratio with the rate of real devaluation from 1990 to 2003. You may recall in this comparison that GDP at constant 2000 dollars grows at the same rates as the GDP at constant local currency units.

"Take the case of Papua New Guinea from 1990 to 2003. Since the country devalued its currency by 51 percent in real terms, its GDP in constant 2000 international dollars PPP grew 12 percent faster than its GDP in constant local currency units. What does this mean? Why should the international purchasing power of the Papuans increase relative to their domestic purchasing power? If anything, it should be lower because they devalued their currency.

"Now look at Bulgaria, where the currency appreciated by almost 40 percent over the same period. The country's GDP in 2000 international dollars PPP grew at only 96 percent of the growth of the GDP measured in local currency. This is counterintuitive and does not portray any aspect of palpable reality. Why should the international purchasing power of the Bulgarians decrease relative to their domestic one while in fact their currency afforded more internationally in 2003 than in 1999?"

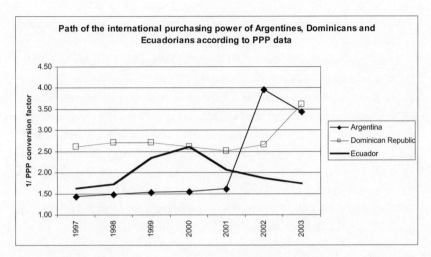

Figure E.1: Path of international purchasing power of Argentines, Dominicans, and Ecuadorians before, during, and after their crises, according to PPP data. *Source:* World Development Indicators, World Bank.

Von Bankrupt then asked rhetorically, "Now, my dear Mephistopheles, please tell me, for what reason, international or local, should the growth rate of Papua New Guinea in constant local currency units be propped up relative to that of Bulgaria in order to compare them in PPP terms? If you are going to make the adjustment, you should do it the other way around, because the Papuans need to work more to service their dollar debts while the Bulgarians need to work less for that purpose. Equally, the Bulgarians could land today in Papua New Guinea and buy 16 percent more Papuan things than in 1990, while the Papuans can buy 16 percent fewer things in Bulgaria.

"Given these adjustments, countries that devalue in real terms *look* better in these statistics than those that do not. That really gives devaluing countries a boost when comparing their GDP with those of others! You can write a book, *Devalue Your Way to Riches*! What do you think, my dear Mephistopheles?"

"Amazing," said the Devil.

Von Bankrupt then said, in a conspiratorial tone, "You realize that you can take the dynamics of the PPP calculations to infinity and increase the output of the Dominican Republic to the same level as that of Sweden by just devaluing in real terms by a sufficient magnitude, don't you? This was the argument that convinced Dema. He dreamed of reaching Sweden's GDP PPP!"

Von Bankrupt laughed. Then he continued, "Using this data was my touch of genius!"

The Devil was really impressed but didn't want von Bankrupt to notice. He was spiraling upward in a whirlwind of self-congratulation. The Devil then asked, "Tell me, then, what is the meaning of the PPP measures?"

"Ah!" said von Bankrupt, "In fact, what the PPP *conversion factors* measure is how the purchasing power of the run-of-the-mill dollars increases domestically when there is a real devaluation. Alternatively, you can say that they measure how expensive the dollar has become for the people earning their incomes in local currency. Then, when these conversion factors are applied to GDP, you get a measure of how much of the country production you can buy with a dollar. For example, if the dollar GDP PPP increases by 20 percent on account of a real devaluation, this means that you can buy 20 percent more of it with one dollar, *if you have it*. But, again, we should remember that people inside the country do not have their incomes denominated in dollars. Instead, they have it denominated in a currency that has depreciated against the dollar, so that getting a dollar is harder for them. This was your experience during your vacations. Certainly, you can buy a lot with one dollar; but getting that dollar means a lot of work for the locals."

"But then you can use the PPP data to measure how cheap or expensive life is in different countries," said the Devil.

Then von Bankrupt turned around to face the Devil and said, in a high pitch, "Not at all!"

Then, in a softer voice, he continued, "Do you realize that the PPP figures do not have anything to do with the purchasing power *of the population*? They do not measure how cheap or how expensive life is for the average resident using the local currency, which is not related to the things a dollar can buy but instead to what their *wages* can buy. Since, my dear Mephisto, real devaluations reduce the real wage in developing countries, you can conclude that real devaluations in those countries do indeed turn the life of their inhabitants more expensive. The proponents of devaluations cannot deny that this is so because the reduction of the real wage is part of one of their most popular arguments: that such reduction would lead to higher employment. Thus, my dear, dollar PPP figures do not have any connection with the reality of the countries. They are useful for travelers with dollars in their pockets, who, by comparing the PPP figures with the current dollar ones can estimate how cheap they will feel each country is."

Then von Bankrupt prepared himself to close his argument. Inflating his chest, he said, "It takes just a moment of thought to realize that if the currency keeps on depreciating in real terms, there would be a moment when the travelers could buy the entire production of the country with a buck-fifty. This is what I promised you would be able to do in Dema Gogo's country. You did that just when the country's GDP PPP was reaching the level of Norway's."

The Devil was happy having von Bankrupt on his team. He embodied the concept he had of a great macroeconomist: assertively ambiguous. "Then, should I understand that the conversion factors are useful to compare the price levels across countries as perceived by people with dollars, but are misleading when applied to estimate how expensive is the life for the residents, and even worse when used to compare the purchasing power of countries as given by their GDP?"

"Yes! Exactly!"

"Thus, for future occasions, should we promote the PPP indicators to compare the growth of income across countries?" asked the Devil mischievously.

"Yes, of course, if you are in the business of buying the entire GDP of countries with a buck-fifty," said von Bankrupt, smiling like a boa constrictor after eating a cow.

"Let's drink to that!" said the Devil, raising his glass.

# Notes

**INTRODUCTION**

1. *Source: Financial Stability in Dollarized Economies*, prepared by the Monetary and Exchange Affairs Department of the International Monetary Fund (IMF) for the Board of Directors of that institution, Washington, D.C.

**CHAPTER 1: THE STANDARD OF VALUE AND THE REVERSED LIQUIDITY TRAP**

1. See Global Development Finance, World Bank. http://web.worldbank.org/WBSITE/EXTERNAL/DATASTATISTICS/

**CHAPTER 2: THE UNFULFILLED PROMISES IN THE FINANCIAL SYSTEM**

1. The sample included all the developing countries for which data existed to calculate the changes in the real exchange rate during the period. It excluded outliers. These, however, were different from those in the sample from 1985 to 1997. The data was taken from the International Financial Statistics of the International Monetary Fund. http://ifs.apdi.net/imf/logon.aspx
2. *Source:* International Financial Statistics of the International Monetary Fund. http://ifs.apdi.net/imf/logon.aspx
3. *Source:* World Development Indicators, World Bank. http://web.worldbank .org/WBSITE/EXTERNAL/DATASTATISTICS/

4. Chilean foreign currency deposits are further discussed at the end of this chapter.

5. *Source:* Central Bank of Dominican Republic. http://www.bancentral.gov.do/

6. The sample shown in the figure eliminates the three top performers in the original sample, which contained the thirty-six countries for which information existed. These were Thailand, Bahrain, and Malaysia. The deletion did not affect the results of the regression but showed more clearly the visual relationship for the other countries.

7. The equation for nominal interest rates is $Y=4.9139X^{-1.5013}$ while for the real rate of interest it is $Y=4.9229X^{-1.5223}$. Y represents the percent of GDP attracted by 1 percentage point in the interest rates. X represents 1 + the rate of nominal devaluation. The $R^2$ is 0.4987 for the first equation and 0.3988 for the second. In both cases, the coefficient is significant to the 99 percent level.

8. *Source:* Moody's Investment Service.

## CHAPTER 3: THE UNFULFILLED PROMISES IN TRADE AND GROWTH

1. Michael Porter, *The Competitive Advantage of Nations* (New York: The Free Press/ Macmillan, 1990).

2. Stephen L. Parente and Edward C. Prescott, *Barriers to Riches*, Walras-Pareto Lectures, Ecole des Hautes Etudes Commerciales, Universite de Lausanne (Cambridge, MA: MIT Press, 2000).

3. The real unit labor costs are a better measurement of the movements in the real exchange rates between two countries than the comparison of the rates of devaluation with the relative inflations of the two countries when discussing the impact on exports and production. It focuses on the real costs of labor, which may vary in different ways than consumer prices. This indicator, however, is available only in a very few developing countries.

4. *Source:* International Financial Statistics of the International Monetary Fund. http: //ifs.apdi.net/imf/logon.aspx

5. The coefficient was −0.41 in the first regression and −0.48 in the second and in both cases they were significant to the 99 percent level ($t = -3.2$ and $-3.95$, respectively). The $R^2$ was 0.14 for the first and 0.16 for the second. The source of the data was the International Financial Statistics. http://ifs.apdi.net/imf/logon.aspx

6. See "Argentina, Another Country," *The Economist*, July 21, 2005.

## CHAPTER 4: THE COSTS OF STABILITY

1. For an example of this line of thought, see "Can This Union Be Saved?" *The Economist*, June 6, 2005.

2. The crowding out may be bigger in some countries than what these figures suggest. For example, the already described National Savings Scheme in Pakistan completely crowds out the private sector from the long-term financial savings market.

3. The spread is estimated dividing 1 + the lending rate by 1 + the deposit rate.

4. The ratio of the banking system credit to the private sector to GDP was 28.9 percent

in Brazil, 44.5 in the United States, and 46.7 in El Salvador. Source: International Financial Statistics of the International Monetary Fund. http://ifs.apdi.net/imf/logon .aspx

5. Normally, I would use the deposit rate for this comparison. In this case, however, the lending rate is more appropriate because this rate is one of the main instruments that the central bank uses to stabilize the economy.

6. At zero devaluation rate, the dollar-equivalent and the nominal rates are the same.

7. Since the spreads between lending and deposit rates in El Salvador are approximately the same as in the United States, the difference between lending rates is equal to the difference in deposit rates.

## CHAPTER 7: THE CURRENCY ORIGINS OF FINANCIAL CRISES

1. *Source:* International Financial Statistics of the International Monetary Fund. http://ifs .apdi.net/imf/logon.aspx

2. The decline in real deposits may create a problem with the intermediation margin because administrative costs increase relative to the financial costs and earnings. This problem, however, is resolved automatically by the market because those margins increase with inflation.

3. See Timothy Lane, Atish Gosh, Javier Hamann, Steven Phillips, Marianne Schultze-Ghatta, and Tsidi Tkikata, *IMF-Supported Programs in Indonesia, Korea and Thailand,* Occasional Paper 78, IMF, Box 6.2, p. 45.

4. Data from the Ministry of the Economy of Argentina.

5. Data from International Financial Statistics, International Monetary Fund. http://ifs .apdi.net/imf/logon.aspx

6. Ibid.

## CHAPTER 9: THE SOLUTION OF CRISES AND THE AFTERMATH

1. David Dollar and Mary Hallward-Driemeier, "Crisis, Adjustments and Reform in Thai Industry," *The World Bank Research Observer* 15, no. 1 (February 2000).

2. Ibid., p. 4.

3. Ibid., p. 12.

4. See Peter R. Fallon and Robert E. B. Lucas, "The Impact of Financial Crises on Labor Markets, Household Incomes and Poverty: A Review of Evidence," *The World Bank Research Observer* 17, no. 1 (Spring 2002): 21–45. The paper is also available on the World Bank's website.

5. Ibid., Table 5.

6. See Gladys Lopez-Acevedo and Angel Salinas, *How Mexico's Financial Crisis Affected Income Distribution,* The World Bank, undated paper available on the Bank's website.

## CHAPTER 10: THE COUNTERFACTUALS

1. Global Development Finance, The World Bank, http://web.worldbank.org/WBSITE/ EXTERNAL/DATASTATISTICS/

## CHAPTER 11: THE CONVENTIONAL OPTIMAL CURRENCY AREA THEORY

1. *Sources:* The World Bank's World Development Indicators for all countries; the website of the State of California for this state's GDP; and the Economic Update of the Partnership for New York City (http://www.nycp.org) for that city's GDP. For the World Bank's data, http://web.worldbank.org/WBSITE/EXTERNAL/DATASTATISTICS/
2. *Source:* Economic Notes issued by the New York City Office of the Comptroller, Vol. XII, September 2004. The report is available on http://www.comptroller.nyc .gov/budget
3. Ugo Panizza, Ernesto Stein, and Ernesto Talvi, "Measuring Costs and Benefits of Dollarization: An Application to Central American and Caribbean Countries," in *Dollarization, Debates and Policy Alternatives*, ed. Eduardo Levy Yegati and Federico Sturzeneger (Cambridge, MA, and London: The MIT Press, 2003).
4. Ibid., p. 171.
5. Ibid., p. 173.
6. Ibid., p. 188.

## CHAPTER 12: TOWARD A REDEFINITION OF AN OPTIMAL CURRENCY AREA

1. David C. Parsley and Shang-Jin Wei, *How Big and Heterogeneous Are the Effects of Currency Arrangements on Market Integration? A Price Based Approach*, Revision of NBER working paper #8468, September 2003, available from the David C. Parsley website at http://www.owen.vanderbilt.edu/vanderbilt/About/faculty-research.
2. See, for example, Andrew K. Rose, "One Money, One Market: The Effect of Common Currencies on Trade," *Economic Policy* 15, no. 30: 9–45 (2000); Andrew K. Rose, "Currency Unions and Trade: The Effect Is Large," *Economic Policy* (October 2001): 449–461; Andrew K. Rose and T. D. Stanley, "A Meta-Analysis of the Effect of Common Currencies on International Trade," 2005. All these and many other papers making the same point are available at http://www.faculty.haas.berkeley.edu/arose.

## EPILOGUE: WERNER VON BANKRUPT ON THE ART OF BUYING COUNTRIES WITH A BUCK-FIFTY

1. The inverses of the conversion factors of Argentina were 1.6 and 4 in 2001 and 2002, respectively. The second is 2.1 times the former. In the Dominican Republic, the inverses were 2.7 in 2002 and 3.6 in 2003. The latter is 1.4 times the former. In the case of Ecuador, the inverses were 2.6 and 1.7. The ratio of the second to the first is 0.66.

# Index

The letter *f* or *t* following a page number refers to a figure or table on that page.